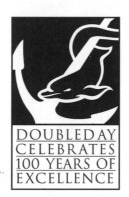

DOUBLEDAY
CELEBRATES
100 YEARS OF
EXCELLENCE

DOUBLEDAY

New York London Toronto

Sydney Auckland

THE
HIDDEN
WRITER

*Diaries
and the
Creative Life*

ALEXANDRA

JOHNSON

PUBLISHED BY DOUBLEDAY
a division of Bantam Doubleday Dell Publishing Group, Inc.
1540 Broadway, New York, New York 10036

DOUBLEDAY and the portrayal of an anchor with a
dolphin are trademarks of Doubleday, a division of
Bantam Doubleday Dell Publishing Group, Inc.

Book design by Marysarah Quinn

Library of Congress Cataloging-in-Publication Data
Johnson, Alexandra.
The hidden writer : diaries and the creative life /
Alexandra Johnson.
p.   cm.
Includes bibliographical references (p. 269).
1. American diaries—Women authors—History and
criticism.   2. English diaries—Women authors—History
and criticism.   3. Women and literature.   4. Women—
Authorship.   5. Creative ability.   6. Women—
Biography.   I. Title.
PS409.J64   1997
818'.03—dc20   96-34066
CIP

ISBN 0-385-47829-1

FOR *my mother* AND FOR *Askold*

Creation often

needs two hearts

one to root

and one to flower . . .

—MARILOU AWIAKTA,
Abiding Appalachia

CONTENTS

CONTENTS

ACKNOWLEDGMENTS

*I*n 1908 Virginia Woolf wrote in her diary that she wanted to show "all the traces of the minds passage through the world; & achieve in the end, some kind of whole made of shivering fragments; to me this seems the natural process; the flight of the mind." In many ways, it's the perfect description of writing a book, especially one about diaries and creativity. If it was the "shivering fragments" of diaries that first drew me to this project, then showing how a creative mind makes its passage into and through the world was always my larger aim. *The Hidden Writer*'s own passage—its being unified into a whole—owes many acknowledgments. The first is to the writers of diaries themselves, both those discussed here and the scores of others I've read over the years. Diaries and journals (terms the writers I've chosen often used interchangeably, as do I) are great working records of creative life. They have sustained me in the long process of writing this book. And I want to thank the judges of the PEN/Jerard Fund Award for their vote of confidence when *The Hidden Writer* was still a work-in-progress. That public encouragement was an invaluable spur to helping me finish it.

No book featuring portraits of writers' lives can be written without the earlier, full-scale biographies that precede it. It is my hope that readers of my book will add the superb biographies listed in the Select Bibliography to their shelves, if they're not there already. But certain ones need special mention here. Quentin Bell's *Virginia Woolf: A Biography* remains, in my mind, a model of its kind, a brilliant weaving of narrative and historical exposition, as is Phyllis Rose's *Parallel Lives*. Antony Alpers's and Claire Tomalin's biographies of Katherine Mansfield are both incomparable; Jean Strouse's *Alice James* is a model of original scholarship and penetrating psychological insight. So too Ernest Simmons and Henri Troyat on the Tolstoys; Deirdre Bair on Anaïs Nin. On diaries themselves, essential books range from Thomas Mallon's *A Book of One's Own* to the more scholarly work pioneered by both Harriet Blodgett and Robert Fothergill.

I want to thank Donald Fanger at Harvard not only for his invaluable help with—and translation of—material on the Tolstoys but for his inspired discussions over the years on literature in general; Linda Simon at Harvard for her guidance in researching aspects of the James family; Kirkcaldy historian David Galloway for his generosity and time during my stay in Scotland and for his help with Marjory Fleming. Research staff at the following collections and archives were invariably helpful in gaining access to original diaries and photographs, as well as other material: the National Library of Scotland for Marjory Fleming's journals and Isabella Keith's letters; the Edinburgh Room of the Edinburgh Public Library for its material on nineteenth-century cultural history; the Berg Collection of the New York Public Library for Virginia Woolf's diaries and May Sarton journals, respectively; the Alexander Turnbull Library in New Zealand for help with Katherine Mansfield; Houghton Library, Harvard University, not only for material relating to Alice James and the James family but also for early diaries by unknown writers;

UCLA's University Research Library for Anaïs Nin's diaries. My gratitude to the estate of Anaïs Nin, especially to Gunther Stuhlmann, and to Rupert Pole for his kindness in granting me access to still-private material. Special thanks also to Alice Vaux, owner of Alice James's diary, for her help and kindness in letting me work with it; Ruth Yeazell of Yale for her scholarship on Alice James's letters; Gavin Grant, curator of the Kirkcaldy Museum, for original artwork on Marjory Fleming; Alison Samuel of the Hogarth Press, London, for tracking down material on Virginia Woolf; the Society of Authors, London, for material pertaining to the estate of Katherine Mansfield.

All that research would have remained raw material were it not for the sustained feedback of Sally Brady and the Tuesday writers' group. This book owes much to their careful reading. I also want to thank Maxine Rodburg, friend and invaluable reader; so too Suzanne Berne, Jessica Treadway, Terri Cader. My aunt, Betty Sanders, inspired my earliest love of books and writing. My gratitude, too, to colleagues and students at both Harvard and Wellesley for their interest in and discussion of diaries over the years.

To my agent, Elaine Markson, a special thanks. My editor, Betsy Lerner, has been a wonderful and steady presence from the start. My thanks also to Pari Berk for her careful reading of the manuscript; and to Bob Daniels for his impeccable copyediting. My husband, Askold Melnyczuk, is owed the greatest debt for his unfailing encouragement, support and patience.

The author has made every attempt possible to trace ownership and copyrights.

PROLOGUE:
FROM
EYE TO I

It is the great quantity of what is not done that lies
with all its weight on what wants to come out of
the soil.

—RAINER MARIA RILKE

I'm standing under a spastic fluorescent light at Osco Drug, stranded in aisle one in the stationery section. I am nine years old. I know just where to find them—next to each other on the bottom shelf. They're often vinyl, with a thin gold key Scotch-taped to the front. I open the diary closest to me, its pages blank, the margins stenciled with flowers like limp medieval illuminations. Stacked next to the diaries are reams of lined composition paper. On such paper I first practiced penmanship, patiently coaxing vowels and consonants, shaping my name from a hesitant into a sturdy diagonal. On this paper I'll soon write essays about Hamlet, brooding. Later still: college applications, love letters, résumés. These will be my passports to a larger world. My eye moves from the composition paper back to the stack of diaries, each with its individual metal key. Staring at the diaries, I wonder why I need the lock in the first place.

Somehow, even at nine, I know I'm searching for clues. To what exactly I can't say, but it has something to do with these two stacks of writing paper. In the meantime, seated amid amber bottles of vitamins, spools of wrapping paper, the powdery smell of aspirin, I wait for my mother. I've brought a book with me, one I carry in my canvas bag since first discovering it. It's written by someone only five years older than I. I love reading the sly way she writes about her family, her body, her budding love life. I can see why the book has been translated into dozens of languages. I read certain passages of Anne Frank's diary over and over. The one dated May 11, 1944, for example: "You've known for a long time that my greatest wish is to become a journalist some day and later on a famous writer . . . whether I shall succeed or not, I cannot say, but my diary will be a great help." Even at nine I hear in her sentences a young girl's dare: a confession and rehearsal of ambition. But only in time will I ask other questions of this diary, this fragment of a document for a fragment of a life. However powerful Anne Frank's diary, it will remind me that the talents went untested. Written in the Secret Annex, the diary exposes a private self that will never realize its public ambitions. No matter how poignantly vital Anne Frank's writing legacy, secretly we say to ourselves, "It's a shame she left *only* a diary."

But on that Saturday afternoon in Osco Drug, I'm thinking about why I'd immediately checked out *The Diary of a Young Girl* after finding it on the school library shelves. It had to do with what had happened only weeks earlier. It was after school, a few class-mates were outside playing in the September air with its sting of eucalyptus. I sat on the floor of the school library, the linoleum cool on my legs, a sticky white rectangle of a Band-Aid on my knee. The book I'd found was the same color as my Schwinn bike, a nervous electric blue. It was part of a Great Biography series subtitled Fa-mous Women. Maybe because my grandmother had gone to Siberia as a nurse during the Great War, I read *Clara Barton, Nurse* with a certain hunger to learn how Barton had founded the Red Cross. Week after week, I'd scan the library shelves for a new Famous Women book. The series, though, had stopped at six, not a single creative life among them. The only other book I could find there was about a girl writing a diary in an attic.

Years later, my adult shelves groaned with the weight of books—novels, anthologies, biographies. While I knew that Charlotte Brontë had a miserable toothache when she began *Jane Eyre*, no one had explained to my satisfaction how that shivering self, Brontë—not Eyre—came to write her books. Or how she imagined that novel's first sentence—"There was no possibility of taking a walk that day"—as her father, that rigid cadaver of a critic, called for his soup from the next room. I still wanted to know: How did Charlotte Brontë *become* Charlotte Brontë? How did Virginia Woolf leap from diary to novel writing? Why did Katherine Mansfield sit in a rented London studio in between trying to write stories, noting "queer this habit of mine. [journal writing] Nothing affords me the same relief. What happens as a rule is if I go on long enough I *break through*." I wanted to know how these and other writers got there— stationed at their desks, willing to work alone, without approval.

Questions start to shape themselves in my imagination: How is creativity sustained? What role does a diary play? Is there a link between the life and the work? When do diarists first notice they're writing stories from a life, not critiques *of* it? How does eye become I?

These are the questions that have haunted me over time, ones that continue to whisper with insistent urgency. The writer's obstacle course—silence, self-censorship, illness, envy, rejection, money, migraines, bad nights, false starts, confidence. What had begun with the two stacks of writing paper at Osco Drug, with the meager Great Biography series, took me on a search similar to those of the writers whose diaries and novels I read. I combed the diaries for clues, for the creative blueprints they held. I was fixed on a series of questions. The first: How does a diarist go from notes to novels, writing, as Katherine Mansfield said, "till I simply exhaust my store"?

Nothing I found showed that shift from private to public voice, from eye to I, more dramatically than a writer's diary. Often a diary is not only a writer's first work but the first draft of creative identity. A living account of what shaped him or her—experiences, reading lists, literary habits—it's above all a barometer of confidence. My second question loomed: What kept the writing underground? What in the writer's psyche or life allowed it to stay hidden? In that respect, those who never got out of the diary, whose creativity was somehow stymied, interested me as much as those who'd broken through to larger creative works. Yet, in the end, it's such writers as Katherine Mansfield and Virginia Woolf whose diaries are the most instructive. They are the most intimate records of a writing self in conversation with itself. There's a thrill as we watch them discovering hidden parts of themselves—concentration, voice, confidence. Most important, in moving from private to public voice, their diaries chart the link between the creativity of the work and of the life. As Phyllis Rose notes in *Parallel Lives,* "Living is an act of creativity . . . at certain moments of our lives, our creative imaginations are more conspicuously demanded than at others." The fascination of diaries, in part, is the various solutions each generation of writers has applied to the knotty questions of private and creative life, of voices coming into being.

The Hidden Writer, seven narrative portraits of writing lives, examines the stubborn evolutionary push of diarists emerging into full creative work over a century and a half. Organized chronologically to show that arc, as well as the stages in a writer's life, *The Hidden Writer* opens with a seven-year-old diarist and ends with a successful writer beginning a diary at sixty. In between, there are genius siblings, feuding spouses, jealous colleagues, passionate friendships, private liaisons.

Each portrait represents a crucial stage in a writer's creativity, from first discovering a voice within a diary to imagining and writing for an audience beyond it. Also at stake are life questions writers grapple with in stubbornly practical terms—how to solve intricate issues of work, money, family, success, rejection and exposure. These seven portraits show the struggle shared by *all* writers. But diaries kept by writing women, still the top sellers and most widely read, show more clearly the social and psychological prohibitions in becoming a writer. They are X-ray glimpses of writers and lives in process. In many ways, the seven portraits here are a time-lapse study of confidence.

Silence, cunning, exile. In *A Portrait of the Artist as a Young Man,* James Joyce coined this phrase to describe a writer's credo. But it is also the perfect description of the problems, the opposite solutions, confronting the diarist. In *The Hidden Writer* my interest is with writers emerging from the shadows, from silence, from the necessary cunning of pleasing others, writers no longer exiled from their own voice. How a diary first sparks a creative voice, only to have it later be in service to another's creativity, is the focus of the portraits of Marjory Fleming and Sonya Tolstoy. With Alice James, growing up within a competitive writing family resulted in her keeping a diary, though illness eventually became a claim to identity when talent was thwarted. Katherine Mansfield and Virginia Woolf provide us with an invaluable record of literary friendship and rivalry. If they used their diaries as springboards into innovative fiction, writing in any form other than a revised diary remained a conflict for Anaïs Nin. In chronicling an outsider's writing career at midlife and in the uncertainties of old age, May Sarton intended her journals for publication from the start.

A writer is a reader moved to emulation, Saul Bellow observed. The search that first began in Osco Drug has taken me on a long odyssey: from young diarist to published writer. Along the way as I read the original diaries—the sharp diagonals from Katherine Mansfield's fountain pen, the spidery elegance of Virginia Woolf's inky sentences, the spirited loops of Marjory Fleming's young hand—I realized I was in the process of putting together a book for the simple reason that I hadn't yet found the one I needed to read. Culling the diaries, letters, memoirs and biographies of these writers, I've tried to provide readers with what would otherwise take them a long time to do on their own. In these narrative portraits I've tried, whenever possible, to let the writers tell their stories in their own words. Ambitious, testy, inspiring, occasionally infuriating, always provocative, each has a great deal to say. What they have in common is far more than keeping a diary. Tunneling their way out into creative life, all shared what every writer first burns with: silence and ambition.

A stack of diaries. Reams of lined composition paper. Private. Public. Hidden voices, hidden talents. Only in time would the relation between these be clear to me. Only in time would I realize that my imagination had long been polishing them as if they were worry beads. Unraveling the riddle these issues posed was somehow part of the questions themselves. It was a search for answers about creativity, both in work and in life, that linked me to a tradition of ongoing questions about writing lives, and what Rilke called "living the questions." When I could answer them fully, I'd know why the writing path, my own and others', hadn't always been a straight one.

By the time I reached college, something had sent my early questions about creativity underground. There they stayed. I read and studied literature—Conrad on self-exile, Tolstoy on war, Dostoyevsky on punishment. Diaries, I was told, were charming adjuncts, often unreliable. Minor. Certainly, some of the world's most famous diaries were notoriously unreflective. On July 14, 1789, for example, as Parisians stormed the Bastille, Louis XVI's diary records only a single word: "Rien!" (Nothing!) In the final weeks just before the October Revolution, Tsar Nicholas II noted cloud formations, temperatures, subtle shifts in weather pressure. Queen Victoria kept diaries from the age of thirteen to eighty-two, but they're as interminable as her empire building, an endless litany of teas and ceremonies under damp English skies or hot colonial suns.

A whispered confidence from a writer's diary that was all the rage in my college years nagged at me. "The false person I had created for the enjoyment of my friends, the gaiety, the buoyant, the receptive, the healing person, always on call, always ready with sympathy, had to have its existence somewhere. In the diary I would reestablish the balance . . . I could let out my demons." The writer is novelist Anaïs Nin. If there was a single image that crystallized my troubled fascination with certain diaries, it was a famous photograph of Nin. Quiet as a geisha, her pale stockinged legs tucked beneath her, she sat inside a Brooklyn bank vault, the repository of her diaries. All around her were hundreds of diaries, those she'd kept from age eleven to woo her absent father and, later, other writers, including novelist Henry Miller.

What had confused me as a child at Osco Drug suddenly became horribly clear. Anaïs Nin, among the century's most commercially successful diarists, had created the spatial equivalent of the diary's lock and key. I thought it strangely redundant that she'd locked up not only her thoughts but the diaries themselves, a form that encourages such conscious secrecy. Staring at Nin's powdered mask of a face, I was reminded of the "pillow books," those small diaries which for centuries Japanese women tucked under their pillows, hidden from their husbands' eyes, as if anything near—or from—a woman's head should be kept hidden from others. Only in time would I learn that Anaïs Nin had a great deal to hide.

Hidden. My questions, still unanswered, were stored in the tiny notebooks I kept in my desk drawer. By the late 1970s, though, centuries of diaries were being published for the first time. Some were famous, like Virginia Woolf's; others unknown, like those of Caroline Fox, the chronicler of eminent writers. As centuries of voices surfaced—ambitious, doubting, testy, distracted, determined—so, with them, did a great deal of information from narrated lives. As a book reviewer, I noticed that while the clever Scottish-born Jane Carlyle, wife of the famous Victorian historian, never got out of a diary, she had a great deal to say about creative life. Studying her husband's creativity like a hawk, in her diary she revealed an outsider who wanted in. The huge sales of published writers' diaries underlined what had always been true: the hunger to find literary role models, writers rooted in daily life. If these diaries sold quickly, it reflected how many contemporary voices were keeping them, trying to find maps for their own work. It's no wonder that in the diary, the form most immune to revision and subtle self-flatteries, writers still continued to invent themselves.

Once the literature of the outsider, by the 1980s the diary was becoming mainstream. But it was what had long kept—and often continues to keep—the writing underground that interested me. The young Charlotte Brontë knew this all too well. In 1837 she wrote the Poet Laureate to ask if he thought her early verses were worth pursuing. "Literature cannot be the business of a woman's life, and ought not to be," was Robert Southey's stiff reply. Charlotte Brontë abandoned poetry, taking up prose instead. How many other gifted voices had wilted under less illustrious censure—disapproval from a spouse, mocking from unsympathetic friends, guilt induced by children? Often a diarist's own powers of self-censorship were enough to make others' chilly disapproval unnecessary. For those working in crevices of time, writing seemed just what others said it was: a hobby, not a vocation, a means of continual self-improvement.

"I would detest to set myself up as an author," Dorothy Words-worth wrote a friend. Yet recalling the hills on a moonless night, she confided to her journal, "It made me more than half a poet. I was tired when I reached home. I could not sit down to reading and tried to write verses but alas!" As she gathered gooseberries or planted her kitchen garden, her brother William freely read her journals. "She gave me eyes," he acknowledged. She also gave him poems. Dorothy possessed of the eye of a naturalist ("a perfect electrometer," Coleridge called it). All those notes she'd made on the spot, including that thankless host of daffodils which has become the bane of every schoolchild's rote memory, William first found in—and borrowed from—her journal. Under the damp slate roof of Dove Cottage, brother and sister were one writer split. In 1802, when William married, Dorothy stopped writing. She was thirty years old. She would live another fifty-two years. Her journal wasn't published until 1941. It has never since been out of print.

In time, I noticed a number of things about the diaries growing on my shelves. Leo Tolstoy had his wife, Sonya, keep a diary, which he alone read. Just decades later the husbands of Katherine Mansfield and Virginia Woolf netted steady royalties from their wives' literary diaries. What had happened so that rivals Woolf and Mansfield offered to exchange and review each other's diaries? What had changed so that the reading public wanted to read someone like Alice James, who never consciously intended to be a writer but whose diary still sells briskly?

Obviously, others were reading for the same information I wanted. They recorded favorite passages into their diaries, imitating the voices in stories of their own. In the process, the fabric of contemporary writing began to change. Novels and stories structured as diaries began to be published. A rich chorus of voices so sorely absent in my own childhood—Maya Angelou, Toni Morrison, Maxine Hong Kingston—would soon fill library shelves for others to find. In fiction, they seized the diary's forum for chronicling and championing the outsider—children, the elderly, the socially marginal trapped between cultures. Later, in memoirs, long-silenced voices were finally heard, providing information about diverse creative lives for whom language or lack of means had made diary keeping just another form of silence.

Writing, as Franz Kafka observes in his notebook, may indeed be "the axe that breaks the frozen sea within," but Katherine Anne Porter is probably closer when she warns, "I have no patience with this dreadful idea that whatever you have in you has to come out, that you can't suppress true talent. People can be destroyed; they can be bent, distorted and, all the philosophy to the contrary, we don't really direct our lives unaided or unobstructed." While I'd long admired Albert Camus' or Thomas Mann's journals for the insights into their novels, it was writers' diaries kept by women that explored the link between the work and the life. "You see for me—life and work are two things indivisible," Mansfield wrote. Unlike her, Henry James and F. Scott Fitzgerald began journals *after* becoming writers, their notebooks adjuncts to work to which they already felt entitled. I began to notice what women's diaries said that others didn't.

"There's no doubt in my mind that I have found out how to begin (at 40) to say something in my own voice," Virginia Woolf wrote, "and that interests me so that I feel I can go ahead without praise." A beginning at forty: a revelation in a writer's diary.

And from Katherine Mansfield: "To be a writer and alive is enough." The razor's edge of possibility in life and writing. "There is no feeling to be compared with the joy of having written and finished a story. I did not sleep. There it was new and complete." Had those words ever appeared before in a woman's diary and been about a story, not just a newborn child?

In the search for creative blueprints, both these writers read the diaries of those who preceded them. Just as Alice Walker would later read Woolf's diaries, so Mansfield and Woolf read the diaries of

George Eliot, Dorothy Wordsworth and Alice James. Searching for patterns, some private creative code that corresponded to one deep inside themselves, they looked for clues these earlier voices had left. As May Sarton notes in *Journal of a Solitude*, "How one lives as a private person is intimately bound into the work." In these diaries the link between the fabric of the life and the work is studied like a puzzle by the writers themselves and by the generations of readers and writers they've spawned.

*D*iaries also chart the underside of a writer's life—the slow drain or premature killing of talent, the shadow of neglect, the chill of self-censorship. While the price of collaborative creativity was high for Sonya Tolstoy, in the case of Marjory Fleming, the seven-year-old Scottish diarist who became the favorite of Mark Twain and Robert Louis Stevenson, talent was simultaneously encouraged and trained out of her from the start. Overshadowed within a writing family, Alice James used a diary and illness as claims to specialness. "Her tragic health," Henry James noted, "was the only practical solution for the problem of life."

Some doubt wormed its way in my mind as I read passages in many of these diaries. An echo. It was the phrase that had sent my questions underground for years. I'd first heard it in college and later as an injunction uttered with tight, practiced smiles by mentors. It was Yeats's uneasy bargain: writers are "forced to choose perfection of the life, or of the work." Wasn't this the cautionary lesson of so many early diaries—the choice had always been for the perfection of the life. Sonya Tolstoy birthing the ninth of her children while trying to write stories; Anaïs Nin, unsolicited, giving Henry Miller her only typewriter when his broke.

I noticed something as I returned to these diaries anew. It was precisely such details, the rich texture of daily life, that infused so much of the fiction women were writing from the 1980s on. Like hidden currents, the two forms—diary and fiction—came together in a creative confluence. Writers like Toni Morrison and Alice Munro began mining in fiction the diary's interior life. The life rhythms the diary had long recorded—continuities of birth, marriage, parenthood; discontinuities of divorce or death—were steadily finding their way into first-rate fiction. As a genre, the diary was often thought minor, but as Alice Walker or Amy Tan revealed in novels, its subject matter was not. From Doris Lessing's *The Golden Notebook* to Carol Shields's *The Stone Diaries*, novels structured as diaries hooked a reading public that believed the material was somehow more truthful—an echo of their own diaries' stories.

A long history of disapprobation has shadowed that creative truth. Early in one of the surviving diaries her husband didn't burn, Jane Carlyle noted, "I remember Charles Buller saying of the Duchess of Praslin's murder, 'What could a poor fellow do with a wife who kept a journal but murder her?' " Indeed, even posthumously, diary keeping is often a dangerous business—Henry James destroyed his copy of his sister's diary; Marjory Fleming's Victorian editors added a sentimentally pious overlay to her diaries; Katherine Mansfield's husband, John Middleton Murry, edited and rearranged scraps of her journals, carefully crafting an image of her as a tragic artist, a cult image that often overshadowed the work.

I was still haunted by those who never got out of a diary. While few writers have faced Anne Frank's brutal restrictions—and certainly all lived longer—in the end, many an early writer's reputation rests on a single legacy: a diary. In vain we hope someone will find a yellowing bundle of poems by Dorothy Wordsworth, or unearth the sharply observed novel Jane Carlyle's talent promised, or the psychological novella Alice James seemed destined to write. Perhaps even a comedy of manners, a domestic farce, by Sonya Tolstoy, whose journals were as epic as her husband's. It is not to be. Not for any of these first voices. For them, clever and sharp-eyed, their creativity remains stubbornly trapped in the possessive case: sister of, wife of, mother of. Well aware of such problems for future writers, Katherine Mansfield wrote, "I am a writer first & a woman second," a stark echo of Charlotte Brontë's "I am not a man nor a woman but an author."

Was all that fine observation wasted? Mere notes, personal jottings, private musings? Creative compromises—half diary, half sketches? "I am 33. Yet I'm only just beginning to see now what it is I want to do," Mansfield noted in her journal. "It will take years of work to really bring it off . . . How unbearable it would be to die—leave 'scraps,' 'bits,' nothing real finished." If diaries are a way of beginning for a writer, they're also a way of not venturing out and finishing a work independent of a diary. Yet the fascination of writers' diaries is the role they play in charting the fluctuations of creative life—not if, but *how* to work. "It strikes me that in this book I practice writing," wrote Virginia Woolf. "I daresay . . . I shall invent my next book here."

Struggling to transform "this loose drifting material of life" in her writer's diary, Woolf observed, "I write variations of every sentence; compromises; bad shots; possibilities; till my writing book is like a lunatic's dream. Then I trust to some inspiration on re-reading; & pencil them into some sense . . . I press to my centre. I don't care if it's all scratched out. And there is something there." If the diary gave her and others a certain stylistic freedom and immediacy—the shock of the telling detail, the thumbnail sketch, the honing of craft—more important, it helped her move from private to public life as a writer. In helping her to train her eye, to form opinions and to imagine an audience wider than herself, Woolf, like Mansfield, shifted from the diary to reviewing. Like many writers since, she transformed her internal censor into a paid public critic. It was not an effortless task. Wrestling with the inner voice that whispered, "Never let anybody guess that you have a mind of your own," Woolf wrote. "Had I not killed her she would have killed me . . . plucked the heart out of my writing."

How many writers, casting a nervous side glance at fame, secretly contemplate their diaries being published? If over the centuries the diary has helped writers discover the *author* in *authority,* confronting the *public* in *publication* still remains an issue for many. In a scene in *The Importance of Being Earnest,* Oscar Wilde struck at the paradox of diary keeping: the simultaneous instinct to be secret and revealed. "Do you keep a diary?" a male companion asks a diarist seated at her writing desk. "I'd give anything to look at it. May I?" Quickly covering its pages, she replies, "Oh, no. You see, it's simply a very young girl's record of her own thoughts and impressions, and consequently meant for publication. When it appears in volume form I hope you will order a copy." If Alice James, Virginia Woolf, Katherine Mansfield and Anaïs Nin all imagined their diaries being published late in life or after their death, May Sarton wrote hers intentionally with publication in mind. Chronicling stages in a lifetime—success at thirty, solitude at fifty, fame at seventy—she brought the diary full circle, back to its original seventeenth-century aim: as a record of conscience and confession.

A vexing question persists: Is what we read in a diary always true? Often using a diary when upset, is a writer more likely to exaggerate a mood, nurse a slight? In her own diary Joyce Carol Oates writes, "We don't think of ourselves in the past tense: we are always present tense: to consciously record the past is thereafter to invent a self to perform in it, consciously and unconsciously—that's where the artifice comes in." Certainly, the posthumous publication of Anaïs Nin's "unexpurgated" diaries set in motion the slow striptease of private revelation, foreshadowing the late twentieth century's lust for public confession.

Today, that paradox thrives in a vast public forum. If nineteenth-century diarists struggled against an erasure of the self, late in twentieth-century life we're witnessing nothing less than a national obsession with it. On talk shows the competition is stiff to reveal the very secrets once so zealously locked away in diaries. And here finally is its wronged heart, the diary as grievance and grudge, a silent publicity campaign for the self. Nin's diaries are often cited for encouraging the worst legacy of diary keeping—its capacity for self-absorption, sloppy writing and confession. Where is the line between exhibitionism and exposure? Unlike a novel, the published diary forces the reader to judge the writer's life as well as the work— ironically, the very fate that has kept many stuck in the safety of a diary in the first place.

"Whom do I tell when I tell a blank page?" Virginia Woolf asked "the blankfaced old confidante" of her diary. Whom is she speaking to? Herself. And to generations of readers and writers searching to map their own writing lives. Our pleasure is watching writers use the diary as a testing ground for talent. After sketching part of a short story, Katherine Mansfield disparages, "Of course I *can't* write that. I'm surprised to have made such a crude note. That's the raw idea, as they say. What I ought to do, though, is to write it *somehow*, immediately, even if it's not good enough to print." Across London that same year, Virginia Woolf wrote, "It is worth mentioning for future reference, that the creative power which bubbles so pleasantly on beginning a new book quiets down after a time, & one goes on more steadily. Doubts creep in. Then one becomes resigned. Determination not to give in, & the sense of an impending shape keep one at it more than anything."

For most of us, if forced to choose between *To the Lighthouse* and volume three of Woolf's diary, which chronicles the writing of that novel, the choice would be easy. The diary is a sketch to the novel's final portrait. But it is the raw nerve of creativity that keeps us reading the diary over and over. Not every diary in this book is in itself great literature, but each sheds light on what goes into the making of literature, into the forging of a creative life. While Woolf's father, for example, declared Marjory Fleming a child prodigy in his *Dictionary of National Biography*, a seven-year-old diarist cannot be judged before her talents fully ripen. But her diary tells us better than any novel how early on a creative voice becomes inhibited. It's a mistake, though, to fix her or Alice James's diary, with its protective camouflage of illness, as a nineteenth-century phenomenon. Sonya Tolstoy's diaries still warn of the danger of abrogating one's creativity.

Today, diaries reflect the fragmented, caregiving lives of both sexes. Virginia Woolf's observation in *A Room of One's Own*, "for women have sat indoors all these millions of years, so that by this time the very walls are permeated by their creative force," remains as much a working metaphor as ever for *anyone* whose voice has still to emerge from a diary. To predict the future of fiction itself is to agree with her that much of its raw material still "lies in old diaries . . . in the lives of the obscure."

As the planet spins toward the millennium, diaries will probably be a constant in the struggle for privacy in a world wired for public information. And as long as there are diaries, there will be people reading them, searching for clues from narrated lives. Into the next century, writers will still eavesdrop on Sylvia Plath as she asks her notebook, wondering if she'll get through all the writing tasks she's set for herself that morning, "Will it come and will we do it? Answer me, book."

1

THE
SHADOW WRITERS

I too am here.

—JANE CARLYLE, *letter,* 1835

Marjory Fleming sketched by Isabella Keith.
(The Kirkcaldy Museum)

*O*n an unseasonably mild afternoon late in the summer of 1809, a six-year-old child with cheeks like mumps sat with her older cousin on a ferry bound for Edinburgh. Cutting across the Firth of Forth, they were making the final seven-mile voyage to the Scottish capital, having traveled from the small town of Kirkcaldy earlier that morning. Shortly after setting sail, Isabella Keith lent young Marjory Fleming her "little glass," a pocket telescope that would help her look back as her native shores receded by the mile. Scanning the brittle blue sky, the tiny brass telescope swung back for a closer view. On that afternoon twenty-two-year-old Isabella wore a high-waisted Indian muslin dress the color of summer wheat. Marjory's coat was gray. To the naked eye, the cousins were no different from scores of other well-heeled young females—possessed of straight teeth, semicorrect French—girls who counted off the calendar in the X of a cross-stitch. But this journey, begun on a clear summer's afternoon, would forever change their fate. Crossing more than a calm patch of sea, they were each beginning an inward voyage that by its end would leave one of them strangely famous, the other languishing in the cool shadows of silence.

The Edinburgh awaiting the two cousins at the other end of their ride was a city galvanized by books. Inspired by the ideals of the American and French revolutions, it was witnessing the last burst of the Scottish Enlightenment, with its belief in the perfectability of the mind. Edinburgh at the start of the nineteenth century had a passion for print, just as the twentieth century later would for information. Booksellers, printers and binderies had long crowded its maze of streets. By 1809 it was a city that smelled of paper. Twelve paper mills operated in Edinburgh alone.

Supplying books for the English market, Edinburgh quickly became Britain's printing center, a city spawning atlases and dictionaries. Here the *Encyclopaedia Britannica* was born, its volumes inching from A to Z, coding the recent revolution in knowledge— philosophy, law, medicine, science. Standing in the city's heart, it was said, one could greet "fifty men of genius and learning by the hand." Lending libraries and literary clubs shot up like wild heather. In 1802 three acquaintances of Marjory's mother had founded the *Edinburgh Review*. Its rival, *Blackwood's Magazine*, later published George Eliot's first words, as well as work of Isabella's future husband, a shy naturalist who wrote brilliantly on the world's most exotic fauna without ever leaving Scotland's shores.

For some, it was an era of possibility and potential. And with Isabella Keith at her side, Marjory Fleming was sailing straight into it.

Seated next to the cousin she'd known barely a month, Marjory squirmed on the hard ferry bench. Her coat made her itch, its stiff collar an "abomination." A knotted napkin full of stale crusts for the gulls sat at her side. As the ferry sliced through slate-dark waters, she knew that in Edinburgh Isabella planned to teach her how to use "semicolings and commoes." Her penmanship was still miserable, easily filling a page with just ten words. The pale older cousin, though, had other plans for the words that tumbled faster than Marjory's scrawl could catch. Isabella prized this child. In taking Marjory to Edinburgh, Isabella would have a respite from caring for her youngest brother. John Keith was a mute. Isabella was keen to coax her small cousin, who at six was still all instinct and improvisation, an explosion of a child whose speech often broke into couplets and perfect rhyme. Just as her own once had.

In leaving Kirkcaldy, Marjory had left behind far more than doting parents and two older siblings. She'd left behind the possibility of being ignored, overshadowed by a new infant sister. In the three weeks Isabella had spent at the Flemings following the christening of their fourth child, she'd immediately been struck by Marjory's quick, sassy intelligence. "I never read Sermons of any kind but I read Novelettes" was Marjory's staunch maxim. Isabella noticed that the six-year-old girl spent as much time in the family's library as playing outside on the knoll of a garden that sloped to the sea. For hours she'd vanish to the ground-floor bookseller, watching "Mr. Parcels," as she called him, wrap books destined for India or distant Scottish shores. The Flemings were a family of avid readers. The birth of a fourth child, though, had taxed the mother's already faint health, and Mrs. Fleming accepted her niece Isabella's offer to watch over the Flemings' most willful but gifted child. James Fleming, an accountant, sanctioned the decision. He was all too aware that his daughter shot to the window whenever the mail coach stopped near their three-story house, bringing news of the world to all-too-quiet Kirkcaldy.

Over the centuries, the tiny linen-manufacturing town had bred its share of eccentrics and geniuses. All had left Kirkcaldy, hungry for wider glory. Living a few doors down from Marjory's High Street house, Adam Smith had wandered Kirkcaldy's sandy shores in his nightdress thinking out *The Wealth of Nations*, his treatise on free-market economy. Architect Robert Adam, the innovative city planner, had been born here, as had the inventor of Standard Time. Like them, Marjory Fleming willingly left behind its quiet cobbled streets, its sandy causeway and ancient graveyard on a hill. Isabella had thought it a shame to ignore a child who'd learned to read by three, the same child she now watched tossing stale crusts to the gulls that trailed lazily behind the ferry.

It would be two years before Marjory Fleming returned to Kirkcaldy. Between 1809 and 1811 Isabella alone noticed as Marjory's hair shaded from auburn to a deep chestnut, her handwriting shaped itself from a looped scrawl to lines as thin as the cut of ice skates. In Edinburgh, Marjory was about to find a life of "perfection," two years, as she'd note in her journal, of "quiet, friendship, books."

Waiting for her at 1 North Charlotte Street were her mother's widowed sister and five clever cousins. Also waiting were three copybooks, their watermarked pages as yet unruled by Isabella's hand. The exercise books, initially meant to guide penmanship, caught instead the first stirrings of a young mind hungry to be released. From 1810 on, Marjory underwent a curious seachange, forsaking children's books for adult ones: Swift, Gray, Burns, Shakespeare. By page fourteen of her journal, she'd record reading Pope; two pages later, she began writing in rhymed verse. A full poem "by the author MF" appeared soon thereafter. In a single year, spurred by Isabella, she'd write 9,000 words, 560 lines of poetry, including a 208-line poem celebrating the life of Mary Queen of Scots. By the time she finally returned home, the cool feel of paper was as natural and necessary as her own breath.

Half a century later, Marjory's story would be stocked in countless Victorian homes, her journals prized by Robert Louis Stevenson. Mark Twain, hailing the mix of "sunshine and thunderstorms," applauded her pluck, the scrappy opinions "every time her pen takes a fresh breath." The poet Swinburne composed an elegy. Hers became the youngest portrait in the *Dictionary of National Biography*, the entry written by its editor, Leslie Stephen. In 1889, as his own daughter, the future Virginia Woolf, hid her first words from her father's prying eyes, he focused on Marjory Fleming. Her journals, he wrote, "show singular quickness, vivacity, and humour, while there is no trace of the morbid tendency too often associated with infant prodigies . . . Her life is probably the shortest to be recorded in these volumes, and certainly she is one of the most charming characters."

Over the next century and a half, though, hers would be a story as wildly jumbled as a child's telling, as curiously distorted as Marjory's own tortured spelling. But behind it lies yet another story: the shadows haunting the corners of creative life—writers of secret diaries, lost letters, manuscripts shelved or hidden deep in drawers. For every diary that survives by stealth or stubborn good luck, there are centuries of voices that have been lost forever. They are the shadow writers—male and female, white and black—voices beat back in the throat. Slave narratives copied out by Quakers or abolitionists whose names appeared on book covers instead. Stories lost because a sheet of writing paper, like salt or shoe leather, was a luxury. Thousands for whom X was a name, a canceled life, signing away its testimony. Stories told into the air, lost as hands stitched or scrubbed or sorted for a living. Stories quietly fading in those who'd lost a continent and, with it, the confidence of an old culture transplanted into the new one that feared its otherness. Words burned by private or public hand. Moments of terrible beauty or grief memorized instead, no trace left of how a voice might have become itself simply by sitting in a quiet room.

For every known story of a writer's life, there is the echoing silence of thousands of others. Over the centuries, many found darkly ingenious outlets for creativity. In China, knot making was perfected as an art, the knots as tight as silenced voices. In Japan, tiny pillow books were hidden under heads at night, safe from other eyes. In the Americas, poems were sealed up in convent walls or sung away as gospel hymns. For much of the world's populace, it would take hundreds of years before their stories surfaced in their own voices. And when they did, it was often first under pseudonyms: from Harriet Ann Jacobs's *Incidents in the Life of a Slave Girl* to George Eliot at the height of her fame. Only in the twentieth century would writers long hidden finally surface, triggering in turn a whole chorus of new voices.

Before then, in a silent creative underground, countless private diaries were kept. Among them was the one Marjory Fleming was soon to start at Isabella's insistence. But on that strangely windless afternoon, as Edinburgh's craggy silhouette finally reared into view, Isabella had no clue that items stored in Marjory's neatly packed trunk—books, a garnet necklace, a child's teacup—would one day be behind thick museum glass. No clue that the writing she was soon to oversee would be preserved in one of the world's great libraries.

In 1809, as the ferry slowed its sail into the port of Leith near Edinburgh, Isabella Keith's destiny was also fixed. The clever older cousin whom Marjory called "beautious Isabella" was still unmarried at twenty-two. Hers was a wintry beauty, the dark hair and pale skin irredeemably plain at other times. Unlike her spoiled, vain older sister, Agnes, Isabella was a fierce reader "always in her room writing." In taking on Marjory's education, Isabella had assumed her social duty guiding a mind other than her own. But being a creative spur took its own form of genius. Like centuries of talented lives, invisible or unsung, hers was a creativity that would spend itself in service to others' gifts—a shadow writer to famous ones. "*I* too am here," later lamented her fellow gifted Scot, Jane Carlyle, wife of the famous historian. For them, diaries became the literature of interrupted life, thoughts scribbled in scraps of borrowed time.

Borrowed time, two summers of it, was all Isabella Keith and

Marjory Fleming had. For Isabella, taking Marjory to Edinburgh was an experiment of sorts. It gave her the freedom to shape and guide a child not her own, a six-year-old girl with a small obstinate mouth and deep-set hazel eyes. A free hand to shape the very image of Isabella's own younger self—before her writing needed to be hidden in locked diaries, and politeness became a catch in the throat. At six Marjory still hadn't learned to hide her gifts. Unlike the cousin she already called Isa, Marjory was fully at war with those activities that kept eyes downcast—intricate needlework or watercolors no one would see.

Stepping off the ferry, Isabella gripped her young cousin's hand tightly in her own. On the pier, waiting for their trunks, Isa still held on to the small hand. An instinct, all thrill and fear, that this child, like a candle or anything that burned too brightly, should not be left unattended.

$\mathcal{T}$he Edinburgh that Marjory Fleming first saw with Isabella Keith was a burgeoning stage set of a city soon to be known as the Athens of the North. Rotundas, mini Parthenons, domed roofs glinting copper-green, were the signature architecture of Europe's newest intellectual capital. From its seven hills surveyors planned bridges, drained bogs, mapped quarries for the whinstone that paved its new streets. Edinburgh was bursting at the seams. The population that would reach over 100,000 by 1811 had long been concentrated in the city's congested late-medieval center, a sooty maze of cramped, winding alleyways thick with taverns. Like a clenched fist relaxing its grip, fingers of new construction fanned at the base of its rocky hill, opening out into New Town.

Isabella Keith's family, like much of Edinburgh's professional classes, had recently settled in New Town, a grid of Georgian squares just north of the center. Home to many of the city's 2,000 lawyers and 1,200 university staff, New Town had become the city's new cultural seat. Up and down George Street wandered learned amateurs and ministers creped in black, their hands slicing the air, debate style. The city, cut off from the Continent by the Napoleonic Wars, had become a haven for cultural exiles. As Napoleon plundered Europe, invading Austria and divorcing his unfaithful Josephine, Edinburgh was growing into a city of instruction: voices thundering from pulpits, echoing off walls in its famous medical school.

Instruction had brought Marjory Fleming to 1 North Charlotte Street, the Keith family home, poised on the edge of Charlotte Square, New Town's centerpiece. The neighborhood was an oasis of greenery rimmed by three-story houses, the facades' classical restraint broken only by a frieze or occasional sphinx. On their carriage ride to Isabella's house, Marjory had taken in the astonishing evidence of Scottish drive: banks easily mistaken for churches, statues lauding individual achievement. Cast in bronze and marble, the rewards of hard work were plain even to a child's eye. So too the city's restless energy, which was curiously like her own. Edinburgh was in the final flowering of the Scottish Enlightenment, the Age of Walter Scott, the novelist, publisher, national and literary promoter who'd figure so strangely in Marjory's story.

One North Charlotte Street was a hive of activity. In the house that smelled of lemon wax and woodsmoke, cousins studied medical texts while Aunt Marianne let canaries fly free as she read. The Keith household was a child's paradise, harboring a pet monkey, two turtledoves, six canaries, two green linnets and a dog named Help. There were no siblings to compete with, only six grown cousins from whom to learn. Maidie, as they called her, quickly flourished in adult company. "This is the first time I ever wrote a letter in my Life," she wrote in her first note home. "Miss Portune a Lady of my acquaintance praises me dreadfully. I repeated something out of

Swift and she said I was fit for the Stage . . . This horid fat Simpliton says that my Aunt is beautiful which is intirely impossible for that is not her nature."

Marjory's tart tongue delighted and horrified the Keith household. Honesty was not always the best policy. Girls her age chattering in the square reminded her of a pig squealing "under the painful necessity of putting it to Death." By contrast, "I am very strong & robust & not of the delicate sex, not of the fair but of the deficient in looks." With eyelids swollen like bee stings, she'd long grown accustomed to hearing the dubious praise that her upper arms were her best feature.

But from the start the Keiths, especially Isabella and her mother, saw beyond the casual accident of genes. Precocity ran deep on their side of the family, a mysterious mental ore. (At nineteen months Marjory's brother William recited verses in public.) In childhood, Marjory's aunt and mother had been encouraged in their intellectual bent by their surgeon father. Confident of Marjory's gifts, Isabella and her mother tucked her into their crowded, ambitious household. Provincialism, they felt, had trapped Marjory's mother, dooming her to hours of quiet teas with dour Presbyterians, women with chins like soft cushions. In Edinburgh, Marjory inherited the Keiths' first-rate library, which Isabella set her free to explore. For the first six months she pillaged its shelves with the same abandon that she dug worms from the garden to feed the linnets. By her first winter she'd committed pages of poetry to memory.

Just before her seventh birthday Marjory began keeping a diary: a forum for her talent as well as for her self-improvement. On its first page she scribbled, "Isabella teaches me everything I know and I am much indebted to her, she is learned witty & sensible." A routine was quickly set up between ten and two. Unrepentant in her horror of math, which she called a "wretched plague," Marjory devoured literature and history. Isabella taught her pupil the story of

Mary Queen of Scots. Within a year Marjory's imagination would recast it into the first of two long historical poems.

In 1810 a child keeping a private diary was rare. Originally intended as a letter journal in lieu of letters home, Marjory's diary soon became something invaluable in itself—a way to trace the growing awareness of her inner life. Words and character were one. Sitting on a small oak stool, journal in lap, Marjory wrote as Isabella sat nearby, often sketching her—the small head bent forward, the bright red shoes still under a white hem. At first Marjory jotted anything that came into her head: yearning to go to London, wanting to see her first play. "Macbeth is a fearful play," she wrote. "I hope I can be content without going." Gray's poetry was jumbled together with a memory of the night before—Isabella suffering a toothache, walking ghostlike in her pale nightgown, "enough to make a saint tremble and me quiver." Within a month of her starting a diary, whatever she was reading began shaping her own pages. "This address I composed myself & nobody assisted me," she declared over and over. Quietly watching Marjory's creativity ferment, Isabella soon began saving the journals, sending letters of her own about Marjory's progress to the Flemings instead.

Since her father visited once and her minister uncle lived nearby, Marjory didn't miss family. Allowed to stay up late reading Gothic novels, she often slipped "into a bed where Isa lies and to my questions she replies, corrects my faults improves my mind." As the two cousins slept head to foot when visiting others' homes, Marjory wrote her journal upside down for Isabella to read. Or noting how on country walks Isabella spiritedly leapt over stone walls, she wrote the entry sideways. Frequent visits to Ravelston, the Keith family's country house, had deepened her love of nature. "I like loud Mirement & laughter. I love to walk in lonely solitude & leave the bustel of the noisy town behind me & while I look at nothing but what strikes the eye." That eye delighted in recording earthly pleasures—

light angling through a canopy of oaks—and at night her ear listened to the swish of copper beech, the same sound as grown-ups' dresses trailing across bare wooden floors. In her journal she also caught the stir of the city: an exhibition of Scottish paintings, celebrations of the King's jubilee, fireworks pinwheeling nightly over Edinburgh.

The world Marjory saw outside her window was far more complex than it appeared. Her future champion, Robert Louis Stevenson, explored its darkest side in his most famous novel, recasting his native Edinburgh as London in *Dr. Jekyll and Mr. Hyde*. In 1810 Edinburgh still had a split personality. While New Town had absorbed professionals like the Keiths, the city also harbored a permanent underclass. Inside its sooty, fog-bound center, houses tilted over crooked passageways, the poor and lower middle classes sharing a common stair. Typhus and smallpox menaced. Everywhere children worked. Those lucky enough to attend school had only four days off a year. As Marjory noted repeatedly in her journals, Isabella was well aware of Edinburgh's social miseries. From the start she made her young cousin conscious of the responsibility of gifts. "I must begin to write serious thoughts as Isabella bids me," Marjory wrote. "I am thinking of how I should improve the many talents I have. I am very sorry I have threwn them away, it is shocking to think of it when many have half the instruction I have."

Inside 1 North Charlotte Street as clocks ticked, the hours regulated in quiet study, a question hovered: Why bother at all? In 1810 one out of six children died before reaching a first birthday. One out of every hundred women died in childbirth. But another mortality shadowed countless nineteenth-century households: the slow suffocation of creative talent. "Genius is a useless and dangerous endowment, which takes [girls] out of their natural state," opined an education book popular in Isabella's childhood. In 1802, a year before Marjory's birth, a published newspaper letter complained:

I am married to a learned wife, and have the misfortune to feel that this very circumstance is a perpetual source of vexation, and may in the end lead to my ruin . . . My wife, instead of attending to domestic concerns, is surrounded by wits. She is a poetess, and spends most of her time composing, transcribing, and correcting. If I bring home a few friends to dinner, the conversation never turns upon mercantile affairs, which would best suit my guests and myself, but on profound topics of literature, which we do not understand.

Edinburgh booksellers' shelves were lined with volumes, their spines stiff with instruction: *The Female Guardian Designed to Correct Some of the Foibles Incident to Girls*, *The Female Mentor*, *Letters to a Young Lady Calculated to Improve the Heart*, Reverend John Bennett's *Strictures on Female Education*. Even the season's most hailed novel, *Self-Control*, published anonymously, was one Marjory noted and the unknown Jane Austen read with envy. Though it sold out within a month, its author, Mary Brunton, wife of an Edinburgh minister, was destined to die in childbirth.

Isabella's quick eye had noted how Marjory had already recorded her cousin James hissing at her, " 'Girl! Make less noise.' " As children in nearby homes stitched samplers praising thrift or fit jigsaw puzzles patterned on Exodus, Marjory poured over the *Newgate Calendar*, the notorious crime blotter, finding it "instructive and amusing." She was mesmerized reading about hangings and narrow prison escapes. Isabella gave her Scott and Shakespeare instead. Fired by the Enlightenment's passion for rational thought, Isabella saved her discipline for ideas as experimental as those of her brother, who told Marjory not to touch magnets during electrical storms. At seven she was poised on the cusp between childhood and her future destiny, an interlude as ripe with potential as the era itself. For this was the age of the genius and the amateur—mineralogists and minister poets strolling side by side. Only time would tell Isabella which her charge was—a genius or an amateur.

In 1810 a long review in the *Edinburgh Review* gave Isabella and its other 7,000 subscribers full license to cultivate a young diarist's mind. Lambasting the cautious author of *Advice to Young Ladies on the Improvement of the Mind*, its reviewer, Sydney Smith, wrote, "If you educate women to dignified and important subjects, you are multiplying, beyond measure, the chances of human improvement, by preparing and *medicating* those early [childhood] impressions . . . which, in the great majority of instances, are quite decisive of character and genius."

What simpler task than training a child who naturally pulled Burns off the shelves, stole from Pope, tried on scores of words instead of new dresses? Between 1810 and 1811 Isabella indulged Marjory's mind as others might sweets, quietly letting minor accomplishments like piano and drawing lapse. As Isabella lost herself in novels the size of her palm, Marjory wrote in the stir of busy rooms, her journal praised and shaped by others' eyes. From the start she wrote for an audience. Unlike thirty-four-year-old Jane Austen, who at that very moment paced her tiny Hampshire garden, nervous about first publication, Marjory never knew writing needed to be hidden when others entered a room.

"It is Malancholy to think, that I have so many talents," she wrote, "& many there are that have not had the attention paid to them that I have, & yet they contrive to [be] better then me." On long winter afternoons the exacting Isabella had finally found a way to check Marjory's notorious temper. She took away the diary. "I wrote so ill that she took it away and locked it up in her desk where I stood trying to open it till she made me read my bible. But I was in a bad humor." Whenever Marjory angrily ripped a page from her journal or threw books down a flight of stairs, Isabella had her consider the "great crime" she was committing against her own future. "I hope there will be no more evil in all my Journal," she wrote, fearing she might get boils like Job. At seven she was ever aware of a possible destiny she saw daily outside her window—the droves of hired governesses pacing Charlotte Square in their thin gray dresses, meek and silently mutinous.

"For my part I would be quite Impatient if I had a child to teach," Marjory confided. With only Marjory, Isabella was saved from the fate of nineteen-year-old Charlotte Brontë, who later rued in her teacher's journal, "If those girls knew how I loathe their company they would not seek mine so much as they do . . . Delicious was the separation I experienced as I laid down on the spare bed & resigned myself to the luxury of twilight & solitude." Isa Keith's patience, though, was legion and Marjory's journals are full of its praises. "I can never repay Isabella for what she has done," Marjory noted, "but by good behaveour."

In the Keiths' high-ceilinged house, where birds flew freely and the pet monkey scampered on shoulders, Marjory was still subject to Calvinist strictures of obedience. In 1810 children still learned the alphabet and catechism together, each new letter accompanied by a tiny sermon. With a tongue and a temper like Marjory's on hand, *d* for *damnation* was ever near. "I confess that I have been more like a little young Devil," she wrote after an outburst. "Isabella compels me to sit down & not rise till this page is done."

Isabella also struggled with Jekyll and Hyde parts of herself. Should she punish or praise a child who increasingly preferred novels to sermons, the thundering drama of the Old Testament to the pieties of the New? "My religion is greatly falling off," the seven-year-old noted, "but as for regaining my charecter I despare for it." Almost daily Marjory repented, transgressed again and continued writing. But a first diary's hidden agenda was slowly surfacing: a forum for self-improvement, less of talent than of a young girl's social behavior. Corrections of grammar soon became corrections of character. By the time she was eight, hesitations wormed their way into Marjory's diary. Unwittingly, Isabella Keith became the first of Marjory's long line of editors. The unblinking eye of criticism. She'd jot "Careless Marjory" in the torn margin of a page, or underline misspelled words in faint pencil. Isabella had given Marjory a journal to find a language for her feelings, aware that in mastering words Marjory was also learning the syntax of goodness. A quick study, she began editing herself. "I acknowledge that this page is far from being well written," she noted, wondering if Isabella was "not tired to death" with her. Marjory Fleming was discovering that every writer has a critic shadowing the shoulder. The drama of her journals is watching who won.

With sermons and instruction darkening all around her, she erupted in her journals—noting herself fidgety in church or staunch in her habit of late-night reading. "Isas health will be quite ruined by me it will indeed." She sprinkled maxims like holy water warding off evil. "We should get the better of our passion & not let them get the better of us." But on April 1, 1811, she couldn't resist grandly writing her older sister, "I am studying much at present and I hope improving my mind—a new cousin of mine offered me marriage." Isabella quickly wrote Marjory's sister that same day, "I cannot say she is in great beauty just now, as she has lost her two front teeth, and her continual propensity to laugh exhibits the defect rather unbecomingly." What Isabella had left out of all her letters, though, was the consequence of her own two-year bookish experiment. As Marjory would soon write the childless Isabella, "I love you . . . with respect due to a mother."

At the end of her Edinburgh stay, Marjory unknowingly tried Isabella's famous patience. At eight she'd discovered firsthand the glorious distractions of love. "A sailor called here to say farewell, it must be dreadful to leave his native country where he might get a wife or perhaps me." An exuberant flirt, she'd become "a loveress."

Isabella, whom Marjory had nicknamed "the Genius Demedicus" after a Medici statue of Venus, was quietly tested. To mention Burns in a diary had been fine, but dull, card-playing locals were quite another story. "In the love novels all the heroines are very desperate. Isabella will not allow me to speak about lovers & heroines," Marjory wrote, adding, "Love I think is in the fashion for every body is marrying." Not quite. Isabella, the coltish older cousin, was still always free on the Keiths' long music nights. No matter how thin the ribbons woven through her dark braided hair, or how luminous her gauze hems, intelligence was clearly a social gamble. "Isabella is always reading & writing in her room, & does not come down for long, & I wish every body would follow her example & they would get a husband soon enough." The child who only a year before had written, "I like to here my own sex praised but not the other," now confided, "Love is a very pathetic thing as well as troublesom & tiresome but O Isabella forbid me to speak about it." "Heroick love doth win disgrace is my maxim and I shall follow it for ever" Marjory jotted, unconvinced.

In mid-July 1811 she finally left Edinburgh, returning home. The baby sister whose christening had first brought Isabella to Kirkcaldy was now two. Just before departing, Marjory had left her journals with Isa. "I am now in my native land," she wrote shortly on her return. Her letters were often written in verse: "O Isa do remember me. And try to love your Marjory." But the clatter of mail coaches on High Street failed to bring Isabella's promised visit. Marjory, who'd grown "excessively fat and strong," was put on a diet. Gone were the long Edinburgh afternoons reading in high-backed mahogany chairs. No more days like the one walking in the country with Isabella as she named twin yew trees Lot and his wife. Marjory's father took over the education Isabella had begun, lessons lasting till eight at night. Kept in crevices of time, her journal was now exclusively used for writing poetry.

On September 11, 1811, Marjory wrote Isabella, "We are surrounded with measles at present on every side." Late in November she contracted them, recovered, only to be bedridden weeks later. Her hair was cropped. The doctor gave her sixpence for being a good patient. On a slate she chalked a poem, "Address to dear Isabella on the Authors recovery." Well enough to go downstairs, she recited Burns to her father. Four days later in the middle of the night, she woke, screaming, "My head, my head." On December 19, 1811, Marjory Fleming died. The cause was listed as "water in the head," meningitis complicated by childhood measles.

The family of surgeons hadn't been able to save Marjory, who died a month shy of her ninth birthday. A lock of her hair was snipped and nestled in her Bible, her bookmark suspended at David's lament for Jonathan. Her mother and aunt in time founded the Royal Society for Relief of Incurables. Her father, grief-stricken, never spoke her name again. "Her poor father unceasingly deplores his loss," Marjory's mother wrote Isabella. "I fear he idolised her too much and was too vain of her talents."

"I have all her writing," Isabella replied, "any of which or even her journals, much as I value all of them, if you wish for them I shall part with but only to her Mother will I ever relinquish the smallest trifle that ever belonged to her." Across the Firth of Forth, mother and cousin exchanged cool, grieving letters. How could it be otherwise? They'd lost the child who'd called each Mother. But it was Isabella, Mrs. Fleming wrote, who'd been "the constant theme of [Marjory's] discourse, the subject of her thoughts, and the ruler of her actions." Requesting Isabella do two watercolors of Marjory from memory, Mrs. Fleming copied out lines from a final poem, "O Isa pain did visit me. I was at the last extremity. How often did I think of you."

The long winter of 1812 gave Isabella Keith time to recall her young cousin: Marjory's whimsical misspellings—learning Swift "by hart" or "flea" the devil. How unripe gooseberries had made her "teeth water," or her ingenious logic in likening a sunset to a "vial of rose oil" or imagining a pineapple a "bright golden geniee." Isabella quietly rued how her own strictness had been a "painful restraint on my affections." But, she wrote, "it is foolish to harass myself with such regrets." Was it her imagination or had she trained the talent back inward? Caution and confession bred like germs late in Marjory's journal. What, after all, had prompted a scrappy, once confident eight-year-old to write, "I will never again trust in my own power. For I see that I cannot be good without Gods assistence. I will never trust in my selfe"?

Late in January 1812, as requested, Isabella sent the tidy parcel of Marjory's journals off to 130 High Street, Kirkcaldy, beginning the first leg of their long odyssey. An aging spinster sister, two men hungry for fame, a zealous widow and well-meaning ministers with locked safes—all would figure in the story. But for nearly half a century the journals sat undisturbed. In the interim, France erupted in civic revolution. Slavery was abolished in Britain. Charlotte Brontë published *Jane Eyre*. Queen Victoria took her first railroad journey. The telegraph system was established. And Marjory's journals waited, a lock of her hair pressed within. Like any curiosity—a minor ruin, a forgotten alphabet etched into the underside of a stone—they had a strange destiny awaiting them. The first was the simplest: they were found.

In 1858 Henry Brougham Farnie, a London journalist who wrote opera librettos on the side, visited his native Kirkcaldy. He was writing a book on Fife, searching for stories. On a quiet afternoon he entered the arched passageway to the Fleming household, probably on his way to tea with Elizabeth Fleming, the sister whose birth had made Marjory's Edinburgh sojourn possible. Marjory's parents were both dead; her brother William had died in India. Elizabeth Fleming was fifty-seven. In the same sitting room where Marjory had last recited Burns, Farnie was the first outsider to be shown her three journals. The clever Cambridge-educated Farnie realized his find. That same year, he published a story on Marjory's life in the *Fife Herald*. He quickly followed it with a booklet based on her life and journals, *A Story of Child-Life Fifty Years Ago*. In the flurry of interest in the "life of a clever little girl," no one noticed he'd subtly changed Marjory to Marjorie, or that he'd given the child diarist the nickname "Pet Marjorie."

Two years later, Farnie's small book landed on the cluttered desk of Dr. John Brown, a distinguished Edinburgh physician. Tired of treating dyspeptic stomachs and spots of gout, he sat in his gaslit Rutland Street study fueling literary ambitions of his own. He'd already published a collection of essays, including the popular "Rab and his Friends," about a doctor and a dog. In 1863, in the guise of reviewing Farnie's booklet on Marjory, Brown traveled to Kirkcaldy to meet Elizabeth Fleming. "I am more and more taken up with Marjorie, and I think I would like to see the originals," Brown wrote. "I do wish you would write me a long letter, telling me her story in your own words."

Who could resist a close friend of Thackeray's and Ruskin's, a mildly melancholic Scot with woolly muttonchop whiskers? Certainly not the aging Elizabeth Fleming. Bored by provincial life, she was thrilled to be wooed as if she still resembled her thin-profiled silhouette on the wall. The spinster studied Brown's thin lips pressed in determination, the eyes keen behind tiny oval glasses. On the spot she decided, correctly, that of the two men, Brown was destined to have the famous career in letters, Farnie to be remembered only as a librettist of light French operettas. She lent Brown the journals, which he whisked back to Edinburgh. In the neat hand that wrote prescriptions, the fifty-three-year-old Brown copied out Marjory's journals, poems and letters. He studied a specimen of her hair, comparing it with Isabella's two portraits of Marjory. His real interest, though, was the anatomy of her voice. In November 1863 he published a long biographical sketch of Marjory Fleming in the *North British Review*, soon issued as a separate book. By including twice as many excerpts from Marjory's journals as Farnie had, Brown raised the stakes considerably for his competitor.

Farnie immediately reissued an expanded edition. "Any further success the little book may enjoy," he flattered in his introduction, owed much to "the kind and genial service rendered by the distinguished author of *Rab and His Friends* who had so happily introduced it and its heroine to a wider audience." Feeling himself fleeced, in *his* next edition Brown spat, "I owe my introduction to Marjorie Fleming—but nothing more." His first edition of 15,000 copies had quickly sold out, spreading her fame—and his—from London to New York. In their feuding literary rivalry, Farnie and Brown parried insults in introductions to each new edition. Mocking Farnie's opportunism, Brown likened him to a shipwrecked fat man who as sailors ate pieces of him "insisted on having the first cut himself."

By 1864 Marjory Fleming had become a small industry.

The reviews were stellar. "Many of the extracts from her diary shew a wonderful precocity," the *London Review* noted. "A noble child-heart," the London *Sunday Times* wrote, "that will do the heart of man or woman to become acquainted with it." After her diary's long silence, the *Bristol Mercury* gushed, "Marjorie's fame will make a greater noise in the world than ever." What had the public on both sides of the Atlantic found so original in these two sketches of a child diarist? While the diary had appeared only in extracts, it was the first published record of what had haunted the century's two great poets, William Blake and William Wordsworth: the earliest stages of imagination. "Children at this age give us no such information of themselves," Coleridge had written while Marjory was busy keeping her diary. "There are many of us that still possess some remembrance, more or less distinct, respecting ourselves at six years old; pity that the worthless straws only should float, while treasures . . . should be absorbed by some unknown gulf into some unknown abyss."

*J*ust as the world was fascinated in 1829 when the first Native American, William Apes of the Pequot Tribe, published his autobiography, so in Fleming they were hungry for reports from the distant shores of childhood. For those weary of the alienating grip of the Industrial Revolution, there was something soothing about what they saw as nobler or purer imaginations. The young Keats had left no journal, nor had Blake or any of the geniuses who in their poetry hungered for the spontaneous imagination of childhood. The world would find in Marjory Fleming not the abstractions of Wordsworth's famous paradox "the child is father of the man," but a rare record of the first stirrings of a real child's voice. Marjory's story coincided with the explosion of diary keeping that had been ignited by the production of affordable pocket diaries. In 1864, as diary keeping became a more common rite of passage, especially for young girls, Fleming's story was still most popular with adults. In her brief life they saw a moral tale of imagination and everything that quietly sought to extinguish it.

"A great many authors have expressed themselves too sentimentally, I am studying what I like," Marjory had written, as if previewing what Farnie and Brown had in store for her with the "Pet Marjorie" craze. But there is another story behind it. In 1864, in his grief as a recent widower, Brown's brain had begun to stir. He knew that Scotland's most famous writer, Walter Scott, had indeed been a friend of Marjory's mother and aunt in youth, and had patterned settings in his Waverley Novels on details from Ravelston, the Keith country home where he and Marjory had each spent time. Brown, taken with Marjory's precocious "turn for expression, her satire, her frankness," concocted a sentimental and utterly false story, one that would eventually doom her diaries.

Using a single letter he'd received from Marjory's sister, in which Elizabeth Fleming mentioned an inscribed but lost book that was "a gift to Marjorie from Walter Scott," Brown spun a wild story. On a snowy November afternoon in 1810, according to Brown, a weary Walter Scott walked with his staghound Maida to the Keiths', a home he visited "almost every day, and had a key." He shouted for Marjory, and "in a moment a bright, eager child was in his arms." In Brown's story, Marjory had become Walter Scott's lucky literary charm, "Pet Marjorie," a child declaiming Shakespeare not for Isabella but at Scott's knee. This "overpowered him as nothing else did," Brown wrote of Scott, who trotted his "wee wife" everywhere before she returned to Kirkcaldy. Except for one inconvenient fact: Marjory never mentioned him, only his poetry, which she loved. Scott never mentioned her either. Not even in his letters when he was terrified his own children might die of the same measles epidemic that killed Marjory.

No one had bothered to notice that Scott's dog wasn't part of his household until six years later. Or that records showed there was no snow in Edinburgh all that November. But by 1864 the story of Marjory as "child genius" and muse to a greater literary talent was set. The moral of diary keeping was clear: creativity is something a young girl should never quite have on her own. As one London newspaper later wrote, "She was the delight of Walter Scott, who was so much attached to her that when he was weary with literary toil he would send for his favourite to amuse him."

Brown had a genius for timing in publishing. In *Marjorie Fleming* he tapped the very nerve of Victorian culture: the cult of the child. Crinolined readers wept over the young Jane Eyre or Dickens's wards and orphans, children cursed with stuttering poverty and social injustices. But how safe to ignore it as fiction. In Marjory's extracted journals they found a real child forever suspended in a summer's afternoon of creativity. They saw their own lost childhoods before creativity had been trained out of them and sexual expression politely channeled into archery or adult interest in photographing small girls. This, after all, was the Age of Alice. Like Lewis Carroll, Brown anticipated the Victorians' obsession with childhood and early death, which bordered on the erotic. In Brown's collected letters, published after his death, was one dated 1860, the same year before he discovered Marjory Fleming. In a letter to Miss Connie Hilliard, aged eight, Brown wrote his young correspondent: "and you know I MUST see your journal." A child's diary was a possible Wonderland of creativity. For in parents' eyes every child begins a genius; adulthood, most know all too well, usually brings other verdicts.

And what did it bring for others in Marjory Fleming's story? "I very often take my little glass and look over at Kirkcaldie," Isabella Keith had written Marjory in November 1811. The southern shore of the Firth of Forth hid Kirkcaldy from full view. But on cool, leaf-scattered days Isabella stood with her small telescope hoping to see Marjory "at play in the fields." The lens of her own social destiny finally came into focus in 1824. Isabella married at thirty-seven—a wild late-life love. Her husband, James Wilson, was a noted zoologist whose writing career she encouraged. She married into a family intimate with Coleridge and Wordsworth, a circle cultivated by her brother-in-law, *Blackwood Magazine*'s most influential, if controversial, critic.

Secluded in their house, Woodville, just outside Edinburgh, Isabella and James Wilson grew a garden lush as a rainforest, etched their initials on the dining room window, thrilled at their astonishing good fortune. "Wife and children! What strange words these seem to be when I think of my former self," Isabella's husband wrote her. Their two children pressed tiny hands against curio cabinets thick with collections of rare birds and boxes of insects. In a secret plan that would have delighted Marjory, Isabella's husband wrote their daughter "to put the grass with the glow-worms' eggs upon [the mantel]," so that they'd shimmer as a surprise for Isabella when he returned from a naturalist's expedition.

But by 1834 Isabella was nearly permanently "shut up in the dim chamber" of the sickroom. Complications from late pregnancies and possible contagion from her husband's low-grade consumption left her an invalid. She took in her husband's orphaned niece, Henrietta Wilson, to help with the care of her two small children. On long summer days, her duties over, Henrietta sat with Isabella. Like Marjory before her, Henrietta realized she was in the company of a superb mind, a woman thrilled to meet Wordsworth, whose portrait hung in the sitting room. With the same "zeal" Isabella showed for her husband's writing career, so, his biographer wrote, she passed on her "very superior understanding and accomplishments of a high order" to Henrietta. Isabella discussed books as Henrietta listened, quietly rearranging the spill of primroses on the invalid's night table.

Isabella Keith Wilson died in 1837, aged forty-nine. She never published a word. Well into the early twentieth century, though, sentences she helped shape were still being read—Marjory's, her husband's, and even the young Henrietta Wilson's. Publishing anonymously at first, Henrietta wrote four books, two published on both sides of the Atlantic. Isabella might well have predicted they'd be meditations on the domestic and the religious. When one's identity was conjugated in the possessive case—wife of, cousin of, mother of—where else was passion to go?

"I have often mused on the probable destiny of Pet, if she had been permitted to live," Henry Farnie wrote of Marjory, "and have arrived at the conclusion that she would have essayed literature in some branch." But, he rued,

> I have the idea, that the woman who has written books worthy of the world's reading—that every such one has lived in sadness and anxiety . . . Who shall doubt this who has read the sad inner-life of Charlotte Brontë . . . *Destiny* called Charlotte Brontë from solitude, from un-opportunity, from sorrow, called her to write. And write she did—she could not help it. So do I think that had Pet lived, her career might have been the same.

"I wanted to speak, to rise—it was impossible," Charlotte Brontë wrote in her journal in 1836, struggling with a teaching career. When finally earning her living by her pen, in her novels she gave voice to those, like herself, long invisible to the world: governesses, spinsters, children. Succeeding as a novelist, she had little need for a journal. Literary passion had its public outlet. Not that a diary's secrecy guaranteed talent's protection. On her eleventh birthday Louisa May Alcott was given a new diary. Her mother's inscription was as indigestible for the future author as the family's experimental diet of unripe apples. "Remember, dear girl," her mother wrote in the new notebook, "that a diary should be an epitome of your life. May it be a record of pure thought and good actions."

Communications. Expectations. Forwardness. Marjory Fleming's steady hand wrote these three words over and over toward the end of her journal. Isabella, no doubt in a fit of frustration, dictated them to the obstinate diarist one weary winter afternoon. Their choice was uncanny. For how one sees those three simple words—communications, expectations, forwardness—determines a writer's relation to the world. Should one seize or hide the talent; push it into the world or keep it locked in a diary? For Twain and Stevenson, the thrill of Marjory Fleming's journal was how she'd preserved the pluck. Till the end of her short life, her words continued to surface like great bursts of oxygen.

But fate is fickle. In 1880 the journals and Isabella's portraits were entrusted to a family friend in Edinburgh, the future Moderator of the General Assembly of the Church of Scotland. While charmed by Marjory's bragging, "I like sermons better than lectures," he locked them in his safe, treasured but obscured. In 1910 they traveled to London, where they sat in another minister's dark safe for twenty more years. In 1930 his widow began the campaign that Marjory's journals should join Scott's and Burns's papers in the National Library of Scotland. Before then a London publisher, working with the British Museum, published her full journals for the first time. In 1934, over a century after she wrote them, Marjory had her own words back as she'd written them. Her star, though, shone fitfully. The new set of reviews praising Marjory Fleming faded in that uneasy interval of peace between wars that Robert Graves called "the Long Weekend."

By the mid-1940s the world itself was darkened by shadows. And it would take the most famous young diarist of all to expose the creative legacy of diary writing. Off Amsterdam's watery maze of canals, a fourteen-year-old girl wrote in her red-plaid diary. Each night Anne Frank deposited it in her father's locked briefcase, safe from other eyes in the Secret Annex. A hidden diary in a hidden attic. In two years, between 1942 and 1944, she transformed her diary from a daily record to one documenting the record of her own developing voice. While she kept a separate journal for reading lists and one for short stories, in her diary her keen eye noted the small human foibles or unexpected generosity of eight people crowded into six rooms.

In her third to last diary entry, she reflected on a book—*What Do You Think of the Modern Young Girl?*—and on the irony of why she still needed to hide her diary. "I have one outstanding trait in my character," she wrote, "and that is knowledge of myself. I can watch myself and my actions, just like an outsider." But in the confines of daily life, "this 'self-consciousness' haunts me, and every time I open my mouth I know as soon as I've spoken whether 'that ought to have been different' or 'that was right as it was.' " In the secrecy of a diary Anne Frank was freed of her own self-censoring. In May 1944 she began to revise the diary, seeing it as source for a book she hoped to write, a book that might reach cities as far away as those on the family's map which marked the Allies' movements.

"I understand more and more how true Daddy's words were when he said: 'All children must look after their own upbringing,' " Anne wrote at the end of her diary. " 'Parents can only give good advice or put them on the right path, but the final forming of a person's character lies in their own hands.' " In her diary, its pages smoothed by her hands, Anne Frank left the world far more than a record of her own character. "I keep on trying to find a way of becoming what I would so like to be and what I could be, if . . ." its last entry read on August 1. *If.* On Friday, August 4, 1944, 10:30 A.M., Nazis stormed 263 Prinsengracht, arresting the Secret Annex's eight inhabitants, deporting them to Westerbork and, later, Auschwitz. Otto Frank's briefcase was used to carry away Nazi plunder. In their haste the Gestapo dumped the briefcase's contents onto the floor, the papers walked over, dismissed as worthless.

In the echoing silence of the Secret Annex's rooms, Miep Gies, Otto Frank's employee, salvaged Anne's diary and papers. Just as she'd helped hide the Annex's two Jewish families, so she now hid Anne Frank's diary. She locked it in her drawer, sealing it in silence as dark as the horror for which there are no words. Anne died in Bergen-Belsen two months before Allied troops liberated the camp. She was fifteen. Only Otto Frank survived. In 1945, on his return to Amsterdam, Miep Gies handed over the familiar plaid diary with its lock. It was, she told him, "the legacy from his daughter."

Alone, Frank read the diary his daughter had once carefully hidden each night in his briefcase. The margins were narrow, the pages dense with words. Her death confirmed by survivors, he read the words no one but Anne had seen. "I know I can write," she wrote on Wednesday, April 5, 1944. In his first-floor office, as he read, Frank learned what no one but Anne herself knew: she had decided to become a writer.

"I want to publish a book entitled *The Secret Annex* after the war," she'd written on May 11, 1944. In the final few months she had revised her diary, changing its style, deleting passages, adding others. By the time of her arrest she'd revised up to March 29, 1944, copying it onto loose sheets. In August 1945 Otto Frank began typing out Anne's words. The diary, later translated into fifty-two languages, is hauntingly suspended in a present tense of possibility. Like all great diaries, it illuminates the past while holding a lens to the future. In Anne Frank's *The Diary of a Young Girl*, a single voice forever reminds the world of the millions whose stories were silenced.

But even Anne Frank's complete diary wouldn't appear in its definitive edition until 1995. In it, a sharp-eyed teenager emerged from behind the familiar icon of hope. Anne's scrappier observations were no longer edited out or softened for public sentiment. Until then, in her most famous entry, "in spite of everything, I still believe that people are really good at heart," readers had found not just a portrait of a young girl but how the world needed to think about itself. In a diary whose writer had been silenced forever, the world projected its hopes, imagining her creative fate, the future books that might have lined shelves. Fifty years later, the world turned to another young girl's diary, that of a thirteen-year-old Bosnian caught in the crossfire of war. "I will try to get through all this, with your support," Zlata Filipovic wrote to the diary, whose international success saved her family. "You're going to be published abroad," she wrote in the diary's final entry. "Have a good journey into the world."

*H*ow odd that journey into the world for some. In the tiny sloping cemetery of Abbotshall, Kirkcaldy, leaves scatter in chill winds. Between ink-dark yew trees, tombstones mark lives lost at sea or in infant mortality, the headstones worn by harsh Scottish winters. Others stones have no names at all, the record of their lives unwritten by wind and sheeting rain. Along the narrow gravel path, toward the far edge of the cemetery, lies the grave of Marjory Fleming. The distant sound of the sea is as muted as the once famous praises of Twain and Stevenson. "Your note about the resemblance of her verses to mine gave me great joy," Stevenson wrote a friend, "though it only proved me a plagiarist." In the twentieth century, though, it is Marjory who still suffers from others' borrowings, contaminated by Brown's invented Scott legend.

From the cemetery's south gate the grave is easy to spot. It rises high amid the others, a sculpture of a child with a diary in her lap. Files of children from odd corners of the world, the vicar will tell you, often come to stare at the statue as large as themselves. They've first seen it in fading newspapers or in editions of Marjory Fleming's diary before it went out of print in the 1960s. Staring at the statue, they linger next to the solitary adult or two, curious how someone can settle so quickly back into the shadows.

Behind her grave, stacked like old library cards, are her two earlier headstones. The first is the plain slate slab erected by her family, bearing only her initials and dates. The second has fragments from her first public tribute. Its epitaph could have been Isabella's: "She continues her journal every day entirely by herself." But Scott's name looms as large as hers. Only the careful eye notices that Marjory's is misspelled.

Sonya Tolstoy on the eve of her wedding.
(Tolstoy State Museum)

2

THE
MARRIED MUSE

Why do you always, when you mention my name in
your diaries, speak so ill of me? Why do you want
future generations and our descendants to hold my
name in contempt . . . You promised you would
strike out the bad words about me in your diaries.
But you did not do it; [are you] afraid that your
glory after death will be diminished unless you show
me to have been your torment and yourself as a
martyr, bearing a cross in the form of a wife?

> — SONYA TOLSTOY, *letter* to Leo Tolstoy

Every man has the wife he needs. She, so I now see,
was the very wife I needed. She was an ideal wife.
. . . yet heathen as she is, she has in her the
possibilities of a Christian friend . . . Will it
develop in her? O Father, help her.

> — LEO TOLSTOY, *Diary*, the next day

All that Sunday afternoon and early into the evening, fits of weeping echoed throughout the Behrs household. Behind closed doors in the cramped Moscow apartment, family members nursed their own private sense of loss. The cause of this muted misery on September 23, 1862, wasn't a funeral but a wedding. In two hours the Behrses' middle daughter, Sonya, who had turned eighteen only the month before, was to wed her thirty-four-year-old suitor. But the sudden departure of this accomplished daughter, a girl partial to poetry and accomplished at Beethoven sonatas, was only part of the reason for tears. As the scheduled eight o'clock service neared, each family member was lost in private contemplation of the man she was about to marry.

Sonya's mother had known Leo Tolstoy since childhood. Only three years older than her future son-in-law, Lyubov Behrs still had the poised beauty that had first attracted Tolstoy when they'd played together as children. At nine Leo had fallen in love with her. In a fit of jealousy, he once pushed her off a balcony for talking to other boys, causing her to limp for a week. The episode, though, had long been forgiven. Still a close friend of Tolstoy's sister, Mrs. Behrs had long hoped that at least one of her daughters would marry the count who owned four estates totaling 5,400 acres. Her husband was less forgiving. The bearded, scholarly Dr. Behrs, physician to the imperial palace, had locked himself in his study. Suddenly indisposed, he'd only reluctantly sanctioned the marriage, still disapproving of how Tolstoy had flirted with, then bypassed, his eldest daughter, Lisa, whom custom dictated he should be marrying today.

As girls, the three Behrs sisters had spent hours in the sunless apartment divining their fortunes in the shapes of melting candle wax. Secretly, Lisa, Sonya and Tanya, the youngest sister, had all set their sights on the same man during the young count's frequent visits between 1856 and 1862. It was democratically mutual. "If ever I marry," Tolstoy told his sister, "it will be one of the Behrs girls." But by 1861 Lisa, passionate about philosophy, indifferent to children, had been eliminated as a candidate. Smiling, others noted, only contorted Lisa's face into "an unnatural" expression. On September 8, 1862, Tolstoy wrote in his diary, "My God! How beautifully unhappy she would be if she were my wife!"

The sister he had decided to marry instead was surrounded at that moment by kneeling women, pins tight between their teeth. Sonya, her eyes rimmed red, stood in the sheer tulle wedding dress as the needlewomen made their last-minute adjustments. Outfitted in a low-necked dress copied from a French original, she had piled her thick black hair high, crowning the long veil with fresh flowers. The most striking of the Behrs sisters, Sonya had large dark eyes, a wide full mouth and a twenty-inch waist. Intelligent but not intellectual, she read voraciously, wrote stories and by seventeen had already received her teaching certificate, passing the examination at Moscow University. Her essay had won first prize. But unlike her clever older sister, whom the family called "the scholar," Sonya had none of Lisa's emotional aloofness. Intense, sensual, often melancholic, Sonya, her father rued, "will never be completely happy." Yet it was precisely her passionate and willful temperament that Tolstoy sensed matched his own. Also, as he wrote, the hidden sensuality crackling through "the slim beauty of her figure," from the pale long neck to her thin wrists.

Leo Tolstoy had been Sonya's childhood hero: survivor of the Battle of Sevastopol, target of police searches for his writing, rescued from a firing squad by the Tsar himself. At eleven she recorded her first diary entry about the high-cheekboned, uniformed soldier whose epic travels and war sketches conjured up mystery and scandal. After one of his visits she tied a red ribbon around the mahogany legs of the chair he'd been sitting in. In late adolescence she copied sentences from his autobiographical novella *Childhood* and wore them tucked inside her chemise. While courted by the cadets and students who constantly filled the Behrs apartment, Sonya was fascinated by this man of paradoxes: a count with hands calloused from manual labor; a writer who'd already run afoul of the state censor; the owner of a 2,000-acre estate, Yasnaya Polyana; a teacher in the progressive school he'd established for the estate's peasants.

But on the eve of their wedding Sonya could not stop weeping. The reasons were as numerous as the wedding gifts that choked the apartment's narrow hallways. The latest incident had happened only hours earlier. Like all pious believers, Sonya was prey to superstition. Tolstoy's visit earlier that morning was an ill omen. Forbidden by custom to see the bride on the day of the wedding, he had nonetheless burst in, overwrought, demanding to talk to her alone. They sat down on the suitcases packed for the honeymoon. The shy dark-haired girl stared nervously at the bridegroom with his chestnut beard and piercing gray eyes: What now?

It had already been a week of extremes, seven nerve-racking days as dizzying as the mood swings that came upon her naturally. Only a week earlier, on September 16, Tolstoy had also burst into the Behrs apartment, thrusting a letter into Sonya's hand as she fetched a shawl. It was the marriage proposal he'd been unable to utter but to his private diary. "Will you be my wife? If you say *yes*, *boldly* with all your heart, then say it, but if you have the faintest shadow of doubt, say *no*. For heaven's sake, think it over carefully." How fitting that their fate be determined, as it would for the rest of their natural lives, by a sheet of writing passing from his hands to hers. Sonya, nearsighted, skimmed it in private and accepted at once. But now on their wedding day it was Tolstoy who was riddled with doubt. He tortured her with questions instead. Was *she* sure? Had her decision been too quick? Yet in his own diary he'd confessed, "On the wedding day, fear, distrust, and the desire to run away."

 he courtship had seemed so simple. On a visit to Sonya's grandfather the previous summer, August 1861, the Behrses had stopped at Yasnaya Polyana. The three sisters and their brother were ushered into a spare ground-floor bedroom. There were only three beds. Improvising one from an armchair, Tolstoy and Sonya stood quietly making her bed, the sheet billowing be-tween them. Two nights later, Tolstoy visited the Behrses. He found Sonya sitting alone in the game room, dressed in white with mauve ribbons streaming down her back. Wiping off the score chalked on the game table's green baize surface, he wrote a series of cryptic letters: *Y.y.&y.d.f.h.r.m.t.v.o.m.i.f.h.* Sonya stared at them as at a ouija board. Stumbling, but with his prompting, she guessed: "Your youth and your desire for happiness remind me too vividly of my incapacity for happiness." The guess was nearly right. Her family, he wrote in another abbreviated sentence, had mistaken his interest in Lisa. In her diary that night Sonya recorded that she had crossed over an invisible threshold. Years later, she recalled that summer, "living those last days of my girlhood with a particularly strange inner light."

The game table incident sat in Tolstoy's imagination for ten years. But like so much directly from their lives, it was grist for the fiction he wrote and she'd copy, offering suggestions. Tolstoy used it in *Anna Karenina* when his hero, Levin, proposes to Kitty. The novel also included the incident that had happened a week before the Tolstoys' wedding day. On September 17, the day after he proposed, Sonya celebrated the Russian tradition of her saint's name day. After the morning's festivities Tolstoy handed her a stack of notebooks. When she slipped into her room that night, her anticipated pleasure quickly turned to horror. Tolstoy had given the impressionable eighteen-year-old his bachelor diaries. A couple should have no secrets between them, he reasoned. She would never quite recover. "How stricken I was by those pages he insisted, in his excessive honesty, that I read," she recalled years later. "Wasted honesty!" The first diary entry by the man destined to become one of the world's greatest novelists began, "It's six days since I entered the clinic . . . I caught gonorrhoea where one usually catches it from." Whoring, gambling, flirting with women, among them her mother's friends, alternated with the diary's homilies on vanity and idleness. She scanned an entry for 1851: "I came to Moscow with three aims. (1) To gamble. (2) To marry. (3) To obtain a post." Most painful were the notations about a nameless peasant woman who had borne his child, both of whom awaited Sonya in her future home.

Reading her future husband's diaries with their moral somersaults—lust and sexual guilt, social depravity and Christian rectitude—she could only recall one of their first walks alone, which had begun their whole romance. "Do you keep a diary?" he asked. She had, since eleven. She had also finished writing a story called "Natasha," based on the idea of three sisters all in love with the same man. The middle daughter dutifully joins a convent so the eldest daughter can marry instead. On August 26, 1862, a month before their wedding, Tolstoy insisted she show him the story. Nervously,

Sonya handed over her notebook. The next day he confided he'd merely glanced at it. Years later, though, Sonya found in his diary what he'd really felt about his own thinly disguised portrait. "What force of truth and simplicity!" he'd written that same night. The story became the embryo for the Rostov family in *War and Peace*, its heroine, Natasha, patterned on a combination of Sonya and her spirited tomboy sister, Tanya.

But that novel was two years away. For now, September 23, 1862, three hundred guests waited in the Church of the Nativity of the Blessed Virgin. Candles glinted off gold icons. A hidden choir intoned Russian hymns. "In his account of Levin's and Kitty's wedding," Sonya later wrote of Tolstoy's use of their own wedding in *Anna Karenina*, Tolstoy "described the whole psychological process"—the groom's equivocation, how the ceremony was delayed until he found a clean shirt, the bride who'd wept all the way to the church.

What was left out, though, was what went through her mind. Through her veil she saw more than a nearly middle-aged man plagued with miserable teeth and bony shoulders. No wedding vow could prepare her for what lay ahead. She wasn't marrying a man. She was marrying a genius—a man who would be known as Russia's other tsar, its moral conscience, a name synonymous with epic. "Epic" would later describe their union: forty-eight years, thirteen children, ten of whom survived, all chronicled in the Tolstoys' dual set of diaries. By the end, seven sets of diaries would be recording the marriage from within the household. The outside world, gossiping about the Tolstoys, would debate if marriage required its own form of genius. But on the eve of her wedding all Sonya Behrs knew was that she was about to become the married muse, wife to a man who, in his own words, left "a bit of flesh in the ink-pot" each day.

An hour before the ceremony Sonya wept for one final reason. Why had she been so foolish? Just before her marriage, she'd taken a match to her diaries and stories, something she'd immediately regretted. Over the years, the Tolstoys' marriage flared with jealousy, sexual and literary passion, willful tempers and the white heat of conflicting ambitions. But all that waited until just after the ceremony.

Watching the needlewomen put the final touches on the tulle dress, Sonya stared at the pins pressing near her flesh, watching as they came so close to her young skin that she didn't dare move or, for the moment, breathe.

*W*hen the six-horse carriage sped past the whitewashed brick pillars stationed at the entrance to Yasnaya Polyana, Sonya Tolstoy was crossing more than the threshold of a new home. As the carriage made its way up the dusty avenue lined with birch and lime trees, she was leaving behind not only the last of her youth but its illusions. Hadn't she long been warned? In her girlhood diary she'd copied a passage from Tolstoy's *Childhood*: "What phase in life can be better than the one in which the two perfect qualities—innocent gaiety and a limitless longing for love—are the only motivating forces in life?" *Fool!* her older sister, Lisa, had scribbled on the opposite page of Sonya's diary. The first test of sentimentality and married life lay ahead. An entry from Tolstoy's 1860 diary still burned in Sonya's memory. "It's no longer the feelings of a stag, but of a husband for a wife," he'd written only two years earlier of the nameless peasant woman who waited at the end of the newlyweds' carriage ride.

At the altar the couple had called out their formal names: Sophia Andreyevna Behrs, Lev Nikolaevich Tolstoy. Over the years, Sonya, as she was nicknamed, called her husband Lev or Lyova. But his fuller identity, she'd only begun to see, was slowly announcing itself. The man sitting next to her in the clattering carriage was a count who'd already exercised his imperial will: demanding their wedding be performed in a week's time, questioning the need for a trousseau. The hastily copied dresses, now packed in the shiny black trunks strapped to the carriage, would not be needed. Sonya's social life was receding by the mile. One hundred and thirty miles southwest of Moscow, Yasnaya Polyana was set deep in the province of Tula. No railway yet existed between Moscow and Kiev, only a sinuous maze of rutted country roads. The grim monotony of provincial isolation that so many of her favorite Russian writers had made their subject had become her new life.

The first night at Yasnaya Polyana, Sonya saw with clearer eyes the house where Tolstoy's aunt awaited them with an icon and the traditional gifts of bread and salt. The estate's main house, a stately white-pillared residence, had long been sold and carted off to pay Tolstoy's early gambling debts. All that remained now were two smaller wings, one for Tolstoy's school, the other for their living quarters. The wings, connected by a courtyard, were a perfect metaphor for their future lives: isolated from each other yet joined by common ground. In marriage, Sonya had become a countess, but the house where she'd spend the next forty-eight years had a spartan shabbiness to it. Palm oil candles ill lit the house, oil lamps used only on special occasions. The unpainted wooden floors had no rugs. Slippers were worn inside to absorb noise. Servants slept in hallways crowded with ancestral portraits. Mousetraps clicked constantly. The garden was rife with weeds; garbage was thrown directly into the paths.

The house Tolstoy had inherited at nineteen echoed with his own ghosts: the early deaths of both his parents, the later ones of two brothers from consumption. Psychic rather than literal orphanhood had left him temperamentally restless, forever at odds with all established order. Even within literary circles he had proven himself

a social maverick, often alienating others with his relentless questioning and stubborn habit of picking arguments. His early bachelor
and soldier diaries augured the challenges ahead for his new wife.
Fiery, iconoclastic, charming, Tolstoy had always been susceptible to
sudden behavior reversals. Their wedding night at Yasnaya Polyana
was no exception. Setting the pattern for much of their married life,
Tolstoy was both consumed and repelled by his own lust. Sonya, the
object of that lust, was torn between her own awakened sexuality
and the bewildering shame it stirred between them. It would come to
unnerve them more than any ghost haunting the hallways.

Once the couple were settled in their new home, Tolstoy made a
decision he'd long regret: that they read and exchange each other's
diaries. Nothing should come between them—no nursed grievances,
no private brooding. No secrets. Sonya's first and deepest impulse
was to please her husband. But wasn't a diary's vow of privacy to
oneself as inviolate as a wedding vow to another? "My diary again.
It's sad to be going back to old habits I gave up since I married," a
lonely Sonya wrote as she opened her adult diary. "I used to write
when I felt depressed—now I suppose it is for the same reason."

Homesick, bewildered by her husband's consuming passion, his
gloomy moods and occasional coldness, Sonya often used her diary
when frustrated or upset. First-year quarrels erupted over different
attitudes on everything, from social life—she missed the boisterous
stimulation of her large cosmopolitan family—to clothing—she
dressed in lace, he in a belted peasant tunic. "It makes me laugh to
read my diary," she'd later write at twenty-four. "What a lot of
contradictions—as though I were the unhappiest of women! But
who could be happier?" But bored early on in the marriage, Sonya
sat in copied French fashions listening to the wind rattle down the
chimneys as her husband took long walks, a gun his only companion. "It is not difficult to find work, there is plenty to do," she rued

in her diary, "but first you have to enjoy such petty household tasks as breeding hens, tinkling on the piano, reading a lot of fourth-rate books and precious few good ones, and pickling cucumbers."

Tolstoy had chosen a wife who didn't shy away from the rigid picture he'd painted of women's duties in his corrosively ironic 1859 novella *Family Happiness*. Independent, willful, capable, Sonya possessed prodigious mental and physical stamina. Early in their married life, the Tolstoys set out to share a common vocation. Utopian farm management soon supplanted his interest in running the estate's experimental school. Another of his sudden enthusiasms, this new manic burst of energy included beekeeping, erecting a distillery and raising Japanese hogs. A fat bunch of keys jangling at her waist, Sonya assumed overseeing both house and office, doing accounts and paying workers.

In December 1862, two weeks after discovering herself pregnant, Sonya came upon a strapping woman, sunburnt legs exposed, scrubbing the entry hall floor. A three-year-old boy played next to her, the spitting image of Leo Tolstoy. Sonya stared at Axinia Bazykina, her husband's former mistress, whom she'd first read about in his diaries. "One blow, I thought, how easy it would be—if only it weren't for the baby." From 1862 until Leo Tolstoy's death in 1910 and Sonya's in 1919, jealousy burned with a dangerous, consuming brightness in their communal diaries. The jealousy, both conjugal and creative, was often retrospective, each spouse haunted by the other's past—her imaginary one, his real one. "I should like to burn his diary and the whole of his past," wrote Sonya. "If I could kill him and create a new person exactly the same as he is now, I would do so happily."

By 1863, a year into their marriage, Tolstoy was buoyed by the security of family life. "I am a husband and a father, well pleased with my fate," he noted soon after the birth of their first son. Tolstoy, orphaned at age nine, had a deep psychic need for family, and, as a writer, an even greater need for the creative freedom family stability provided. Subconsciously, he'd adopted the maxim of his contemporary Gustave Flaubert: to write well, one must think like a radical and live like a bourgeois. The steady, certain rhythms of family life were the backdrop against which he was safe to take greater risks seated at his desk. Gone was the restless pursuit of vocations. It was as if some difficult question had been solved, focusing his mind on writing as his primary identity. "Never before have I felt my mental and moral capacity so free and so fit for work. I have plenty of work." And Sonya? While the Tolstoys entered a period of domestic happiness, a settled vocation still proved elusive for her. A year into their marriage she was juggling motherhood and managing the estate that Tolstoy had largely left in her capable hands. She also steadily made improvements in the dark, drafty house and tamed the garden.

"My wife is not playing with dolls," Tolstoy wrote fellow writer Afanasy Fet in 1863. "Don't misjudge her that way. To me she is a valuable assistant." By 1864 Sonya found herself rectifying more than her husband's ill-fated farm schemes. In the same vaulted, ground-floor room where she and Tolstoy had improvised her bed during their courtship, Sonya was soon to make the invisible bed she would lie in the rest of their married life. The room, now a family nook, still had several iron rings screwed to the ceiling, remnants of its early days as storage room for hanging saddles and cured meat. It was here that she'd first begin her true vocation: reading, copying and commenting on what would become *War and Peace*. In this small den, between 1864 and 1869, the Tolstoys first worked together: he during the day, she at night. The late 1860s would find Tolstoy at the zenith of his creative powers, spilling over into *Anna Karenina* from 1873 to 1877, and establishing him as one of Russian literature's most original voices.

Late into the night, long after the household was asleep, Sonya quietly worked. "She used to sit in her small drawing room off the zala [living room] at her little writing table, and spend all her free time writing," her son Ilya later recalled. "Leaning over the manuscript and trying to decipher my Father's scrawl with her shortsighted eyes, she used to spend whole evenings at work, and often stayed up late at night after everyone else had gone to bed." A compulsive editor of his own writing, Tolstoy often invented whole new scenes in the cramped corners of a page, scribbling down margins and between lines. The next night Sonya would find the clean copy she'd given him that morning crosshatched with illegible corrections. In final draft, *War and Peace* ran roughly three thousand manuscript pages. Sonya Tolstoy copied it seven times.

Sonya, though, was more than an obedient scribe offering minor corrections of grammar. An astute reader, she offered key suggestions, often foreshadowing what critics would notice. "I shall never forget," Tolstoy later thanked her, "how one day you told me that the whole historico-military side of *War and Peace*, over which I labored so hard, was coming out badly, and that the best part would be the psychological side, the characters and the pictures of family life. It couldn't have been truer, and I have not forgotten how you were able to see that and tell me." In *War and Peace*, Tolstoy caught the heroic in its minute moments, the abstract sweep of history encoded in the telling human detail—a soldier stumbling on a battlefield, missing home; a sister holding an icon before her dying brother which he refuses to kiss. As Tolstoy imagined these scenes, the heroic of the everyday quietly went on in his own home: Sonya keeping her husband's mornings free from all household noise, copying his manuscripts by candlelight, often using a magnifying glass to decipher his small, cramped scrawl.

Fame and wealth descended on Yasnaya Polyana as inevitably as the apple blossoms that showered the orchard beyond the Tolstoys' front door. In the first decade of their marriage, as Tolstoy centered himself fully in the public eye, Sonya increasingly found herself in the moon-dark orbit of private life. Between 1863 and 1888 she gave birth to thirteen children, all but three surviving. The last was born when she was forty-four and Tolstoy sixty. Idealizing the traditional domestic life he'd craved as a child, Tolstoy in his novels set up parallel narratives contrasting the possibilities of family life. In *Anna Karenina*, for example, marriage and motherhood were embodied by its two main female characters: an alluring adulterer and a saintly domestic drudge. In the Tolstoys' own marriage, Sonya's sexual fatigue in the face of constant childbearing baffled and irritated her husband. His belief in tradition sparked further marital conflict, beginning with their first child, over her difficulty in breastfeeding. Her nipples painfully cracked, she was chastised by Tolstoy for temporarily turning to a wet nurse. "Make him write a story about a husband who tortured his sick wife and forced her to nurse her child," Sonya's physician father wrote. "He is a great master at speechifying and literature, but life is another matter." But Tolstoy's autocratic passion for principle prevailed. Wanting to please her husband, Sonya nursed children for the next twenty-five years.

The year of the Tolstoys' courtship had coincided with Tsar Alexander II's emancipation of the serfs, a cause Tolstoy would champion further as a social visionary. Yet, for a wife, freedom advocated outside the home did not necessarily translate inside. As early as 1863 nineteen-year-old Sonya confided in her diary, "I am a piece of household furniture . . . When the machine is working properly it heats the milk, knits a blanket, makes little requests and bustles about trying not to think." Her hips and waist thickening, hormones fanning mood swings, Sonya periodically suffered fits of hysteria: the weeping and jealous rages that her husband would later use against her. And while the Tolstoys remained devoted to the idea of marriage, tensions mounted in the household between the creative and the procreative, between the value given to conceiving books and that given to birthing children. The split was further fissured by the suicidal intimacy of shared diaries. For the greater part of their marriage, the Tolstoys lived a simultaneously open and secret life—in person and in the diaries. What couldn't be said over the breakfast table surfaced like anonymous neighborhood gossip in the other's diary, sabotaging the very thing a shared diary was meant to supply: an avenue of communication. Paranoia instead prevailed. Sonya observed, "Lyovochka has said nothing and has not made the slightest allusion to my diary. Has he read it?" Worrying about his own temperament when not writing, Tolstoy wondered aloud in his diary, "Where is it—my old self? . . . I have become petty and insignificant. And, what. is worse, is it has happened since my marriage to a woman I love. Nearly every word in this notebook is prevarication and hypocrisy. The thought that she is still here now, reading over my shoulder, stifles and perverts my sincerity . . . I must add words for her because she will read them. For her I write what is not true, but things I would not write for myself alone."

Tolstoy saved his own marriage from resembling characters he couldn't control by creating fictional ones he could. Beginning late in 1865, Tolstoy kept no diary for thirteen years. There is no more significant pause in the history of writers' diaries. Immersing himself entirely in works of genius, he produced *War and Peace* and *Anna Karenina*. On April 17, 1878, he resurfaced, noting with breathtaking casualness, "After thirteen years I want to continue my diary." Sonya, busy dawn to dusk copying manuscripts, correcting proofs and nursing children, had also let her diary slip. While domestic discord often occasioned her to take up her diary, Sonya was beginning to leave an intimate portrait of shared and auxiliary literary life. Like rock crystal forming on a string, her diary slowly thickened with clusters of social detail. Births, deaths and marriage intermingled with crises large and small—nursing a fevered child through scarlet fever, burying him weeks later, battling state censorship of Tolstoy's work. Sonya revealed the hidden human drama behind her husband's brisk notational diary style. Over the years, her diary offered snapshots of frost-filled nights at Yasnaya Polyana; of harvesting mushrooms in birch-dense forests; of a growing family seated outside at a long table in late summer, the linen cloth whitening as dusk settled all about them.

At twenty-five, seven years into her marriage, Sonya had borne four children and acted as midwife to Tolstoy's longest novel. Her jet black hair shot with its first strands of silver, a child suckling her sore breasts, she needed only to look back on the diary of first-year married life to find she'd long ago diagnosed her own psychic challenge. "Sometimes I long to break free of his rather oppressive influence," she'd written in 1862. "I have begun thinking his thoughts and seeing with his eyes, trying to become like him, and losing myself." The husband who holed up undisturbed in his study until three in the afternoon often immediately walked the estate, hunted or rode into the supper hour. Early in their marriage, while Tolstoy was away, Sonya had written the first of several keys to her adult diary:

> I am so often alone with my thoughts that the need to write in my diary comes quite naturally . . . Now I am well again and not pregnant—it terrifies me how often I have been in that condition. He said that for him being young meant *"I can achieve anything."* For me it means *I want and can do anything.* But when the feeling passes, other considerations come into my mind, and reason tells me that there is nothing I either want or can do beyond nursing, eating, drinking, sleeping, and loving and caring for my husband and babies, all of which I know is happiness of a kind, but why do I feel so woeful all the time, and weep as I did yesterday? I am

writing this now with the pleasantly exciting sense that nobody will
ever read it, so I can be quite frank with myself and not write for
Lyovochka.

appiness of a kind. Copying favorite passages of Tolstoy's
fiction into her childhood diary years earlier, had she
imagined the dull animal calm of long days indoors, sewing or
caretaking, that had become her life at Yasnaya Polyana? While
Tolstoy's writing often proved a more challenging rival than any
real-life mistress, Sonya contained her irritation at being neglected
by grafting her ambition onto his. She gauged both his moods and
the caliber of his writing with the same intuitive accuracy as if
reading a child's fevered forehead with her hand. Managing the
estate largely on her own from 1868, she possessed an astute business
sense, and within a decade and a half she would create for herself the
covert role of unofficial literary agent. Focused on how to promote
Tolstoy's work, battle the state censor and circulate new work by
private subscription, by the late 1880s Sonya had become indispensable, moving from secretary and copy editor to self-appointed publi-
cist. Her motive for her new role wasn't just a vicarious pride in
fame, but the need to find an enriched inner life of her own. As early
as 1864, when copying *War and Peace*, she wrote, "As I copy it, I
live through a whole new world of ideas and impressions. Nothing
has such an effect on me as his ideas and his genius. This is something quite new in me."

The shift from helpmeet to cohort would not please everyone. In
transferring her ambition onto her husband, Sonya would be accused
of a kind of spiritual plagiarism, using her husband's inner life as her
own. But hadn't Tolstoy subtly done the very same to her? On long
provincial evenings she had watched her childhood and the Behrs
family be re-created in *War and Peace*. "You think you are not

earning your board," Tolstoy joked with Sonya's younger sister, Tanya, a frequent houseguest and the model for Nastasha in *War and Peace*. "I am constantly using you as material." In *Anna Karenina*, Tolstoy drew even more directly on his courtship and marriage to Sonya. "The writer takes out of his life the best that is in it, and puts it into his work," Tolstoy wrote Afanasy Fet. "His work is therefore beautiful and his life—bad." The novel's huge critical acclaim brought with it a lack of psychological privacy, the life offered up for literary vivisection. What rights, if any, does a subject in a writer's work have? Foreshadowing the Tolstoys' bitter battles over ownership and copyright of diaries and writings, Sonya struck a psychological bargain: as creative subject, she surrendered all control of her life, but marriage to the author allowed her to be part investor in the work.

"As I was reading Pushkin's life the other day," Sonya wrote in February 1870, "it occurred to me that I might render a service to posterity by recording not so much Lyvova's everyday life as his mental activities." In addition to her diary, she wrote a short story, "Sparrows," and compiled French and Russian grammars to teach her children. Sonya, though, once again found herself pregnant. On February 12, 1871, she went into premature labor, almost dying before delivering a sickly girl. Puerperal fever set in. After three days of delirium, she woke to find her husband standing by her bed. "I've failed you again," Sonya whispered, ashamed. To offset the fever, her head had been shaved while she was unconscious. But at that moment it was he who somehow seemed changed.

In the last year, almost imperceptibly, an anguished restlessness had gripped Tolstoy, forcing him in the time ahead to question the very point of the work he—and she—had spent nearly a decade sacrificing everything to. All those days of literary partnership. The incessant shoring up of Tolstoy's confidence, listening to work being read aloud, praising, offering suggestions, soothing nervous tensions, seeing him through fitful depressive cycles. Suddenly it all seemed up for negotiation. "A shadow has passed between us," Sonya would write several months later. As if to confirm her immediate instincts, she listened to the thin cry of a newborn, her fifth, howling in the darkened room.

From her window Sonya Tolstoy had a view of the three small graves. During the winters of 1873 and 1874, the Tolstoys lost three children: two boys and a girl. Tolstoy's two maiden aunts, the final link to his own childhood, had also died. The dark sum of those losses triggered in him a morbid phobia and obsession with death. By 1878 the forty-nine-year-old writer and his family were living a bewildering paradox. *Anna Karenina* was earning fame and huge revenues. Sonya and the children were utterly devoted to Tolstoy, a boisterous clan scheduling their lives around him. Tolstoy, though, took little pleasure in any of it. As spent by literary success as by family losses, he questioned the fundamental meaning of life, igniting a spiritual crisis that had been brewing since early adulthood. The novelist who'd written with such passionate subtlety on the human condition increasingly found himself obsessed with remedying its suffering. Between 1877 and 1881 he embarked on a spiritual quest, traveling to monasteries for guidance, haunted by the suffering from famine and social inequality he'd witnessed among Russia's vast peasant class.

"Lev is working," Sonya wrote her sister, "but alas! he keeps writing religious tracts until his head aches." Sonya inconveniently found herself now married to a budding spiritual genius as well as a confirmed literary one. She watched him plunge into a life of Christian piety and self-purification while openly rebelling against the institutionalized doctrines of the Orthodox Church. Quietly she wondered if his quest for moral salvation merely exchanged one form of dogmatism for another. But in the winter of 1878 Sonya, the "skilled nurse of his genius," still imagined the crisis passing like an illness that had temporarily descended with sudden gravity. As she blotted his new essays, prepared for the birth of another baby, spooned quinine to older children, in her diary she monitored his— as well as her own—internal debate over worldly ambition. Between 1878 and 1879 she completed and published the first biographical essay on Tolstoy. But even as he was finishing *Anna Karenina*, Tolstoy began deriding novel writing as a morally bankrupt occupation. Alarmed by his "artistic suicide," Sonya lamented his obsession with social activism at the cost of his literary career. "There is something lacking in my life, something that I loved, and that is Leo's literary work . . . I'm a true writer's wife, so greatly do I take his writing to heart." Psychologically, it was as if she were already a widow. At thirty-five she circled around what she couldn't quite admit in her diary: she was out of a job.

From the early 1880s on, the Tolstoys' diaries charted a couple on a collision course. The enlargements they'd made to Yasnaya Polyana had already proved too small for the growing family. Beginning in 1882, they wintered in Moscow so that their older children could be properly educated. The extended fiscal responsibility of two homes coincided with Tolstoy's increasing aversion to wealth and owning property. The bourgeois life that had once fed his work now suffocated it. The Moscow house was a hive of activity—five tutors, a host of governesses, uniformed servants, guests for musical concerts. Sonya's crowded drawing room, astir with the cultural evenings she'd long missed, was in stark contrast to Tolstoy's monk-like study. Increasingly, a steady stream of disciples, drawn from his visits to Moscow's slums and prisons, cut through the drawing room on their way to his study. Tolstoy was augmenting his print audience with a literal one, scores of moral seekers, their boots tracking mud over the family oriental carpets.

Sharing the breakfast table with a saint wasn't easy. Tolstoy's vegetarianism required two separate family menus, and his new hobby of cobbling shoes dulled conversation. "How can I turn like a weather-cock in every direction?" Sonya wondered of his urgings that the family share in his conversion. Caught between her devotion to his genius and the struggle to keep up with its newly minted moral demands, she confided, "I cannot prove to him how deeply I love him—as deeply as I loved him 20 years ago—for his love oppresses *me* and irritates *him.*" Tolstoy's joyless credo of self-abnegation divided the couple more than any conflict over the trappings of bourgeois life ever could. By 1883 distractions for Tolstoy included the family itself. The sermonizing that Sonya argued flawed his novels was now aired daily around the hissing samovar. Their son Ilya provided a mirror-image portrait of the tensions in family life: "From the fun-loving, lively head of our family he was transformed before our eyes into a stern, accusatory prophet . . . We would be planning an amateur play, everybody was animated, chatting away, playing croquet, talking of love. Papa appeared and with one word, or worse, with one look, everything was spoiled . . . The worst was that he felt it too."

Her husband had abandoned his career as a novelist, but, in a literary crossover, Sonya found herself assuming and excelling at its management. It was no longer just to her diary that she confided her despair at Tolstoy's stalled literary career. She made no secret of how she agreed with novelist Ivan Turgenev, who on his deathbed had recently written Tolstoy, "My friend, go back to literature!" Between 1879 and 1884 as Tolstoy churned out *Confession*, his apologia for abandoning the church, as well as *What I Believe*, Sonya bore three new children. But she'd also found another outlet for her energies. Borrowing money from her mother, she began a publishing office in a converted shed near their Moscow home. By 1885 she'd dedicated herself to producing a full-scale edition of Tolstoy's writing, including the new religious works. To understand the intricacies of publishing, she'd traveled to St. Petersburg to consult with Anna Dostoyevsky, widow of Russia's other great writer. Once her husband's secretary, in midlife Anna Dostoyevsky had established a thriving business, serving as literary watchdog to his work after his death. Sonya had fourteen years of literary experience to draw on. Sleeping five hours a night, she planned the edition, corrected proofs, placed ads in papers and, in 1885, traveled again to St. Petersburg to battle the censor. The successful enterprise, originally sanctioned by Tolstoy, soon met with his chilly disapproval. Buoyed by her newfound confidence, Sonya countered, "I have accepted the idea of *fulfilling* my duty in my relation to you as a writer, as a man requiring first of all his freedom, and therefore, I demand nothing of you."

Once jealous of each other's pasts, the Tolstoys were now ferociously jealous of their divergent visions of the future. "I'm distressed that such intellectual powers should be wasted on chopping wood, tending samovars, and stitching boots," she wrote. He spit back, "There can be no agreement and no loving life between us until you come to what I have come to . . . a life devoted to God and to other people and not to one's own pleasure." In their diaries the Tolstoys' visions for each other's lives exposed a core vanity about their own. If Tolstoy had successfully transformed Sonya into the mother he'd never had, the faithful bearer of children and midwife to his creative career, she often treated him as a son who'd disappointed her with choosing the wrong profession. An air of injury hung over the Moscow and Yasnaya Polyana households. He raged that she trivialized his conversion as religious zealotry; she despaired that her unwillingness to commit to a life of poverty was mistaken for abject material greed.

Dueling in their diaries, the Tolstoys deepened a schism over the literary and social welfare of their family. By 1886, midway in their marriage, the squabbling had crystallized over one issue: ownership and copyright of the novels, essays and private diaries. The royalties from Tolstoy's hugely lucrative earlier novels was the family's principal capital. Why, asked Tolstoy, should he keep writing popular novels just to pay for a privileged lifestyle he'd not only come to abhor but regarded as a social evil? How, reasoned Sonya, furiously protective of her family, could their numerous children's educations and futures be safeguarded? "If I'd been left in poverty with the children," Sonya later reflected in her autobiography, "I should have had to work for the whole family—to feed, do the sewing for, wash, bring up children without education. Leo, by vocation and inclination, would have done nothing else but write."

And write he did, steadily producing articles and essays, helping to fill the over ninety volumes he'd leave by the end of his life. With the household kept quiet each day until he'd finished work, Sonya still shielded him from all distraction, but her eye was vigilant for signs that he might return to novels. In a kind of literary cottage industry, Tolstoy's eldest daughters, Masha and Tanya, joined Sonya in copying out their father's drafts. Tolstoy, often feuding with his sons, had long favored his daughters, who in assuming Sonya's tasks potentially became her rivals. One by one, the children were being won over, vying for their father's infrequent attention by the separate dramas of their conversions. In sympathetic alliance, his eldest daughters donned peasant dress, visited the poor and toiled at manual labor at Yasnaya Polyana. Sounding as much the exasperated provider as the harried housewife, Sonya used her diary as a safety valve, venting her creeping paranoia as the family sided with or rebelled against her dogged pragmatism. "Everybody in this house—especially Lev Nikolaevich, whom the children follow like a herd of sheep," she rued on October 25, 1886, "has foisted on me the role of *scourge*. Having loaded me with all the responsibilities for the children and their education, the finances, the estate, the housekeeping, indeed the entire material side of life—from which they derive a great deal more benefit than I do—they then come up to me with a cold, calculating, hypocritical expression, masked in virtue, and beseech me in ingratiating tones to give a peasant a horse." Only the Tolstoys, it seems, could have produced children who pestered their parents to get *rid* of all shiny new material distractions. But as Tolstoy noted in his famous opening to *Anna Karenina*, happy families are all alike, but unhappy ones are each unhappy in their own way. The Tolstoys were no exception. From 1888 on, peace was just a brief tribal truce.

As Leo had been the hero of Sonya's childhood, she had once been the muse of his early adulthood. No longer. In her husband's eyes, the literary angel had become an avenging demon, a willful, nagging opponent prone to hysterics. Xantippe to his Socrates. The woman who'd lived his theories of motherhood and family duty had, at forty-four, settled into a dowdy domesticity. Sitting opposite her at the long summer table at Yasnaya Polyana, wicker chairs creaking, Tolstoy rued their sad collective fate: "she suffers and causes me pain like a toothache." His novelist's eye, ever keen, couldn't fail to take in Sonya's slackening jawline, the doughy, matronly cheeks, the hands plump and puffy from twelve pregnancies. Just as their separate bedrooms were stark contrasts—hers covered with icons and family portraits, his a whitewashed cell—so their bodies mirrored their psychic estrangement: Sonya's wide hips bracketed from births, Leo's thin frame carved with a gaunt, determined asceticism. Only their diaries continued to bulge in unison. Particularly Sonya's. From 1888 on, her diary assumed epic proportions, totaling some half-million words by her death in 1919. As if already preparing her defense in history's eyes, she minutely chronicled the complicated pattern of their working relationship, the spiraling moods, conflicted ambitions, tortured devotion.

All her married life Sonya had been almost pathologically jealous of any woman who might rival her in Tolstoy's affections. She'd been caught unawares, then, charmed even, by the sympathetic young visitor who first came to call in 1883. Vladimir Chertkov hailed from the same privileged background as Tolstoy. The son of a famous general, he'd spurned his aristocratic birthright and early army career, swept up by Tolstoyan social activism. Unlike the majority of Tolstoyans, who numbered in the thousands by the mid-1880s, Chertkov was a socially polished convert: educated, articulate, seemingly at ease in the leisured world both he and Tolstoy had renounced. The thirty-four-year-old bachelor with thinning hair and fastidious grooming habits quickly gained access to the inner circle of family life. Only slowly did Sonya notice that his organizational skills were equal to his strategic hunger to become Tolstoy's chief disciple—his spiritual son. With messianic devotion, the humorless, formidably controlled Chertkov insinuated himself in Tolstoy's life, becoming his de facto confidant and secretary. As he praised Tolstoy as a social visionary, recording the great writer's every word, Sonya realized she was finally staring at the rival she'd feared all her life. By 1888 Chertkov, whom Sonya called the "dark shadow," had already laid his plans.

Like a ward who'd suddenly found himself legally adopted by his benefactor, Vladimir Chertkov inherited a situation ripe with social possibility. Since the early 1880s the Tolstoys had feuded over the family's future security. In 1883 Tolstoy gave Sonya power of attorney, nine years later divesting himself of Yasnaya Polyana and other holdings, dividing his estate into ten equal shares, living thereafter as a guest on his own property. However, a thornier issue of ownership remained. Increasingly convinced that the copyrights of his works belonged to the public domain, Tolstoy sought to unburden himself of them. In 1883 he made a verbal contract with Sonya that all copyrights before 1881, including those for *War and Peace* and *Anna Karenina*, belonged to her, and that she could publish future editions at will. Yet to Tolstoy, Sonya's keen business acumen seemed safer when confined to managing Yasnaya Polyana. By 1886, with Tolstoy's active blessing, Chertkov had set up a rival publishing company, mass-producing cheap pocket editions of Tolstoy's religious writings. While targeting the indigent audience Tolstoy aimed for, the inexpensive booklets sold twenty million copies in six years, undercutting Sonya's more expensive full edition, offered as a complete set.

Then, in 1889, to Sonya's delight, Tolstoy once again turned his talent to fiction. But it would be a novella she soon wished he'd never begun. The year before, Tolstoy had sought to divest himself of one more mortal yoke: sexual relations. Just as he'd given up tobacco, alcohol and meat, so after twenty-six years of marriage he sought to rid himself of the impulse that had cursed his life with contradictory behavior. While weary of pregnancy, Sonya, at forty-four, feared severing the only sure cord that continued to tie Tolstoy to her. Amid their fractious bickering, Tolstoy began *The Kreutzer Sonata*, a brilliant manic confession of a man, who, suspecting his wife of infidelity, kills her. Tolstoy's disciples would claim the novella was triggered by the writer's own jealousy over Sonya's platonic, love-starved friendship with composer Sergei Taneyev, who had briefly supervised her piano playing. But the seeds for this story about the disillusionment of romantic love were present as early as his 1859 novella *Family Happiness*, as well as fully cultivated in his two later famous novels. Diminishing matrimony as merely "legalized lust," *The Kreutzer Sonata* was Tolstoy's scorching tract against marriage. Symbolically, it killed off Sonya, who, aflame with fury and shame, nonetheless continued to copy out the majority of the manuscript.

The public, not just Sonya, registered a groundswell of shock. Condemned by the church, debated on the street, replicated and distributed illegally after it was banned, *The Kreutzer Sonata* became a cause célèbre. With its shockingly censorious views on marriage and sex, the novella threw the Tolstoys into the goldfish bowl of national gossip. In drawing rooms across Russia, readers construed Tolstoy's assault on marriage as an unbridled attack on his wife, the inevitable postscript to his famous lines in *War and Peace* when a world-weary aristocrat warns Tolstoy's hero, "Never, never marry, my dear fellow! That's my advice: never marry till you can say to yourself that you have done all you are capable of, and until you have ceased to love the woman of your choice and have seen her plainly as she is." Sonya, tongues wagged, had overstepped her wifely place. In a private interview with the Tsar in 1891, she'd persuaded him to lift the ban on *The Kreutzer Sonata*, allowing it only in her full edition. But the public stir also spotlighted Tolstoy's own moral fallibility, since the novella, an invective against sexual love, was conceived shortly after the birth of his thirteenth child.

By 1891, though, Tolstoy's celebrity status had silenced most critics. In his spiritual crisis the nation had found a mirror for its own deep alienation, the moral disaffection of the intelligentsia, the social despair of the peasantry. Tolstoy remained one of Russia's lone free voices, a moral conscience battling the political and social repression that had only worsened since Tsar Alexander III's ascension in 1881. As Tolstoy societies and chapters sprang up throughout Europe and America, fan clubs were fewer at Yasnaya Polyana. Left to cope with the quiet infamies of daily life—unpaid bills, toothache, moody children—Sonya sighed, "I feel as though I had been caught in a trap and the task of running this Christian household is the greatest curse that God has sent me. If spiritual salvation consists in killing the life of your neighbor, then Leo is certainly saved."

Left alone in the cooling shadows of family life—sewing puppets, quelling hurts—Sonya watched as Tolstoy independently created his world family, the ever-adoring one guaranteed never to abandon him. While after the death of her four-year-old son in 1886 her diary would remain blank for nine months, she too was slowly becoming a blank shadow in her husband's diaries. While devoting herself fully to the unrelenting miracle and assault of Tolstoy's talent and temperament, from 1884 on, Sonya watched as the pronoun "she" replaced her very name in his diaries. As her publishing and domestic skills deepened, Tolstoy saw Sonya keeping less a diary than a résumé. In 1890 she noted the sheer crush of daily life:

I have to worry about my children's illnesses and studies, my husband's medical and (more importantly) his mental state, his older children's affairs, their debts, jobs and children, the sale of the Samara estate, and the plans—which I have to get hold of and copy for buyers—the new edition and Volume 13, which contains the banned *Kreutzer Sonata* . . . the proofs for Volume 13, Misha's nightshirts and Andryusha's boots and sheets; I must be sure not to default on the household expenses, I must see to the servants' passports, make sure the jobs are done on the estate, keep the accounts, copy them out . . . And for all this I am directly, inescapably responsible.

But Sonya had defaulted in her responsibility to one crucial aspect of her life. If hers was a genius for management, it was also a genius, she'd finally begun to see, for letting her own talent and personality be subsumed. "How I regret," she wrote at forty-six, "that my perpetual emotional dependence on the man I love has killed all my other talents—my energy too: and I had such a lot of that once." The "silent friend" of her diary was one of the few places where she created "my own spiritual world, independent of Lyovochka's crushing sermons." But the self-confidence a private diary could confer was constantly undermined. Her husband's eye could pick the diary like a secret key. And when, in 1890, Sonya sketched a story, "Who Is to Blame"—her response to *The Kreutzer*

Sonata, told from the wife's point of view—she allowed Anna Dostoyevsky and others to dissuade her from publishing it.

Sonya came to depend on her and Tolstoy's shared diaries like a habit. In 1890, tired of her making copies of his diary for posterity, Tolstoy deprived her of the bond that had joined them: he locked his diaries away. She often saw them unguarded. "I read his diaries on the quiet, and tried to see what I could bring into his life which would unite us again," wrote Sonya. "But his diaries only deepened my despair." No wonder. Just as Tolstoy had once done with Sonya, he and Chertkov cemented their spiritual bond by sharing their diaries, something the men had unofficially done since 1886. "I suffer because my wife does not share my convictions," Tolstoy confessed to Chertkov. "Never have I entreated her with tears to believe in the truth or told her all simply, lovingly, softly; yet here she lies beside me and I say nothing to her, but what ought to be said to her I say to God." Chertkov, now able to quote specific passages about Sonya, widened the rift between husband and wife by stoking Tolstoy's vision of a solitary pilgrim's life. Should a woman who called disciples "uneducated loafers" be fit to manage a literary estate? whispered Chertkov. Neither man needed to mention her recent hysterics, fueled by the onset of menopause, by caring for ten children and a publishing enterprise. But by 1891 Sonya neared mental breakdown as she openly fought to protect her husband and her family's security from a humorless, sycophantic fanatic. At stake was more than the vast international business Tolstoyanism had become. At stake was her whole life, past and present.

As real as her battles were with Chertkov, Sonya's inner demons were far subtler. The contest of wills in the Tolstoys' diaries went far deeper than issues of copyright and authorial control, or even of the relationship of a great creative talent with his satellite secretary. It struck at the heart of the political balance of power, the struggle between muse and master, in married and literary life. In the first

decade of their marriage, Sonya had been the ideal muse and helpmeet, a small ever-present supply of fresh oxygen. She'd performed
her duties well: buffering Tolstoy from the dissonance of his own
internal voices, calming, steadying, shoring confidence. The muse-
helpmeet is a writer's psychic safety net, allowing him to walk the
tightrope of ambition. In welcoming and praising the ongoing work,
the literary helpmeet offers a private rehearsal of public success. But
unlike Dorothy Wordsworth, who freely lent her journal for her
brother's poems, Sonya Tolstoy's years of blind devotion were numbered. It wasn't just that she failed to make the shift from literary to
social disciple in Tolstoy's eyes. She'd become as sharply real as the
carping voices in his own head. Capable of criticism and comments
of her own, Sonya was no longer all adoration, no longer Tolstoy's
charm against the fickle inconstancies of his own inner life. She was
guilty of that stubborn, forgivable sin in all marriages: she wanted
something back. By midlife she refused to be the patron saint of
literary wives, the shining model after whom generations of writers
genuflect in tiny, unread prefaces—"to my wife, without whose
help . . ." But fate, Sonya guessed, would not be as generous.
"Now I am cast aside as of no further use," she rued at forty-five,
"although I am, nevertheless, expected to do impossible things."

Sonya watched as much in the Tolstoy household was cast aside.
On September 16, 1891, Tolstoy declared in a published newspaper
letter that the copyrights to all his work, except the pre-1881 ones
Sonya owned, was now held by the public domain. Anyone, decreed
the sixty-three-year-old author, was free to use, translate or reprint
his later writing. Fearful that he'd destroy his diaries, Sonya saved
every scrap of paper that fell her way. Unfortunately, Chertkov had
not only the same goal but far more access to Tolstoy's papers,
including the loan of Tolstoy's current secret diaries, which he copied. Between 1891 and Tolstoy's death in 1910, Sonya and Chertkov
became competing reverse archaeologists, uncovering layers of pre-

cious material before it ever got buried. The drafts to Tolstoy's final novels, *Resurrection* and *Hadji Murad*, as well as his story *Diary of a Madman*, were carefully preserved. But Tolstoy's "evil twin," as Sonya called Chertkov, eyed more than the glory of the master's words. He wanted sole control of them. In 1909 Tolstoy made him executor of his literary estate.

But the cool sting of betrayal would come less from Sonya's rival than from within her own household. Flesh of her flesh, the Tolstoy children were busy keeping their own diaries. There was a great deal to record: the devastating loss of Sonya's youngest, favorite child in 1895; her growing hysteria that Tolstoy would similarly abandon her; her halfhearted suicide gestures, trying to abandon him first. But one child, Tolstoy's most ardent disciple, seemed obsessed by her parents' painfully divided goals. Sasha, as Alexandra Tolstoy was nicknamed, was Sonya's secret guilt. In 1884, in despair at finding herself pregnant for the twelfth time, Sonya had taken scalding baths and jumped from a high chest of drawers, the only time in her life she'd consciously tried to miscarry. The child she had tried to abort twenty-five years earlier now planned to rid herself of the mother who she felt had never favored her. As played out in the tumultuous late summer of 1910, the secret course of events would take away Sonya's life: her job, her husband, her spirit.

On July 1, 1910, Sonya, near hysteria, demanded that Chertkov return her husband's diaries. He refused. Two weeks later, Tolstoy, acting as peacemaker, dispatched two of his children to retrieve his own diaries. Sonya immediately secured them in a state bank vault. What she didn't know was that Sasha, from whom Sonya grabbed the forbidden diaries, had sided with Chertkov and the increasingly tight cabal of Tolstoy's inner circle. Yasnaya Polyana plunged into gloomy warfare. As Tolstoy's secretary noted in *his* diary, "The samovar boiled cheerily on the table, the bowl of raspberries stood out like a bright red patch on the white table cloth, but those sitting around the table looked as if they were serving a prison sentence." For Sonya, the conflict over diaries had focused her mind with merciless clarity: losing control of the literary estate meant being condemned to a life sentence, seen merely as Tolstoy's long-suffering wife. Nothing more. But in their forty-eight-year marriage both Tolstoys had been transformed by the process of a collaborative creativity. The seventeen-year-old "little girl in a yellow dress" who'd first visited Yasnaya Polyana in 1861 had become, four decades, thirteen children and a publishing company later, a woman still able to draft her autobiography and an occasional story while daring to critique her husband's writing. "Get rid of the weight of responsibility? Throw it off?" Sonya wrote in 1906. Not without a fight.

Years of confession in shared diaries, though, had poisoned the Tolstoys' marriage, leeching it of the trust necessary to heal the growing final rift. On the morning of July 14, 1910, Tolstoy drafted a letter assuring his wife of his love, absolving her of any guilt, but asserting his implacable conviction that his was the path of the solitary pilgrim. Their children referred to the "letter of intent" as "mama's reference from her employer." A week later, Sasha Tolstoy guided her then eighty-one-year-old father to a tree stump in a nearby village forest. Amid a small circle of witnesses Tolstoy signed a secret new will. All copyrights, including those prior to 1881 owned by Sonya, went into the public domain. In a separate document Chertkov had drafted, Sasha was made the literary estate's new executrix, himself its official administrator. While she'd live to bitterly regret it, Sasha felt that the writings and diaries, now out of her mother's hands, were finally safe as a rescued child.

On October 27, 1910, a month after their forty-eighth wedding anniversary, Tolstoy woke to the familiar sound of "Sonya Andreyevna, searching, probably reading" in his study. Waiting till Sonya fell asleep, Tolstoy woke Sasha and told her of his decision to flee. Six days later, as her private train approached the remote station of Astapovo, deep in the province of Ryazan, Sonya found herself part of a scene destined to become more famous than any Tolstoy ever created in his novels. Inside the stationmaster's four-room cottage, her husband lay dying of pneumonia, surrounded by disciples and three of his children. Just as Sasha had kept her mother from Tolstoy's writings, so she now forbade Sonya to enter or disturb her dying husband's room. Shut outside the cottage crowded by hordes of disciples and world press, Sonya had her every move recorded, her life frozen into the frames of public newsreels. In dark theaters all around the world, people would soon be able to stare at Tolstoy's future widow, a sixty-six-year-old woman—dazed, dowdy, numbed by grief and shame.

But one image, a still photograph as vivid as any diary entry, indelibly caught her fate. Sonya standing on her tiptoes, peering through the dusty cottage window, her hands cupped to her face, looking in on the life she had devoted herself to. Like the newsreel cameras that clicked and whirred, at that moment did her life—not just his—flash before her? Conflicting pictures from her diary, her life's other work. Which one was she to believe as most truthful? From 1887, at age forty-three:

> Many people blame me for not writing my diary and memoirs, since Fate has put me in touch with such a famous man. But it is hard to break away . . . and most of all, to find any time to do it.

Or from 1891, at age forty-seven:

> I cannot help secretly exulting in my success in overcoming all the obstacles, that I managed to obtain an interview with the Tsar, and

that I, a woman, have achieved something that nobody else could have done!

In 1905, twelve years before the revolution that Tolstoy had anticipated and she lived to witness, Sonya Tolstoy published a cycle of prose poems entitled *Groans*. While everyone could guess the author, she published it under the pseudonym "A Tired Woman."

Alice James sketched by Henry James.
(Houghton Library, Harvard)

3

THE
HIDDEN WRITER
IN A
WRITING FAMILY

Full many a flower is born to blush unseen,
And waste its sweetness on the desert air.

—THOMAS GRAY

What an awful pity it is that you can't say *damn*.

—ALICE JAMES, *Diary*

*L*eamington, eighty-five miles northwest of London, suffered a double fate. Since it was both a provincial and a spa town, silence settled its streets all too early in the afternoons. In 1855 and 1862, after Dickens had given readings, the local paper rued that large audiences were "not common things" there. At dusk the only sounds were often the muted clatter of cane bath chairs being wheeled down the wide Regency streets. Unlike spas on the Continent, small cities unto themselves, Leamington was not an invalid's emporium of white fountains, those tiered fantasies of stuccoed swans and smiling sea nymphs. Nineteenth-century Leamington had none of the intense Continental competition for fashion. No elegantly garbed women, their hats plumed like ailments, thin gossamer trails of complaint: neuralgia, backache, a spot of gout. Those who visited were leisured, largely English, sensibly dressed in tweeds or black silks. Daily walks meant a shuffle to the safety of local tearooms. Waters had bubbled in Leamington since Roman times. After their discovery in the eighteenth century, their medicinal properties had attracted a parade of dyspeptic pilgrims.

Continental Europeans usually weren't tempted. To take waters in England seemed singularly redundant.

Eleven Hamilton Terrace, like so many guesthouses catering to spa visitors, was a Regency terrace house situated in the center of Leamington. Inside, the rooms were comfortably spacious: high ceilings, brass warmers gleaming near the fireplace, tables draped with paisley felt cloths. Rooms to nap or read in. In the spring of 1889 an American sat at the second-story window, a leather-bound volume open on her lap. Beside her was a tiny bottle of sepia ink, the same color as autumn leaves that tumbled outside on mild English afternoons. The only sound in the room was the scratch of the pen.

May 31st, 1889.

I think that if I get into the habit of writing a bit about what happens, or rather doesn't happen, I may lose a little of the sense of loneliness and desolation which abides with me. My circumstances allowing nothing but the ejaculation of one-syllabled reflections, a written monologue by that most interesting being, *myself*, may have its yet to be discovered consolations. I shall at least have it all my own way and it may bring relief as an outlet to that geyser of emotions, sensations, speculations and reflections which ferments perpetually within my poor old carcass for its sins; so here goes, my first Journal!

How was it possible that a first journal, that private training ground for so many young girls, had not begun until now? Alice James was forty. No one, with the exception of her closest friend, Katharine Loring, would know she was keeping a journal. Certainly not her family. Especially not her family. It was important that this writing be kept private. *I shall at least have it all my own way.* That wouldn't be possible with her older brothers. Their keen, appraising eyes would probably scan the diary's first sentences for clues to why she had come to sit by herself in a foreign country, at odds with her own body. Wouldn't her brothers, so different in temperament but so alike in their public success, see this first journal entry as exactly what it was: an anthem of ambition and ambivalence? They'd pick up its phrases like a scent. Her eldest brother, William, the psychologist, would ferret out the warring impulses of a thwarted self. *I think that if I get in the habit of writing a bit about what happens, or rather doesn't happen* . . . Her brother Henry, with literary ambitions long his own, might pause over Alice's wish that *a written monologue by that most interesting being,* myself, *may have its yet to be discovered consolations.*

Looking up at the second-story window of 11 Hamilton Terrace that May afternoon, the casual passerby would have seen a woman's face staring down. It was a face easily missed in a crowd, irredeemably plain, a high-forehead, full-cheeked face. The eyes, though, flickered—witty and caustic. To someone standing below that south-facing window, the momentary impression could have seemed an imagined fancy, a trick of light. But the woman's eyelashes were light-colored as if scorched from the thoughts beaming behind those deep brown eyes.

*H*ow had an American, three months shy of her forty-first birthday, come to sit alone in a damp spa town in central England? In the spring of 1889 Alice James had already been residing in England for five years. It was not the first time she had crossed the Atlantic, nor the first she'd found herself settled in foreign lodgings. The steamer trunk, the casualties of lost or wrinkled linen, the window open on formal foreign gardens, were long familiar. A "rootless and accidental childhood" spent as "hotel children" had been the result of her philosopher father's determination to give his children a progressive education. Travel, culture and leisured studies, often with him as tutor, were the golden formula for intellectuals in training. Between 1855 and 1860 Henry James, Sr., a mild eccentric idealist, devotee of free will, believer in visions, carted his children from New York to Europe to Newport before finally settling in Boston. The family restlessness surfaced even earlier in the parents' marriage. Each of the five James children was born in a different place: William, Henry and Garth at separate New York addresses, Robertson in Albany, the ancestral seat. Alice, the youngest and the only girl, was born at 54 West Fourteenth Street in New York on August 7, 1848. When she was six, the family embarked on the first of two long European sojourns, shuttling among France, England, Switzerland and Germany.

The ship crossings, private hotels and hired tutors had been funded by a family fortune made in property a generation earlier. The Irish ancestors who had flourished in Albany by the 1830s were "an extravagant, unregulated cluster . . . handsome dead cousins, lurid uncles, beautiful vanished aunts, persons all bust and curls." The family's literal wealth was soon put at the service of developing the family's spiritual fortunes. A friend and admirer of Emerson, Henry Sr. believed in the strategic investment of individualism in each child. "This character or disposition cannot be forcibly imposed," he warned, "but must be freely assumed." The solution was to surround his children "as far as possible with an atmosphere of freedom." One of the ironies of Alice James's childhood was that a fortune amassed in real estate speculations financed so rootless an adolescence. The James children grew up studying foreign maps, sorting timetables, memorizing the value of the strange coins jingling in their pockets. Thumbing through stacks of foreign dictionaries, Alice and her brothers learned an invaluable lesson early in life: the verb "to be" is irregular in almost every language.

"What enrichment of mind and memory can children have without continuity & if they are torn up by the roots every little while as we were!" Alice wrote her brother William years later. Yet a deeper psychic discontinuity had been at work in the James family from the very start. Rebelling against his own Calvinist childhood, Henry Sr. had turned to drink as a young man. His restlessness led to his dropping out of Princeton Theological Seminary. At thirty two he suffered a nervous crisis that sent him retreating into the mystical works of Emanuel Swedenborg. The man Alice James would call Father spent his days rooted in his private study, grappling with problems of free will. His wife ministered to her husband's visionary whims with seeming selflessness. Yet Mary Walsh James's compliance with her husband's idealistic travel schemes masked a stern will often mistaken for efficiency. A cool, controlling disciplinarian, she played brisk family nurse, a foil to her husband's lifelong role as overprotective parent. Her keen eyesight, erect spine, and capable limbs constantly reminded the family that she alone was uncursed by the nervous James genes. Quietly triumphant in health, Alice's mother soon became indispensable to the husband and children whose neediness assured her the upper hand. For like a game of telephone, the secret of nervous collapse would subtly be passed down the line of children, one by one, until it finally rested with Alice, the child Henry Sr. forgot to mention when he described taking his "four stout sons" to Europe.

By the time the family arrived in Europe in 1855, a tacit pattern had been established: any rumor of illness or malaise in their children would be met by their mother's silent impatience and their father's belief in moral willpower. The spiritual crisis Henry Sr. had suffered as a young man had brought him to the brink of psychic breakdown. Years later, he described the exact nature of the episode. Terrorized by "some damnèd shape squatting invisible to me within the precincts of the room," he had been visited by the shape of evil itself. The brief hallucination had left him "reduced from a state of firm, vigorous, joyful manhood to one of almost helpless infancy." Nonetheless, he was "determined not to budge from my chair till I had recovered my lost self-possession." Unblinking, he stared down the "influences fatal to life." This episode would have lasting consequences for how he raised his children. Alice's father believed in the salvation of moral willpower, the willingness to examine and master the dark corners of horror in oneself. The man whose right leg had been amputated after a boyhood accident was determined that his own children stand firmly on their own two feet.

With the ambitious idealism of an intellectual set that included Emerson, Thoreau, Thackeary and Carlyle, Alice's father eyed his children's lives as open-ended narratives, the plots as yet undetermined. As the James family crisscrossed Europe, sailing Lake Geneva's placid surface, viewing the Alps, picnicking in Boulogne, Henry Sr. slowly, subtly, began to shape his children's characters. "Our parents," wrote Henry Jr., "had for us no definite project but to be liberally 'good.' " Yet bright Christmases in London and summers lolling outside Paris couldn't disguise the flaws in Henry Sr.'s social utopian views. However cloudy their father's lectures against competition and selfishness, by adolescence all five James children knew in their bones that life's goal was excellence, even if it meant achieving it at the expense of one another. By the time the European educational experiment was over, his children had learned a single lesson by heart: a belief that the success of one sibling almost superstitiously translated into the inevitable failure of another. Only seven years later, Alice would sum it up best: "Your sister her having so little mind," she wrote her brother William, "may account for your having so much."

In 1860 the Jameses returned to America, to Newport, on the eve of the Civil War. As the nation braced for battle, North against South, brother against brother, so the James siblings began a private fraternal war: a covert competition over their father's ill-defined notions of success. William was eighteen, Henry seventeen, Alice twelve. Their father had set them the abstract goal "just to *be* something," inconveniently omitting the what and how. As Alice's brother Henry rued, their father's worldly indifference to his children's "special and marketable talents and facilities . . . couldn't but often cause impatience in young breasts conscious of gifts." Already Henry was "a devourer of libraries, and an immense writer of novels and drama"; William, in his father's view, was "very devoted to scientific pursuits, and I hope will turn out a most respectable scholar." In almost a postscript to his nomadic European experiment, their father wrote, "Our chief disappointment has been in regard to Alice who intellectually, socially and physically" had been at "a great disadvantage compared to home." In Newport, her hair cautioned into a tight curl, twelve-year-old Alice had resumed her eclectic education, memorizing dates and points of etiquette from a teacher who would later commit suicide.

In 1864 the family moved to Boston, settling permanently in Cambridge. Within two years they had established themselves at 20 Quincy Street, a stone's throw from the ancient oaks and shady eaves of Harvard Yard, where two of Alice's older brothers were to attend college. By then a tacit pecking order had been established among the siblings. William would go to medical school, Henry briefly to law school. Alice's two other, unfavored brothers had already dutifully enlisted in the Civil War. (Sitting out the war, William and Henry Jr. spent their Cambridge years suffering psychosomatic ailments, unconsciously mimicking the battle wounds they thought were their civic duty.) One by one, the brothers prepared to enter the world. Competition, though, has no citizenship.

"He is a native of the James family," Alice observed of her brother Henry, "he has no other country." But how to assert oneself when the competitive arena is the circumscribed world of the family?

"The quiet little sister," Emerson's son remembered, "ate her dinner, smiling close to the combatants," those older brothers brandishing knives, debate style, to score points. Outshouted, outshone, Alice sat in the cooling shadow of her brothers' world. Like them, she read voraciously, spoke perfect French, was a gifted linguist and a witty raconteur. By nineteen, though, she had slowly come to realize that, for her, good works meant sewing bees or charity work for indigent women. "All the world seems to be getting married," she wrote in 1867 of the one other good work still available to her. As her circle of women friends, drawn from Boston's great intermarrying academic families, got engaged, Alice waited patiently on her sofa, reading books such as Thomas De Quincey's memoir *Confessions of an English Opium-Eater.*

Wandering Cambridge's shady streets just as she once had Newport's rocky promontories, Alice James quietly passed from girlhood to maturity. Yet as her brothers studied for graduation, Alice struggled with the most basic rite of passage: the full emotional shift from girlhood to adulthood. She stubbornly resisted the family's hidden message that had shadowed her since puberty. It was a message about identity so firmly encoded in memory that she recorded it in her diary in a single snapshot:

I had to peg away pretty hard between 12 and 24 . . . absorbing into the bone that the better part is to clothe oneself in neutral tints, walk by still waters, and possess one's soul in silence. How I used to recall the low grey Newport sky in that winter of 62–3 as I used to wander about over the cliffs, my young soul struggling out of its swaddling clothes . . . How profoundly grateful I am for the temperament which saves from the wretched fate of those poor

creatures who never find their bearings . . . who never dimly
suspect that the only thing which survives is the resistance we
bring to life and not the strain life brings to us.

Silence. Neutral tints. Resistance. Her credo, finally registered in
her diary at forty-one, would be hard-won. Alice James would use
her diary to examine the long odyssey spent rejecting available models of identity and vocation around her, struggling to find new ones.
Ever her father's daughter, she too craved the clean slate of an
invented self. But what thimbleful of destiny awaited a plain-faced,
intelligent but untrained girl, soon to shuttle between Boston's intellectual salons and the sickroom? Her father had anointed her "heiress of the paternal wit and of the maternal worth." From birth, the
clever, quick-witted Alice identified with her intellectually driven
father and brothers. Her body, though, destined her for her mother's
role of quiet passive power. Split in mind and body, Alice suffered a
breakdown in the fall of 1867. At nineteen she had struck a darkly
ingenious compromise: her ailing body was a femininely accepted
means of garnering some of the attention lavished on her older
brothers. Illness would be her unique route to expressing herself. If
the body was the battlefield on which the young Alice James played
out thwarted ambition, her diary would later be its tiny Gettysburg
of creative resistance.

As the James siblings reached their twenties, life inside the "inner sepulchre" of 20 Quincy Street revealed the real legacy of their
European years: too many hours for self-scrutiny, a permanent sense
of displacement. In time, the split childhoods spent crossing foreign
borders would translate into their final adult subject matter: for William, the dual sides of the psyche; for Henry, riding the cusp between American and European identity; for Alice, the creative split
in mind and body. But as young adults, they found their interrupted
upbringing exerting a dark pull: a psychological sense of struggle, an

anxious hanging back and a failure to commit. Like one of their father's titles, *Substance and Shadow*, a thin shadow of doubt over identity and vocation had trailed each of the five James siblings well into adulthood.

Tight-knit, generous, competitive, Alice and her brothers took turns assuming the protective camouflage of illness, its safety and delay from parental expectation. Their father had cautioned against "narrowing" their interests in life, but he'd nonetheless linked identity and vocation in their minds. As he published book after book, and filled the house with the nation's leading intellectuals, his children saw that the mind *was* identity. The father afflicted with a slight stammer nonetheless had been clear in conveying that they were to be extraordinary using their minds. As Alice's brother Henry concluded, the task was to transform "simply everything that should happen to us, every contact, every impression and every experience" into their very own form of self-expression.

William and Henry, born only fifteen months apart, scrambled to imitate their father's professional life. Henry barricaded himself in his room, writing. William restlessly pursued medicine. In 1867–68 William and Alice suffered parallel nervous collapses, each plagued by suicidal thoughts. Alice had spent the previous winter in New York undergoing "motorpathy," an exercise treatment for nervous disorders. But by 1870 William was a newly minted M.D. within reach of his first Harvard teaching appointment. Henry was on the threshold of publishing his first novel. The news that Alice had returned from her New York cure "fat as butter," wrote William, was "well fitted to tranquillize anxiety & annual pity but not to kindle enthusiasm or excite envy." At nineteen Alice James had become a professional invalid. The demon that had stalked her father as a young man, paralyzing him with fear, bidding him not to move from his chair, had found its final companion. By the spring of

1868 Alice had assumed the seat her father—and brothers—had vacated.

What had happened? Why had the once robust daughter of Boston intellectuals, a playmate to Emerson's children, taken to her bed? Why were a strange set of nervous ailments eclipsing the already fading promise of marriage and motherhood? The answers would wait for her diary. For the next eighteen years Alice settled in the clapboard Quincy Street house. After her mother's death in 1882 she cared for her grieving father in a smaller house on Boston's Beacon Hill. Caring for her father until his death only ten months later further limited her freedom to explore the world just outside her window—the blocks of salmon-colored brick houses, the green expanse of the nearby Common. Since the 1860s, Boston had been a hothouse of social ferment and intellectual causes: abolitionism, women's suffrage, spiritualism, utopian reform, movements Henry seized on for his novel *The Bostonians*. With an invalid's meager appetite, Alice had only but sipped the city's wider possibilities. In 1884, her parents dead, her brothers scattered, she confronted the ghost of her own life, its failure yet to achieve her father's injunction "just to *be* something." In her own eyes, she had failed to achieve either her mother's domestic role or her father's intellectual mantle. Years later, she recalled the scene in her diary:

In those ghastly days, when I was by myself in the little house in Mt. Vernon Street, how I longed to flee in to the firemen next door and escape from the "Alone, Alone!" that echoed thro' the house, rustled down the stairs, whispered from the walls, and confronted me, like a material presence, as I sat waiting, counting the moments as they turned themselves from today into tomorrow.

In 1884 she left America for Europe, ostensibly to visit her brother Henry, who had settled in England nearly a decade earlier.

Before packing, the thirty-six-year-old Alice James had ample occasion to order family photos of herself. At six, staring directly at the camera, she is outfitted in a dark tiered cape, her tiny hands clasped as if in prayer. With its trimmed white lace collar, the cape has something faintly ecclesiastical about it: Alice as a tiny cardinal. Grim, alert, panicked, determined, the facial expression is already set. At nine, her brown hair parted and pulled tight at the scalp, she poses in a Parisian studio, hat in hand, her posture ramrod straight. In Newport, dressed in a soft tartan plaid dress, she is seated reading a letter. In profile, her smooth fourteen-year-old face doesn't yet hint of hours spent in the sickroom, headaches menacing the forehead so often bent over an open book. By twenty five Alice James no longer looks directly at the camera; she is caught instead at a slightly oblique angle, in quarter profile, a cross strung tight at her neck. In a sketch Henry did in 1872, Alice is seated at a writing desk, busy, her back turned on the observer. In all the photos, though, a single feature catches the eye. It is her head. It is large, disproportionate, ballooning from her body as if the cranium itself were about to burst.

In 1888, a year before she started to keep her journal, Alice James received a letter from her eldest brother, William. *"Your* letters," he wrote, "show no effect from the fluffiness and wooliness of your environment, and your character seems to grow more and more like that of the young girl-heroine of whom I read many years ago in a Boston story-paper, and whose charms were summed up in the phrase, 'she was like bottled lightning.' "

In the spring of 1888, as Alice sat swaddled in blankets in Miss Clarke's rooming house, she imagined herself anything but a heroine. Plain, unmarried, middle-aged, her body untouched except by the cool, sterile fingertips of doctors, she'd arrived in England seasick, carried to shore by two sailors. Fearing overdependence on Henry, the brother she was closest to and who watched over her first in London, she eventually headed for Leamington Spa. Since 1886, her world had been two large rooms, a north-facing bedroom, sunlit all morning, and a sitting room where she spent afternoons on a chaise, a shawl draped over her shoulders, a scratchy rug around her knees. On fine spring days, the drapes were drawn to shield headachy eyes, the fireplace heaped with coals to warm feet chilled from poor circulation. "I cannot make out," she'd later ask her diary, "whether it is an entire absence or an excess of humour in Destiny to construct such an elaborate exit for my thistle-down personality."

In the long hours in Leamington, Alice occupied herself with the one activity the James family had trained her in: serious reading. Raised by a father who hated all religious rituals, she was now surrounded by a nurse who slipped her books on the early Christians and a parson downstairs who offered to read spiritual homilies. Shunning both, she relied on the public library. To her nurse's horror, she spent her Sundays reading Zola. Between 1887 and 1888 Alice had been busy. She'd assembled a commonplace book, copying out quotations and passages from the sophisticated array of her reading: Tolstoy, Montaigne, Carlyle, Cervantes, George Eliot. In handwriting as precise as a surgeon's knife, she copied out a description of Eliot's heroine Maggie Tulliver that could have been Alice herself: "a creature with blind instinctive yearning for something that wd. link together the wonderfull impressions of this mysterious life and give her soul a sense of home in it."

Having stared at dozens of sickroom walls since she was nineteen, Alice James had long known that her task, like that of all the James siblings, was to find a home for one's gifts, uncork the lightning. But talent, like lightning, seeks grounding to discharge its power. After years of chronic indecision and anxiety, William was well on his way to pioneering moral psychology; already Henry was destined to be one of the century's greatest novelists. Alice's two other brothers had fared poorly. One would die an alcoholic failure; another, die young, his identity eclipsed by his older brothers'. The "steady flame which has illuminated my little journey," Alice would muse in her diary, "altho' it may have burned low as the waters rose, had never flickered out." But almost. Keeping the flame of her own identity steady hadn't been easy. There were breakdowns at nineteen and at thirty. A host of treatments—hypnosis, massage and walking cures—continued to take their toll. In England, Alice applied an electric battery to her head as if to jumpstart it.

On May 31, 1889, she abandoned the book comprised of other people's quotations and started her diary. She also began clipping newspaper stories of social injustices—mistreatment of children, the inequities of the British class system, the struggle for Irish independence. Pasted into her diary, the clips psychologically mirrored her own story writ large: her struggle as a child for independence within the James sibling class system. In a sitting room that smelled of English damp and other people's dinners, she reflected on illness, silence, *being* silenced. "The difficulty about all this dying is that you can't tell a fellow anything about it, so where does the fun come in?" she'd ask in the fourth to last entry in her diary.

Under a ceiling light shaped like a pawnbroker's sign, three frosted glass balls, Alice sat reflecting on the poverty of her own life. "I have seen so little that my memory is packed with little bits . . . childish impressions of light and colour come crowding back into my mind . . . for a ghostly moment." And: "How funny it is to remember these trifling things but it is a joy to bring back the past in any way and I shall put down everything I can think of in this precious reservoir." As her inky fingers shaped sentences, she could hardly have imagined her diary's real legacy. In it, Alice James would leave the world a working record of creative ambivalence, of will and ambition ferociously at odds, of incandescent intelligence and wit unnaturally constricted. Written with the safety of distance, decades later and thousands of miles from home, the diary detailed the psychic price of bottled-up gifts. Future generations would prize the courage with which she chronicled the mind's private struggles with ambition, failure and vocation. For like the ghostly séance raps William experimented with, or the symptoms Henry gave his numerous invalid heroines, tics and spasms had been Alice's private creative code: a telegraphed message, written on the body first and later on the page, of a voice struggling to speak and be heard. In her diary she provided a glimpse of the internal policing instinct that silences even the most gifted voice trying to write without full permission.

Just as Jane Austen had written some of her minutely observed novels in the nearby spa city of Bath, hiding them from outsiders, so in 1889 Alice James took up her diary in Leamington—to magnify her tiny world. "The well perceive not the tiny flowers of observation and impression which spring up on the field of restricted vision," she confided in her diary. "How grateful I am that I actually do *see*, to my own consciousness, the quarter of an inch that my eyes fall upon." On occasions such as the Fourth of July, Alice had herself wheeled out to the countryside in a bath chair by an often inebriated helper, Somers, warning him not to charge the grazing cows. Forgetful of her "palpitating heart and jumping jack stomach," she paused at the lush orchards of Hawkes Farm. "I lay in a meadow until the unwrinkled serenity entered into my bones." On good days, she lay in a meadow, alone, "absorbing like blotting paper" the freedom all around her. Instinctively, in likening herself to blotting paper, she'd found a writing image that conjured overflow, as if still mopping up a mistake.

"If I can get on to my sofa and occupy myself for four hours, at intervals, thro' the day, scribbling my notes and able to read the books that belong to me," she noted in her diary, it would "clarify the density and shape the formless mass within." Shaping sentences helped define the life so unlived till now. Keeping a diary had given Alice James occasion to reflect on the curious parallelism of her condition: an American in exile, marooned on an island, stranded on the small raft of her bed.

> It's rather strange that here, among this robust and sanguine people, I feel not the least shame or degradation at being ill, as I used at home among the anaemic and the fagged. It comes of course in one way from the conditions being so easy, from the sense of leisure, work reduced to a minimum and the god *Holiday* worshipped so perpetually and effectually by all classes. Then what need to justify one's existence, one is simply one more amid a million of the superfluous.

Finally released from family competition, from the pressure "to justify one's existence," she started to examine the forces long at work in her psyche, the voices that whispered *no*.

The diary, begun to counter loneliness, soon became a forum for shrewd psychological self-assessment. Like a photograph sharpening in developer solution, Alice's diary slowly revealed a pattern: the "complicated eluding" she had engaged in to avoid the "multifold traps set" for her undoing. In the quiet hours of Leamington and later in London, she studied just how the traps had been set. As the parson, Bible in hand, shuffled outside her door and the nurse nodded off to sleep in a quiet corner, Alice probed the riddle of her invalidism:

> William uses an excellent expression when he says in his paper on the "Hidden Self" that the nervous victim "abandons" certain portions of his consciousness . . . altho' I have never unfortunately been able to abandon my consciousness and get five min-

utes' rest. I have passed thro' an infinite succession of conscious abandonments and in looking back now I see how it began in my childhood, altho' I wasn't conscious of the necessity until '67 or '68 when I broke down first, acutely . . . As I lay prostrate after the storm with my mind luminous and active and susceptible of the clearest, strongest impressions, I saw so distinctly that it was a fight simply between my body and my will, a battle in which the former was to be triumphant to the end.

Looking back on her childhood, her memory worked two clues, both involving the life of the mind: "When the fancy took me of a morning at school to *study* my lessons by way of variety . . . the most impossible sensations of upheaval, violent revolt in my head overtook me so that I had to 'abandon' my brain." Remembering long hours inside watching her father write his books she wrote, "I used to sit immovable reading in the library with waves of violent inclination suddenly invading my muscles taking some of their myriad forms such as throwing myself out of the window, or knocking off the head of the benignant pater as he sat with his silver locks, writing at his table." Throw herself out a window or kill her father, who wrote freely at his table? The choices were impossible. Instead, ever conciliatory, she turned the murderous impulses inward, allowing herself to sit in the library but not add to its shelves.

As Alice sipped spoonfuls of thin soup in Leamington, her brother Henry often had tea with Sir Leslie Stephen, a Victorian intellectual and paterfamilias to rival his own. Nearly forty years later, Stephen's daughter, the future Virginia Woolf, would use imagery as violent as Alice's to describe killing off the internal voices that whispered "never let anybody guess that you have a mind of your own." Alice, unfortunately, wouldn't live to read "Professions for Women" or *A Room of Own's*, in which Woolf imagines Shakespeare having a gifted sister. Both essays would have shed light for

Alice on the casual accident of her fate. If the lottery of destiny had given the Brontë family four gifted sisters and one favored wastrel son, the Jameses were the exact reverse: four sons and an unfavored but gifted sister. Yet the novels and poetry of the three surviving Brontë sisters, long familiar to Alice, were as unimaginable a task as creative vocation itself. "Nurse asked me whether I should like to be an artist," she wrote, "imagine the joy and despair of it! the joy of seeing with the trained eye and the despair of *doing* it." *Doing*. It's as if the sheer thought sent the word fainting into italics, an activity Alice's body had mimicked since childhood.

A child destined to keep diaries listens perhaps most intently to parents' whispers rather than their words, the hesitations and pauses where the praise or encouragement so wished for might have been. Alice James's diary is silent on the whispers in the James family. But there had been many. Could her father's published definition of his ideal child have been lost on her? In *The Nature of Evil*, he declared: "I desire my child to become an upright man, a man in whom goodness shall not be induced by mercenary motives, but by love." The adored and adoring father who "used to spoil our Christmases so faithfully for us," showing the gifts in the forbidden closet, later proved himself a spoiler in a more serious way. "The very virtue of woman," he wrote in *Putnam's Monthly*, "disqualifies her for all didactic dignity. Learning and wisdom do not become her." Alice's New York physician, Dr. Charles Fayette Taylor, concurred: "Give me the little woman who has not been 'educated' too much, and whose only ambition is to be a good wife and mother . . . Such women are capable of being the mothers of men." And what did her own mother have to say to Alice, who, having survived her first breakdown, regretted not seeing William before she left New York. Mary James admonished her daughter: "There is no wisdom in indulging your selfish regrets in the matter, but accept cheerfully the fact, that life is made up of changes and separations from those we love." But how can one be selfish when there's hardly enough of a self to go around in the first place?

Invisible sentences, blank spaces, a line suddenly breaking off. Often these are a diary's most intriguing places, the spot where the eye lingers longest. What's not written in Alice James's diary is nonetheless present on every page: as an invalid, she'd tell the world her gifts were invalid. With its genius for metaphor, the body expressed what her creative mind had left blank all those years: that fainting was normal when the target of ambition kept spinning out of her hands; that hysteria was appropriate when one was asked to choose mind *or* body; that nervous attacks mimicked an identity under siege. Like her namesake's, Alice's body shrank or fattened as she found herself in the perpetual Wonderland of her family's and the world's contradictory messages. "How sick one gets of being 'good,' how much I should respect myself if I could burst out and make every one wretched for 24 hours; embody selfishness," she'd write. Late in her diary Alice slowly began reflecting back on "that hideous summer of '78, when I went down to the deep sea, its dark waters closed over me and I knew neither hope nor peace." In 1878, after suffering a nightmarish year of breakdown, thirty-year-old Alice had requested her father's permission to end her life. With devastating ironic candor Henry James, Sr., tried dismissing it. "I told her," he later wrote, "she had my full permission . . . only I hoped . . . she would do it in a perfectly gentle way in order not to distress her friends." Over a decade later, with biting irony, Alice recorded in her diary another incident showing how her nervous condition might distress others. The subject of her only published letter, signed "Invalid," it concerned an American matron looking for rooms at Miss Clarke's. Informed there was an invalid in the house, the woman said, " 'In that case perhaps it is just as well that you cannot take us in; for my little girl, who is thirteen, likes to have plenty of liberty and to *scream* through the house.' " In middle age,

Alice still civilized fury into italics. "It is an immense loss to have all robust and sustaining expletives refined away from one," she lamented. "I wonder, whether, if I had had any education I should have been more, or less, of a fool than I am." Half a century later, poet Marina Tsvetayevna posed the question for all the world's gifted Alices. "What am I to do," she asked, "with all this immensity in so measured a world?"

 s Alice sent up faint smoke signals of her long suffering, women from her same privileged intellectual background had been busy. Outside their Boston doorsteps, on shady cobbled Mount Vernon Street or in nearby Concord, women had taken up pens the way men of their generation had seized bayonets in the Civil War. Louisa May Alcott, daughter of another social utopian father, wrote for publication. So too Harriet Beecher Stowe and Sarah Orne Jewett, whose shelves included Marjory Fleming's diaries. Daughters of New England intellectuals, home-tutored, self-taught in writing, they'd managed to produce bestsellers: *Little Women, Uncle Tom's Cabin, The Country Doctor.* How? Or how, for that matter, forty years earlier, had the Brontës and George Eliot labored under dull northern English skies, shifting from private diaries to public creative work? But, for the moment, that's getting ahead of the story.

Like her contemporaries, Alice James was born into a culture that prescribed rest for women who hungered for intellectual activity. If the nineteenth-century social contract advocated education for men as a course in maturity and self-control, higher education, as Alice's doctor opined, made "the woman of our modern civilization" into "the bundle of nerves which she is." The spa, the sickroom, the sanitorium, functioned as a kind of creative laboratory for women's misplaced energies. The facts are simple. In 1883 at the Adams

Nervine Asylum for "nervous people who are not insane," for example, all thirty beds were occupied by women. That same year, Alice underwent her rest cure there, the tiny Boston asylum received 371 applications, drawn largely from the leisured upper middle class. Outside, the asylum was webbed with a maze of wooden porches, its Victorian Gothic roof speared with lightning rods. Inside, where silence reigned except for black medical bags clicking shut, patients were left alone with the very "cure" that had brought them there in the first place: more isolation.

In 1873 Alice James had finally found the sympathetic guide she would need to lead her through illness, someone she first met through the Society to Encourage Studies at Home, a correspondence course to promote "the habit of study" in all classes of American women. Katharine Peabody Loring was a Boston Brahmin whose erect posture only emphasized her plainness. In photos, she conjured the reform-minded women Alice's brother Henry mocked in his novel *The Bostonians*, women with faces like a scold, as if someone were invisibly mangling Latin declensions before them. At twenty four Katharine was a teacher for the Society. She looked the part of head history tutor: crinkly light brown hair drawn into a bun, a glint of Yankee common sense beaming behind frameless glasses, high-necked dresses with a minimum of entrapping ribbons. In 1875 she asked Alice to become a history tutor, the subject that had interested Alice most since childhood.

"I wish you could know Katharine Loring," wrote Alice. "There is nothing she cannot do from hewing wood & drawing water to driving run-away horses & educating all the women of North America." Alice only partially exaggerated. A prodigious reader, Katharine learned braille so that she could still read in bed with the lights off. Her organizational skills proved legendary. With Julia Ward

Howe, author of "Battle Hymn of the Republic," she'd founded the Saturday Morning Club of Boston, a social and literary discussion group. With Julia Ticknor, a cured invalid, she'd not only founded the Society to Encourage Studies at Home but was instrumental in establishing the Harvard Annex, the future Radcliffe College.

Katharine's charitable skills were never off duty. For years she'd been nurse companion to her younger sister, Louisa, who upstaged Katharine with the fatal romance of being both beautiful and consumptive. Katharine soon also took on her ailing friend Alice James, acting as travel companion on short New England excursions in 1879–80 and on a European trip in 1881. In competing arias of complaint, Alice and Louisa, bitterly jealous over Katharine's attentions, vied for who was the sickest. Alice won. Katharine was beleaguered by family duties of caretaking. In an ironic bid for freedom from her own suffocating family, by 1884 Katharine alternated taking care of a petulant sister with taking care of her gifted friend Alice James, first in Boston, later in England. Just as Wordsworth had his Dorothy, Tolstoy his Sonya, so Alice James had Katharine Loring: confidante, nurse, creative ally. The encouragement she'd never found in her mother's doughy, mock-maternal face, Alice at last found in Katharine's uncompetitive goodwill. Instinctively, long before the dying Alice wrote that "moral discords and nervous horrors sear the soul," Katharine understood fully when Alice described her heart as "the bewildered little hammer."

While Alice's stint as a history tutor was short-lived, in her diary a decade later she began a correspondence course with herself: a self-education in vocation. Surrounded by a coterie of productive, working women—a nurse, a maid and Loring herself—she began to examine the possibilities of work as identity. Being a victim, Alice soon saw, wasn't what anyone around her considered a useful occupation. "Yesterday Nurse and I had a good laugh," she wrote of an incident in which the nurse helped her dress. As Alice's mind was "flooded by one of those luminous waves" of original thinking, she wondered why the nurse had "no inherited quarrel with her destiny of putting petticoats over my head." Who would want to be inside your head, the nurse vehemently replied, someone with "a sick head-ache for five days!" What faced Alice James in 1889 was her father's original injunction—to seize responsibility for her own life in terms of some form of work or self-expression. "When will women begin to have the first glimmer that above all other loyalties is the loyalty to Truth, i.e., to yourself, that husband, children, friends and country are as nothing to that."

In 1890 Katharine moved Alice from Leamington to London. Establishing themselves near Henry in South Kensington, they later settled in a small house in Kensington's Campden Hill. From her spacious sitting room, Alice spied poppies, nasturtiums and sweet peas in the "good scraplet of a garden." The inhabitants also flourished. Of the housemaid they'd promoted and hired away from Leamington, Alice wrote, "The truly thrilling thing to see is the simple soul of Louisa shedding the chrysalis of the drudge and learning to flutter her wings." The description, in many ways, applied to Alice herself. Cocooned in mohair shawls, she'd transformed her diary in just over a year from a document of complaint to a complex record of intellectual life. "What determines the *selection* of memory, why does one childish experience or impression stand out so luminous and solid," she'd earlier asked her diary. "The things we remember have a *first-timeness* about them which suggests that they may be the reason of their survival . . . I remember so distinctly the first time I was conscious of a purely intellectual process." Recalling a disastrous picnic in France in 1856, Alice remembered herself at eight seated next to a disfigured guest as two of her brothers ground their heels into her shins. Consoling her, Henry Jr. deadpanned, "This might certainly be called pleasure under difficulties." In Henry's droll remark Alice first grasped the power of irony.

"The substance and exquisite, *original* form of this remark . . . came to me in a flash . . . I can also feel distinctly the sense of self-satisfaction in that I could not only perceive, but appreciate this subtlety, as if I had acquired a new sense, a sense whereby to measure intellectual things."

In her diary Alice James finally claimed the James life of the mind as her own, belatedly measuring her own intellectual achievement and that of other women. "I was greatly touched a little while ago with Constance Maud's talk about her music," she wrote, recalling a Leamington visitor. "She wants to devote herself to it seriously as a profession but as she is a daughter and not a son her tastes are set aside . . . Her compositions are very good, they say, and original, isn't it too bad?" Stranded on her sofa reading the seventeenth-century memoirs of the Abbess of Hereford's sister, Alice copied into her diary that the abbess knew " 'every language and science under the sun and she corresponded regularly with Descartes'; she was also very handsome, but her nose was apt to grow red . . . when this misfortune overtook her, 'she used to hide herself from the world.' Dear friend, how I feel for you! . . . for which of us has not a red nose at the core of her being which defies all her philosophy."

In London, Katharine became a whirlwind of social activism, attending marches, organizing educational teas. Alice sat inside, recording: "How amusing it is to see the fixed mosaic of one's little destiny being filled out by the tiny blocks of events." As she reflected in the sun-drenched sitting room, listening to the rooks in nearby Holland Park, an idea slowly surfaced in her subconscious: that her diary might have future readers. After all, she already had one reader. Illness had often forced Alice to dictate her diary entries to Katharine. From December 31, 1890, on, the diary was kept entirely in Katharine's sharply precise handwriting. Just as Dorothy Wordsworth had sat at William's side in their small hearth-warmed kitchen at Grasmere, so Katharine, head bent, expression neutral, recorded Alice's words, including those about Katharine herself. "I am on my knees to her perpetually not to bewilder the natives with her jokes," Alice dictated, noting how Katharine's candid humor often startled the British.

Unlike the diaries kept by the Wordsworths or the Tolstoys, a diary kept by two was now one shared by equals. Alice James's diary was the dividend of a "Boston marriage," a common social arrangement between intellectual women who were single because their men had been felled in the Civil War, or out of rebellion against the strictures of nineteenth-century marriage. The diary was Katharine Loring's vote of confidence in Alice James, and Alice's in herself. And with this small intimacy, the history of the diary inched a half step further: sharing diaries, the writer could imagine an audience wider than herself. Alice tried out this kind of ventriloquism. "These confidences reveal to you, dear Inconnu," she addressed the diary's unknown future reader. "While I think of it I must note, lest unborn generations should think me a plagiarist," she stage-whispered about an idea of hers she'd found confirmed in a book, "this proves conclusively what I have always maintained against strenuous opposition, that my Mind is Great!"

*B*ut another destiny awaited Alice James, one she had been preparing for all her life. Late in May 1891 her London physician, Sir Andrew Clark, confirmed a malignant tumor. At forty-three Alice had breast cancer. On May 31, the anniversary of starting her journal two years earlier, she wrote, "Ever since I have been ill, I have longed and longed for some palpable disease . . . but I was always driven back to stagger alone under the monstrous mass of subjective sensations." Told by scores of doctors to recover or die, "I have been at these alternations since I was nineteen and I am neither dead nor recovered." With the curious dark logic of someone who once believed she had no place in life, death was a liberating solution, a surcease, as illness had long been, from the nagging claims of creative identity. "To him who waits, all things come! My aspirations may have been eccentric, but I cannot complain now, that they have not been brilliantly fulfilled."

In their own way, they would be. In her diary Alice James honed a style as unique as her aspirations: detached, ironic, at once satiric and reflective. She chronicled her impending death as if it were someone else's. Propped up in bed, she recorded with black humor notarizing a will, planning the funeral, seeing that her urn not end up "a parlour ornament for William's new house." Oddly, the specter of death didn't deter her from looking for possible creative models. "It is reassuring to hear the English pronouncement that Emily Dickinson is fifth-rate," Alice mused, "they have such a capacity for missing quality." She copied a favorite Dickinson stanza into her diary:

> *How dreary to be somebody*
> *How public, like a frog*
> *To tell your name the livelong day*
> *To an admiring bog!*

Alice's quick eye had earlier been puzzled by the "faint spark of life" in George Eliot's posthumously published journals, among the first to appear by any famous woman writing in English. "Whether it is that her dank, moaning features haunt and pursue one thro' the book, or not, but she makes upon me the impression, morally and physically, of mildew, or of some morbid growth . . . something damp to the touch"

It's not surprising that Alice preferred the work of a social recluse over a social rebel, a spinster like herself over a woman living with a still-married man. But Alice's disappointment in George Eliot's journals masks the still unanswered ones in her own. Why were Eliot's—or Charlotte Brontë's—adult diaries so negligible, hastily kept adjuncts to novels? How had some nineteenth-century women managed not only to write but to imagine a creative life wider than the diary? For the obvious reason that they had firsthand experience of the larger world. All had to go out into the world to earn their living. After the death of her sullen, controlling father, Eliot worked as an editor and translator in London. Brontë, after a failed attempt to start a school, gambled on a writing career over the eclipsed life of a governess. Louisa May Alcott worked as a seamstress, teacher and governess in addition to writing to support her chronically impoverished family. Harriet Beecher Stowe wrote to support a husband and seven children. In entering the larger social forum of work, each experienced a larger possible identity: the freedom and responsibility of income, the public testing of competence and confidence. And with each new public step, the writing itself enlarged: from letters and diaries to reviews, essays, novels. *Authorized* to earn a living, they were freer to earn it as writers. While every one of them, from Eliot to Stowe, suffered from depression, moving into public voices testified not only to literary but to life genius, negotiating the hurdles of ambition and competition that had kept Alice James bedridden so long.

*I*n the winter of 1892, as Alice lay dying, her head cratered in a pillow, a short story appeared in the *New England Magazine* that uncannily paralleled Alice's nervous career. Its author, Charlotte Perkins Gilman, a niece of Harriet Beecher Stowe's, had been treated for neurasthenia in 1886 by Philadelphia's Dr. Silas Weir, pioneer of the rest cure for nervous women. Freud, as early as his 1895 *Studies on Hysteria*, found much of interest in Weir's theories of unconscious hysteria and sexual repression. As therapy, though, Weir advocated rest for Gilman, exhorting her to "never touch pen, brush or pencil." In her autobiography Gilman recalled, "I went home, followed those directions rigidly for months, and came perilously close to losing my mind." Instead, picking up her pen, she wrote a classic in American literature. "The Yellow Wall-Paper," published in January 1892, explores a young mother forbidden to work or write by her physician husband and her family in order to cure postpartum "nervous depression." Isolated from her baby, bedridden in a former child's nursery, she undergoes the infantalizing routines of milk and rest cures Alice James knew. Her only outlet is a diary she keeps "in spite of them," exhausted by "having to be so sly about it." She confides if she "had less opposition and more society and stimulus," she might be cured. While the story's character succumbs to madness, in real life, writing liberated its author. Opting for work over rest, travel over seclusion, Gilman later became an economist and social activist, author of the international bestseller *Women and Economics*, advocating financial equality between the sexes. Gilman died in 1935, a year after part of Alice's diary was published. Had she read the diary, with its championing of social justice for children, the poor and women, Gilman would have glimpsed a fellow spirit, and been pleased no doubt when Alice noted, "I am impatient for the moment when the knitting of a good stocking will be thought of as 'worthy work' as the painting of a flimsy sketch."

*D*ying, though, would be Alice James's final expertise. It, along with her diary, would distinguish her in the James family. Both showed her how "one's wavering little individuality stands out with a cameo effect" and that "all the abortive little *stretchings out*" had been at the heart of the journey. But the creative "stretchings out" had come too late. The "unholy granite substance in my breast" meant "the months have slipped away and the sofa will never more be laid upon, the morning paper read, or the loss of the new book regretted; one revolves with equal content within the narrowing circle until the vanishing point is reached."

In July 1891, two months after the tumor's discovery, Alice received a letter from William James. While praising her "fortitude, good spirits and unsentimentality," the brother she idolized confided:

> I know you've never cared for life, and to me, now at the age of nearly fifty, life and death seem singularly close together in all of us—and life a mere farce of frustration . . . Your frustrations are only rather more flagrant than the rule . . . How many times I have thought, in the past year, when my days were so full of strong and varied impression and activities, of the long unchanging hours in bed which those days stood for with you, and wondered how you bore the slow-paced monotony at all, as you did! You can't tell how I've pitied you. But you *shall* come to your rights erelong.

Thanking him for his "fraternal letter," Alice summed up her final year. "It is the most supremely interesting moment in life . . . months so full of interest and instruction." She then bitingly noted, "I will venture upon the impertinence of congratulating you upon having arrived 'at nearly fifty' at the point at which I started at fifteen! 'Twas always thus of old, but in time you usually, as now, caught up." Admonishing him for underlining "the tragic element" in her life, she noted that life's obstructions "have indeed only strengthened the sinews to whatever imperfect accomplishment I may have attained . . . So when I am gone, pray don't think of me simply as a creature who might have been something else . . . I have always had a significance for myself."

Six weeks before her death Alice had asked Katharine to have the diary typewritten. Sailing home to Boston, Katharine handed on Alice's ashes, but not the two-volume diary. For nearly another two years neither Henry nor William knew of its existence. Katharine perhaps suspected that the diary would be a shock. It was. In 1894, though, she presented Alice's brothers with privately printed copies. "In our family group, girls seemed scarcely to have had a chance," Henry rued after reading the diary. Alice's words, so often about her brothers' talents, sounded from beyond the grave. On Henry: "Tis a sad fate . . . that he should have fastened to him a being like me . . . the beautiful patience with which he listens to my outpourings on *Questions* (Heaven forbid that I should ever be so base as to descend to *Subjects*)." And: how "thrilled and touched by the implication . . . that he cared for my opinion as an opinion." On her delight for William's good reviews: "William has had four requests already to translate his book into German." Alice had always been William's creative shadow, the reminder of breakdown before the steady nurturance of work, marriage and fatherhood released him from his own private demons. William read his sister's diary while alone on vacation. Only two years before her death he'd written her after her only letter had been published, "You must continue to contribute now that you've made the plunge. I am entirely certain that you've got a book inside you about England, which will come out yet." He must have paused, though, seeing that, even at the end, Alice viewed publication as "the family serpent." Still conflicted over competing directly with her siblings, she boasted of their accomplishments and her own darkly unique one. "Within the last year [Henry] has published *The Tragic Muse*, brought out *The American* and written a play, *Mrs. Vibert* . . . combined with William's *Psychology*, not a bad show for one family! especially if I get myself dead, the hardest job of all."

Neither brother lived to read the praising reviews after Alice's diary was published—partially in 1934 as *Alice James: Her Broth-*

ers—Her Journals, an effort brought about by her niece Mary Vaux, and then fully in 1964 as *The Diary of Alice James.* "Alice James's diary," one critic declared, "is vigorous, frank and brilliant." One of the "neglected masterpieces of American literature," wrote another. And yet another: "In some of her insights, some of her assessments of nineteenth-century humbug, Alice James went beyond either of her eminent brothers." But in the spring of 1894, after first reading the diary, Alice's brothers steadily composed their own reviews. "The diary," William wrote Henry, "produces a unique and tragic impression of personal power venting itself on no opportunity . . . It ought some day to be published. I am proud of it as a leaf in the family laurel crown." Henry replied, "I have been immensely impressed with the thing as a revelation of a moral and personal picture. It is heroic in its individuality, its independence—its face-to-face with the universe for and by herself—and the beauty and eloquence with which she expresses this, let alone the rich irony and humor constitute (I wholly agree with you) a new claim for the family renown. This last element—her style, her power to write—are indeed to me a delight."

Not quite. Henry, Alice claimed in her diary, "embedded in his pages many pearls fallen from my lips, which he steals in the most unblushing way, saying, simply, that he knew they had been said by the family, so it did not matter." While gossip recorded in his own notebooks was creative fodder for stories, *his* gossip in Alice's alarmed him. "Intensely nervous and almost sick with terror about possible publicity," he feared others reading what he'd privately confided about them to Alice. Henry destroyed his copy of Alice's diary. But not before writing William that "her tragic health was . . . the only solution for her of the practical problem of life." If Alice's body was hostage to nineteenth-century conflicts of thwarted ambition, the sharp, iconoclastic voice she'd found in the diary heralded the independent voices to come from the 1890s on—Kate

Chopin, Ellen Glasgow, Edith Wharton. But perhaps none more so than the savage social irony of fellow invalid Flannery O'Connor, who wrote that illness "is always a place where there's no company, where nobody can follow."

"I might pose to myself before the footlights of my last obscure little scene," Alice had written at the end. "I have come to the knowledge within the last week or so that I was simply born a few years too soon." The diary so full of theater metaphors—stage, footlights, comedy, farce—dimmed its lights. "Ground slowly on the grim grindstone of physical pain," Alice resisted a final, lethal injection of morphine. Inside her, the cancer spread with a fluency she hadn't allowed herself in life until too late. "These long pauses don't point to any mental aridity," she wrote; "my 'roomy forehead' is as full as ever of germinating thoughts, but alas the machinery is more and more out of kilter. I am sorry for you all, for I feel as if I hadn't even yet given my message." On March 4, 1892, the day before Alice James died, Katharine Loring took dictation. "Moral discords and nervous horrors sear the soul," Alice slowly dictated. She knew that her words were "completely under the control of [Katharine's] rhythmic hand, so I go no longer in dread." "This dictation," Katharine wrote afterward, "was rushing about in her brain all day, and although she was very weak and it tired her much to dictate, she could not get her head quiet until she had it." In the diary's postscript Katharine's steady hand recorded, "All through Saturday the 5th and even in the night, Alice was making sentences."

Alice James, with Katharine Loring, writing from her sickbed in Leamington. (Houghton Library, Harvard)

Katherine Mansfield in 1913 just after the publication of her first book. (Alexander Turnbull Library)

4

A PUBLIC

OF TWO

We've got the same job, Virginia, and it is really
thrilling that we should, quite apart from each other,
be after so very nearly the same thing. We are, you
know; there's no denying it.

—KATHERINE MANSFIELD to Virginia Woolf

What a queer fate it is—always to be the spectator
of the public, never part of it. This is the reason
why I go weekly to see K[atherine] M[ansfield] up at
Hampstead, for there at any rate we make a public
of two.

—VIRGINIA WOOLF, *Diary*

*J*anuary 12, a Friday. The night before, it had rained heavily in London, but the forecast for this second weekend of 1917 predicted a clear winter's night. Ice, thin as a watch crystal, sheeted the Thames. On the half-hour train ride from Waterloo Station to the suburbs, the two dinner guests had ample opportunity to rehearse those last-minute miseries of social expectation: would the night be a success; would one's partner bore and embarrass; was the hostess more subtly dressed, already possessing the edge? They'd soon know. It was only a short walk from the tiny station at Richmond, down Eaton Road, to Hogarth House. The Woolfs dined at seven-thirty. By the time Katherine Mansfield and John Middleton Murry arrived at the Woolfs' doorstep, their skin would be mottled, not just from the cold but from the anxious flush of being so prompt for this first dinner.

For years the two women had narrowly missed meeting. Just two months earlier, though, their overlapping worlds of Bloomsbury and literary bohemia had finally met. On the five-minute walk from the station to Hogarth House, Katherine Mansfield had time to go over what she already knew about Virginia Woolf. All those details gleaned from late-night literary gossip with a set of friends Mansfield forever felt herself on the fringe of: Lytton Strachey, the stoop-shouldered, acid-tongued biographer who'd first introduced the two women; economist John Maynard Keynes, from whom Mansfield currently rented. At the heart of Bloomsbury's collective lore were images of Virginia Woolf's childhood, images Katherine Mansfield had no trouble conjuring: the famous father, Sir Leslie Stephen, celebrated scholar and man of letters, editor of the *Dictionary of National Biography*; the leafy silence of their Hyde Park Gate home, its dusky interiors ruffled only by the tissuey sound of pages being turned. The Stephens were a Victorian intellectual dynasty: related to Thackeray by marriage, descended from a long line of judges, writers and publishers. Favorite sons were groomed for Cambridge. The two ethereally beautiful Stephen sisters had inherited their left-over books. In photos, it was a household of children all wearing the elliptical half-smiles of ancient statues. From the nursery, Virginia Woolf had known the pantheon of her father's friends—Hardy, Tennyson, James—whose dark-bound volumes lined the library like the shiny backs of beetles.

Such a far cry from the sun-squinting New Zealand of Katherine Mansfield's "*wasted, wasted* early girlhood," a childhood of stiff crinolines and cream teas in the murderously hot colonial sun. The fat, neglected middle daughter of socially ambitious parents, she'd stuttered early on. Her father, a self-made banker, was a distant man with a fetish for the mimicked correctness of English life. Ignoring the daughter in steel-rimmed glasses, her mother had missed the often disobedient eyes. After being shipped off to boarding school in London, Katherine, on her return at age seventeen, was determined to lose more than the weight, the stutter, the steel-rimmed glasses. She'd strip herself of the fear of authority: father and fatherland. In 1908, at nineteen, she returned alone to London to improvise an independent life. But in the nine years since then, her first forays into adult freedom had occasioned a reckless string of acts that had long ago thinned to regrets. So many of them.

How very much couldn't be talked about tonight: the impetuous marriage at nineteen to a music teacher eleven years her senior whom she'd left the same night; the pregnancy by another man; the miscarriage; the lovers; the abortion. And now her current liaison with critic John Middleton Murry, with whom she'd lived since 1912. Perpetually scraping money together, she and Murry had long led a nomadic existence, since flats for unmarried couples were hard to come by in London. Only two weeks earlier she'd complained bitterly about the battery of addresses they'd shared in the past five years. "ALL those flats ALL those rooms we have taken and withdrawn from." It wouldn't change until she finally secured a divorce this next year. She couldn't discuss *that* tonight. None of it. Secrecy, she'd later advise Murry. "Don't lower your mask until you have another mask prepared beneath—As terrible as you like—but a mask."

Turning down Eaton Road from the station, the couple, like dozens of guests before and since, had been directed to look for "the 2nd house on the left at the join" of the cross street. Suddenly it loomed before them: the ludicrous aptness of the Woolfs' address. Paradise Road. Of course. Once again Katherine Mansfield found herself, as she would over and over, "a little colonial walking in the London garden patch—allowed to look, perhaps, but not to linger." But on that first night it's hard to imagine her not lingering for a moment outside the Woolfs' eighteenth-century townhouse. As she stared at the ancient brick of Hogarth House, its mullioned windows lit in the chill night, the comparison with her hostess wasn't lost on Katherine Mansfield. It was there from the beginning: the sting of jealousy, envy for the conditions that allowed for a creative life. Stability, a devoted husband, a room of one's own. Income.

Inside Hogarth House, Virginia Woolf waited that night much as she had so many evenings since first moving into the house in 1915. She felt "mute and mitigated" in Richmond, doomed to social exile imposed by her husband, Leonard. Suburban life, with its neutering quiet, left her "baffled and depressed." If only her guests knew how she secretly envied their freedom, to be in the stir of things, "not on the verge of them." Paradise Road indeed. It was enough to mock all the small domestic failures—how she often stitched her hems together with safety pins, or how she'd once cooked her wedding ring into a suet pudding. She couldn't mention that tonight. Or how, two years ago after a breakdown, four strapping nurses had monitored her in this very house. Or, a year and a half before that, how her now watchful husband had narrowly missed her swallowing Veronal. Or, earlier still, the breakdowns at thirteen and twenty-two, triggered by "the oriental gloom" of her childhood home—the procession of deaths: her mother, her half-sister, and, finally, her father, whose life, had he lived, "would have entirely ended" hers. Not for dinner talk: the nursing homes, the afternoons of madness, the birds outside the window spouting obscenities in Greek.

It all waited that night of January 12, 1917: the table set for five, the spoons heavy in the hand, the kind of silver that's only inherited. The cook, Nelly Boxall, prepared the meal, steam webbing her chin. The fifth guest, Katherine's cousin Sydney Waterlow, who'd unsuccessfully proposed to Virginia in 1910, was often late. Virginia Woolf waited instead for the first sound of the woman who had "dogged my steps for three years." Outside, that very woman stood on the threshold, her breath feathering the January night air.

Two women seated at a suburban dinner. On this evening and the ones that followed it, they eyed each other discreetly between bites of haddock. Netting impressions of the other,

Katherine's wide, dark brown eyes momentarily met Virginia's gray-blue ones, hooded like a falcon's. That night they took in what others, staring boldly, normally saw when looking at each woman. Virginia Woolf: tall, patrician, her skin fragile at the temples, her collar bones shimmering like ivory calligraphy above the square-necked dresses she usually preferred wearing. By contrast, the newcomer, Katherine Mansfield, was petite, her dark hair swept up like an artist's model's, the thick curtain of bangs so shiny one might see a reflection. Sensual, wary, bohemian, she had the shock of the new about her: the penchant for black, for silver stockings and, later, for sleekly bobbed hair. But the first impression of all who encountered her was the pale mask of a face, the thin lips pressed tight. To Virginia, Katherine soon seemed "of the cat kind: alien, composed, always solitary & observant." In Virginia, Katherine sensed the instinctive distance of someone born in a cool climate.

At that first dinner, though, neither was fully aware of how much they shared in common: authoritarian fathers; mothers lost to death or invalidism; the isolation of illness; the toll of time wasted. Each had lost a brother—Katherine's in World War I; Virginia's, after a trip to Greece in 1906, typhoid beckoning in a glass of clear water. Both women, subtly sparked by the other, would soon write about these lost brothers and childhoods. In doing so, each would finally find her own voice, the quest that until now had proved so elusive. Sitting at opposite ends of London, both writers used their diaries and notebooks not just to spark memory but, creatively, to forge this new transition, catching the shape of consciousness itself, ways of expression in stories and novels that had yet to be.

Virginia Woolf was thirty-four; Katherine Mansfield, twenty-eight. Neither had yet quite arrived.

That was soon to change. Four months from now in the same dining room, their lives would be altered forever, and with them, the fate of the modern short story and novel. Late in April 1917 a hefty crate arrived containing the printing press the Woolfs had bought for their new publishing venture, the Hogarth Press. On this same dining room table Virginia Woolf would learn to print, her long fingers nimbly setting inky blocks of typeface. After publishing her own short story first, she brought out a sixty-eight-page story by Mansfield, celebrated at another dinner in October 1917.

But at this first dinner neither understood how long the other had struggled to become a writer. Virginia's first novel, *The Voyage Out*, had been rewritten ten times over seven years. The failed drafts filled an entire cupboard. The day after it was published in 1915, Woolf had suffered a severe breakdown. Katherine's first book of stories, *In a German Pension*, had been written after suffering a miscarriage. Published in 1911, it had long been out of print. Ashamed of the collection, Mansfield argued even years later against its reprinting. "I really can't say to every ordinary reader 'Please excuse these horrid stories. I was only 20 at the time!' "

Seated at a suburban dinner party, who imagines the future beyond dessert? From this first night on, though, the creative lives of Virginia Woolf and Katherine Mansfield were paired in an intricate dance as friends, rivals and catalysts in each other's work. While 1917 began a friendship "founded on quicksands—marked by curious slides and arrests," Virginia could have been speaking for both when she later wrote of Katherine, "a woman caring as I care for writing is rare enough I suppose to give me the queerest sense of an echo coming back to me from her mind the second after I've spoken."

On that clear, icy night in January 1917, as the darkness pressed at the windows, could either woman imagine her new acquaintance replacing, as Virginia wrote, the "blankfaced old confidante" of her diaries and notebooks? Friendship as a living diary. Could either imagine how those diaries, proving ground for the talent, would soon become great working records of creative life, the first kept by women—not if but *how* to work? Or how for her future books she'd use, in the words of Virginia's husband, "the diary as a method of practicing or trying out the art of writing," determinedly exploring "the day-to-day problems of plot or form, of character"?

The conversation at this first dinner party, though, went unrecorded, the evening noted only in Leonard Woolf's meticulously kept diary. His diary, however, held no hint of the dramas soon to unfold: that one of the women had only seven years left to live. That, dying, she promised to send her diary to the other, who would review it, posthumously, four years later. That each of the husbands made small fortunes off their wives' diaries, which they'd publish. That each man saw the private diaries as parallel creative records to the stories and novels, providing generations hungry for blueprints of creative life with "an unusual psychological picture of artistic production from within." That the only time the diaries and notebooks were not in print was when Virginia Woolf and Katherine Mansfield were writing in them.

After a future social occasion Katherine told Virginia that the fun of any party was watching it with her. "All parties are cursed," she'd remarked, "if one cannot remain invisible at them." But on January 12, 1917, invisibility still plagued each of the women, "trained to silence" since childhood, as Virginia noted. How to become visible as writers, "to speak, invent, comment"? The race began: in public with each other; in private with themselves in their diaries and notebooks. In the seven short seasons left between them, time ticked, nervous as a pulse, as each monitored her slow progress:

Katherine: "I am 33 yet I am only just beginning to see now what it is I want to do. It will take years of work to really bring it off."

Virginia: "There's no doubt in my mind that I have found out how to begin (at 40) to say something in my own voice; & that interests me so that I feel I can go ahead without praise."

*O*n February 1, 1917, less than a month after the Woolfs' dinner, Katherine Mansfield inserted yet another Yale key into a new lock. 141a Old Church Street in Chelsea was a studio flat with a huge north-facing window illuminating the narrow space. Glass doors overlooked a small back garden. In the late afternoon, columns of dusty sunlight fell on the mantle on which sat a small borrowed Buddha, its lips set in implacable calm, the learned indifference to circumstance. This "address of my nunnery" was Mansfield's twelfth residence since arriving alone in London in 1908, determined to live off an allowance of £100 a year, the rest supplemented by her wits. "I'd far rather sit in a furnished room in a hotel & work than have a lovely flat & feel that the strain of money was crippling," she'd recently written her companion, John Middleton Murry, who'd taken separate rooms in nearby Redcliffe Road.

Once again Mansfield found herself trying to find her voice in a makeshift room determined by others' lives—walls bald from missing prints; carpets worn by the trafficked footprints of strangers; cupboards full of mismatched plates chipped by other hands. But with its curtained bedroom and tiny balcony kitchen above it, it would do nicely as a writer's room. "It is the only life I care about—to write[,] to go out occasionally and 'lose myself' looking and hearing and then to come back and write again. At any rate that's the life I've chosen." In her journal she noted small pleasures: the solitary meal, a book propped before her, blowing crumbs from its pages, falling asleep on the wide settee as treetops brushed the windows.

"Now really, what is it that I want to write? I ask myself. Am I less of a writer than I used to be?" she'd wondered only the year before. In 1917 she reflected hard on what she'd accomplished as a writer so far: a collection of well-received stories she now thought thin, sketches and stories published first in light magazines like *Idler*, then almost exclusively in the serious, avant-garde *New Age*. Then there was also the accomplishment of who she'd become in less than a decade in London. "My life as I see it up till now, complete with all its alarms, enthusiasms, terrors, excitements—[is] in fact the nature of an insurrection." A social rebel since childhood, she'd long rejected the narrowness of her bourgeois background, a life destined for unrelieved leisure. Born Kathleen Mansfield Beauchamp in Wellington, New Zealand, in 1888, she'd arrived in London in 1908 reinvented as Katherine Mansfield. Like everything her parents gave her, even her surname was subject to a kind of spiritual pawning. The subtle shift from Kathleen to Katherine was also more than a blurring of the past. It was one of the host of possible selves she'd tried on—Katie, Kass, K.M., Katharina, Tig—just as she'd literally tried on the occasional cameo role as a film extra to make pocket money. To the outside world she epitomized the New Woman— independent, sexually liberated, often reckless—someone who'd accented her flat once with chrysanthemums stuck into a prop skull, and who'd worn black to her doomed first wedding at a London registry.

But it was the "driving necessity—the crying need" to write that had brought her to London and to the attention of its numerous literary circles. Since her mid-twenties she'd moved on the fringes of Bloomsbury, the privileged if daring circle of painters and writers, many who had been friends of Virginia Woolf's brother at Cambridge. Katherine's sharp tongue and capacity to shock were both criticized and admired by the set known for its sexual and artistic freedom. In Bloomsbury, gossip was a blood sport and Katherine had been fair game since 1916. There was her dalliance with Bertrand Russell, her notorious capacity for flattery and treachery, for both lying and blistering honesty. Bloomsbury's mock emperor, the brilliant and languid biographer Lytton Strachey, secretly admired

Katherine's quick native intelligence and gift for storytelling. "Decidedly an interesting creature," he'd first written Virginia about Katherine, "very amusing and sufficiently mysterious." Secretive, impulsive, insecure about her colonial background, Mansfield had just enough vulnerability to be of interest in a kind of social experiment. "She spoke with great enthusiasm about the Voyage Out," he wrote Woolf, "and said she wanted to make your acquaintance more than anyone else's. So I said I thought it might be managed. Was I rash?" In Strachey's eyes, Katherine Mansfield and Virginia Woolf were just enough alike in ambition and talent for it to be stimulating—and uncomfortable.

But Katherine Mansfield was no colonial waif. Long aware of the creative capital her outsider status held, in 1917 she applied its edgy vitality to the first of a series of brilliant stories written in her London flat. In a half dozen temporary addresses, rooms with tables doubling for meals and work, her keen eye mercilessly dissected the customs and privileged worlds she'd often felt excluded from. Increasingly focused on frictions in marriage and class, she first turned to her own lost past. "Oh, I want for one moment to make our undiscovered country leap into the eyes of the Old World." That country wasn't just the New Zealand of her birth, but the uncharted terrain of her imagination.

Since her brother's death in 1915 she'd been mining a wave of memories of the childhood and country she'd left behind: the shimmering arc of Wellington harbor, the wooden houses with their red iron roofs, the hills silhouetted by "big dark plummy trees massed together." A single memory haunted her—the move she'd made at age five to the country, before returning to the security of the family's square white house with its pillared veranda. "The Aloe," first begun as a novel in 1915, sought to capture more than the subconscious inner life of children unsettled by a move. It contained the germ of all Mansfield's future work: the subtle estrangements be-

tween spouses, the insecurity of family, the haphazard improvisa-
tions of ordinary life.

For nearly two years Mansfield had wrestled with finding a new
shape to tell a story. "I want to write," she noted, "almost certainly
in a kind of *special* prose." Unmoored from home and homeland,
she'd invent a prose style mirroring that haunting disconnection.
She'd produce a bold new style: the poetry of discontinuity. Inching
the short story into modern life, she'd soon explore the self's shifting
core, as treacherously changeable as childhood itself. "The Aloe,"
later retitled "Prelude," was written as a series of snapshots connected by voice—a young girl wandering through the echoing emptiness of her old house; a cook hiding a grease-splattered book that
interprets dreams; a child watching a pet duck killed for supper, its
feathers soaked with blood. "The Prelude method," she'd later call
it. "It just unfolds and opens."

In 1917 Katherine Mansfield sat alone in her quiet studio, revis-
ing the story she'd first begun two years earlier. "I am a recluse at
present," she wrote Bertrand Russell, "& do nothing but write &
read & read & write—seeing nobody & going nowhere." In her
journal she mused on the price of this self-elected exile. "Even if I
should, by some awful chance, find a hair upon my bread and
honey—at any rate it is my own." The voice too would soon be her
own, a voice born in temporary rooms, illuminating all those outside
the thin walls of human safety—loners, children, servants, marital
exiles. "By the way," she'd soon write Murry, "isn't *Furnished
Rooms* a good title for a story?"

"*O*ur press arrived on Tuesday," Virginia Woolf wrote her sister at the end of April 1917. "I can see that real printing will
devour one's entire life. I am going to see Katherine Mansfield, to
get a story from her." It would be the first of several visits to

Mansfield's Chelsea studio. Over the seasons, she'd see the studio's work table crowned with various arrangements—in summer, saucers of dark ripe figs from the garden; in autumn, fresh quinces or vases of Michaelmas daisies. On that first visit, though, Virginia Woolf had come to talk work. The Hogarth Press, initially conceived by Leonard Woolf as a hobby for Virginia, a soothing activity after hours of writing, almost immediately became a serious business venture. The Woolfs were interested in publishing unknown but talented writers, in building a reputation as an innovative modernist press. By summer Katherine had submitted "Prelude," a story whose title fittingly signaled the start of the prickly professional friendship between the two women. The obstacle race to become known writers quickened with that first visit to Mansfield's studio, its yellow curtains lifting in the breeze as if beckoning each writer: *Hurry.*

Virginia Woolf, in a sense, had also invented herself in a series of solitary rooms. Born in 1882 into a "literate, letter writing, visiting" family and cultural world, she too had rebelled against the suffocating social constraints she'd inherited. The third child of a second marriage, she'd been fortunate in having parents suspicious of the solemn pieties of late-Victorian life. Her philosopher father, Leslie Stephen, was a scrappy, freethinking agnostic; her mother, Julia, a tireless social activist. Competition was stiff amid the boisterous clan of eight siblings, all clamoring for attention from a mother zealously driven by social ministry and from a father shrouded in scholarly solitude. "As a child," Virginia wrote nearly forty years later, "my days . . . contained a large proportion of this cotton wool, this non-being." The nursery, the library, the top-floor bedroom, quickly became her private sanctuaries. In the quiet corners of the Hyde Park Gate house, she converted its voluminous privacy into hours of scribbling, imitating her father and his industrious circle of famous friends who crowded the drawing room at teatime.

By age five she was inventing a story every evening for her

father. By nine she was producing the family newspaper. By fourteen she'd begun her first diary, hiding it from prying eyes in the covers of her father's logic treatise. The question of sibling competition had solved itself early on. Virginia would be a writer; her older sister Vanessa, a painter. With their brothers sent off to school and university, the two sisters with identical initials "formed together a very close conspiracy," working side by side on the top floor at Hyde Park Gate.

But the free-spirited childhood quickly halted after their mother's sudden death in 1895. From thirteen to twenty-two, Virginia, along with Vanessa and their half-sister, Stella, devolved to the dutiful role of caretaker, consoling their widowed father, whose sullen, grief-soaked tirades terrorized the sisters. With their father's death in 1904, the two surviving Stephen sisters were finally freed from the genteel expectations of Hyde Park Gate. "By nature, both Vanessa and I were explorers, revolutionists, reformers. But our surroundings were at least fifty years behind the times." In October 1904 they moved to 46 Gordon Square, in the then unfashionable borough of Bloomsbury. The move left behind far more than the narrow, shuttered house stranded in a cul-de-sac. For Virginia, it ended nine nightmarish years scarred by three family deaths, the first of her breakdowns and her half-brother's sexual gropings. The move also marked the end of a dark apprenticeship—learning to offset the depressions in the diaries, letting her subconscious work the losses like worry beads. It also began the long apprenticeship of learning to write fiction. She'd search for ways to voice what haunted her imagination: her mother's selfless vitality; her father's lonely, gloomy brilliance; the undertow of mental collapse. "A shock is at once in my case followed by the desire to explain it," she'd later write. "It is or will become a revelation of some order . . . It is only by putting it into words that I make it whole; this wholeness means that it had lost its power to hurt me."

At twenty-two, having survived a breakdown after her father's death, Virginia found herself in an adult paradise: unchaperoned, free to write, ensconced in her first real workroom. In Gordon Square's airy, high-ceilinged rooms, she and Vanessa worked. On Thursday evenings there was the social and intellectual stimulation of her brothers' college friends, among them her future husband, Leonard Woolf. Between 1907 and 1912 the circle of open minds met informally. Lytton Strachey's acerbic essays, *Eminent Victorians*, fired the first salvo at the social heroes of their parents' generation. Social independence, mental freedom and artistic experimentation were Bloomsbury's new bywords.

As a writer in training, though, Virginia had inherited her father's Victorian zeal for work and intellectual curiosity. Unlike Katherine Mansfield, who'd spent three years at Queen's College in London's Harley Street, Virginia had educated herself in her father's huge library, hungrily devouring books. While Bloomsbury sharpened her naturally analytical mind, her real literary education had been watching her father undertake his huge project, the *Dictionary of National Biography*. His biographical sketches, particularly of writers' lives, were models for the reviews and essays she'd write from 1904 on. At twenty-two she often visited the nearby British Museum, entering its domed reading room like "a thought in a giant's head," or sat undisturbed at home, surrounded by books found in the scores of local second-hand shops. Inside Gordon Square the young writer with a face of an etched Victorian cameo, chestnut hair and gray-blue eyes first felt the bite of modernism. Soon after her marriage in 1912, she began thinking about creativity and writing lives, especially the prolific life of Anon., who, like herself, had long "written up in all those rooms, too humble to be called libraries, yet full of books, where the pursuit of reading is carried on by private people."

On her way to Katherine Mansfield's solitary studio, though, that late afternoon in April 1917, it was another writer's work that had temporarily brought relief from the tedium of her own. She was in the middle of writing *Night and Day*, a "stone-breaking" second novel. Terrified of criticism, the psychic freefall after finishing *The Voyage Out*, she'd sought a safe, conventional narrative about marriage. Unlike Katherine, who'd improvised a modern life in still largely Victorian London, Virginia had accepted a life of twin beds, sexual passion sublimated into a working creative partnership. The new novel examined the tempting split between marriage and solitary creative life, "this astonishing precipice on one side of which the soul was active and in broad daylight, on the other side of which it was contemplative and dark as night."

By the summer of 1917 Katherine Mansfield and Virginia Woolf, writers born in opposing hemispheres, had allied themselves in work. In late June, Virginia told her sister that Katherine had "a much better idea of writing than most"; Katherine, in turn, wrote a mutual friend about Virginia, "I do like her tremendously," noting "the strange, trembling, glinting quality of her mind." In August, Virginia invited Katherine to her rented country house in Sussex. During the weekend Katherine delivered "Prelude" and Virginia first showed her what would become "Kew Gardens," her impressionistic story about couples strolling in a park. On her return to London, Katherine praised Virginia's new style, so eerily like her own in "Prelude." In reviewing the story when it was published in 1919, Katherine focused on the tight originality of craft. Whereas the "note-books of young writers are their laurels; they prefer to rest on them," Woolf's story was "so far removed from the note-book literature of our day . . . filling all that is within her vision with that vivid, disturbing beauty that haunts the air."

But even in 1917 the air was haunted by the disturbing beauty of their own discoveries as writers. Independently, each had invented a similar prose style, one that sought to map and mirror consciousness itself. Each was quarrying characters' inner lives—Virginia, the mind recording an ordinary day; Katherine, the anatomy of heartbreak. In between the acceptance of "Prelude" and its publication late in 1918, the two writers had time to reflect on unspoken questions each had sparked in the other. When does the thrill of mutual recognition subtly give way to the chill of competition? When is shared creativity poisoned by personal criticism? When does the room suddenly seem too small?

For Mansfield, the praises the Woolfs heaped on "Prelude" at a dinner in October 1917 were undercut by their delays in publishing. Virginia's final verdict on Katherine's story, much of it typeset herself on the treadle press, was summed up in the new diary she'd begun keeping. "I myself find a kind of beauty about the story, a little vaporish I admit, & freely watered with some of her cheap realities, but," she noted with competitive praise, "it has the living power, the detached existence of a work of art." At that dinner, a year before three hundred bound copies of "Prelude" crowded Hogarth House's top floor, Virginia had pulled a trial proof sheet to show Katherine. It suspended between the two writers' hands: a manifesto, a contract, a truce.

That truce was tested as Woolf and Mansfield soon entered identical professional forums as writers, critics and partners within competing literary marriages. The nettle of competition, though, temporarily dislodged itself at the end of 1917. As Virginia typeset "Prelude," Katherine sat in her damp studio flat plagued by high fevers, aches and a dry, racking cough. In 1918 a spot darkening her right lung was confirmed as tuberculosis. After visiting a frail Katherine, Virginia noted, "Illness, she said, breaks down one's privacy so that one can't write." That shattered privacy included the first of sunny winters in Italy and France, scores of doctors, some seven in all, and a host of cures. But just as a writer slips off a public mask in the privacy of a diary, so between 1918 and 1919 Virginia and Katherine first faced the vulnerability beneath their clever banter.

By November 1918 Virginia was making weekly visits to Portland Villas, the Hampstead house Katherine had moved into shortly after her marriage to John Middleton Murry earlier that year. Virginia, in a kind of crossover, assumed the role of initiator, bringing cigarettes, flowers, coffee, freshly baked breads. The visits, "religious meetings . . . praising Shakespeare," centered on their love of books and writing, the bright consuming flame of shared ambition. "I wonder why I feel an intense joy that you are a writer," Katherine told Virginia, "that you live for writing—as I do. You are immensely important in my world." In her diary Virginia echoed, "I find with Katherine what I don't find with the other clever women, a sense of ease and interest which is, I suppose, due to her caring so genuinely if so differently from the way I care."

Curious about a life so unlike her own, Virginia Woolf trekked to the tall, narrow house off Hampstead Heath with its cascading views of London below. Inside sunlit rooms the color of a "pale shell," she'd find Katherine seated next to a writing table cluttered with milk and medicine bottles. Katherine, a brilliant mimic with a pitch-perfect ear, often rallied to shock and amuse Virginia. "She's had every sort of experience, wandering with traveling circuses over the moors of Scotland," an astonished Virginia wrote a friend, alluding to Katherine's once joining a traveling opera troupe to be with a lover. Conversation, while intense, wasn't always intimate. The most private things, barely touched on in their diaries, remained conversational hedges—Virginia's insane half-sister, banished to the top floor of their childhood home; the shame of her half-brother's sexual fumblings; her celibate marriage. So too Katherine's shame at suffering early on from gonorrhea; her loneliness with Murry; her fear of, and desire for, pregnancy.

Skilled at probing to the core of characters' inner lives, Woolf and Mansfield often couldn't crack the surface of each other's. Katherine irritated Virginia with her cavalier claims of independence, that marriage was no more consequential than hiring a cleaning lady. And there was the odd relationship with Ida Baker. A former classmate and munitions worker, Ida served as Katherine's long-suffering housekeeper and companion on foreign trips. Ida's dull, worshipful nature, so willing to do Katherine's domestic bidding, made Portland Villas a strange nest. Privately, Virginia often found Mansfield "inscrutable." Katherine, terrified of lowering her mask, soon worried in her diary, "True to oneself! Which self?" By 1919 their pattern of wooing and withdrawing had a deeper cause. Because of Katherine's frequent travels and brave-faced letters, Woolf misread the seriousness of Mansfield's illness. Katherine's silences became Virginia's imagined slights. After Katherine returned from seven months in Italy, for example, Virginia noted, "K. is back I suppose; & I amuse myself with playing at the silly game—who's to take the first step."

The "durable foundation" Woolf sought with Mansfield was more subtly undermined by the envy coiling deep in each writer's psyche. In the gray-facaded Hampstead house Katherine had nicknamed "the Elephant," neither writer spoke of the real elephant in the room: their own discomfort with tolerating each other's successes, real and imagined. Years later, Virginia Woolf confessed, "We were both compelled to meet simply in order to talk about writing. This we did by the hour. Only then she came out with a swarm of little stories, and I was jealous, no doubt; because they were so praised." But in 1919 Virginia sat across from a visibly "husky & feeble" Katherine, fighting off her own consuming disease of envy, wishing success had happened to her first.

Alone with her notebook in her top-floor study, Virginia later wondered, "Is the time coming when I can endure to read my own work in print without blushing & shivering & wishing to take cover." In their private struggles both writers turned to diaries to shield them from the world's judgments. "I must be private, secret, as anonymous and submerged as possible in order to write," Woolf noted. Within their writing rooms, stubbing out a cigarette or ignoring a tea spot widening on a sleeve, both grappled daily with the problem Virginia posed to her diary: "Whom do I tell when I tell a blank page?" Often it was Katherine. But the stubborn habit of silence, born of writing in isolation, kept many of the discoveries each was making from 1919 on confined to their journals. In solitude, they wrote for an audience of one, determined to break through to the wider public just beyond the study walls.

"Unpraised, I find it hard to start writing in the morning, but the dejection lasts only 30 minutes," Virginia noted. "One should aim, seriously, at disregarding ups and downs; a compliment here, silence there." The silences that were their friendship's loss quickly became their journals' gain. Stories weren't lost in thin air over tea, polished and reduced to anecdote. Unknowingly, in their separate diaries Katherine Mansfield and Virginia Woolf held an ongoing conversation, recording the fluctuations of creative life. While Katherine, pulling a diary deep from a pocket, wrote on a succession of trains or in foreign hotel rooms, both writers used diaries as sketchbooks, producing lightning-quick portraits, the shock and immediacy of a recorded scene. "It strikes me that in this book I practice writing; do my scales; yes and work at certain effects," Virginia later wrote, "and shall invent my next book here."

While Katherine had burned the "huge complaining" diaries of her youth, after publishing a first story at nine, she'd "been filling notebooks ever since." The struggle—"*can* I be honest? If I lie, it's no use"—was solved by inventing herself as a writer in her journals, moving from confession to concrete observation. Like Woolf's, her adult journals thickened with reading lists, story titles, character names. As haphazard as her social life, Mansfield's journals were an odd whirlwind of notebooks, ledgers, exercise books. Drafts of letters mingled with shopping lists, thumbnail sketches, details for future stories. "My sciatica!" Katherine jotted. "Remember to give to someone in a story one day." Illness, envy, heartbreak—everything had its use. "It's very strange, but the mere act of *writing anything* is a help. It seems to speed one on one's way."

In 1919 Virginia Woolf reread her diaries, amused at how they'd grown "almost a face," their marbleized covers neatly lining her study shelves. For twenty-seven consecutive years her diaries, written at "rapid haphazard gallop," fed a creative intelligence that swallowed life whole: incisive, acid-etched portraits of friends, sketches of London, the stir of its streets. Writing in blank volumes patterned with Italian paper, she acknowledged, "I can trace some increase of ease in my professional writing which I attribute to my casual half hours," a diary propped on her knee after tea. Her diary became a hidden savings account for a planned future memoir. Netting "this loose, drifting material of life," Woolf imagined her diary as a deep old desk. In it, she hoped that memory "sorted itself and refined itself and coalesced, as such deposits so mysteriously do, into a mould, transparent enough to reflect the light of our life, and yet steady . . . with the aloofness of a work of art."

At opposite sides of London, Virginia Woolf and Katherine Mansfield privately took their sentences like hurdles. Even in diaries it meant the discipline of not letting "the pen write without guidance." "I have a passion for technique," declared Katherine. "Out of technique is born real style . . . There are no short cuts." Refining a story begun as a raw idea in the journal, she noted, "I choose not only the length of every sentence, but even the sound." Across London, Virginia scribbled, "I write variations of every sentence; compromises, bad shots; possibilities; till my writing book is like a lunatic's dream." Almost as if an echo answering her, Katherine wrote, "What happens as a rule is if I go on long enough I *break through.*"

Two years into their friendship both writers, yet again, were about to break through, their work appearing in professional forums each had inherited. In January 1919 John Middleton Murry assumed the editorship of the *Athenaeum*, the influential literary weekly. With their husbands, Katherine and Virginia each now had a public forum—the Woolfs', the Hogarth Press; the Murrys', *Athenaeum*. Each drew from a similar pool of writers—E. M. Forster, Bertrand Russell—while also publishing each other. In May 1919, for example, the Hogarth Press published T. S. Eliot's *Poems*, Virginia's *Kew Gardens* and Murry's *The Critic in Judgment*. Murry, in turn, used Virginia as a reviewer, but was careful not to eclipse Katherine, who'd become his regular weekly critic.

"Katherine is now in the very heart of the professional world—4 books on her table to review," Virginia watched as Katherine shot before the public eye, producing over a hundred reviews in eighteen months. Their private weekly meetings had finally found a public audience, neatly transforming their inner critics into paid reviewers. Katherine initially was the most helpful, working through Woolf's ideas on George Eliot or sharing excitement over Chekhov's letters. Independently, each used reviewing fiction to shape new ways of writing it. In the privacy of their rooms they read as critics and creators, searching often in reviewed diaries for Woolf's "moments of being," small details that suddenly render ordinary life extraordinary. Angered by an introduction to Dorothy Wordsworth's journals where an editor questioned the need to record tiny details of daily life, Katherine tartly jotted in the margin, "There is! Fool!" Late in 1919 both writers had begun to mine the territory of new, original work—Virginia laying the groundwork for her essay series *The Common Reader*; Katherine, for her brittle modern stories. "I do believe the time has come for a 'new word' but I imagine the new word will not be spoken easily," Katherine wrote. "It is a hidden country still."

If they now literally shared the same jobs, Bloomsbury, with its killer instinct for gossip, became a Greek chorus of attacks, pitting the two against each other. Success had divided them into literary camps animated by others' social insecurities. Murry dismissed Bloomsbury as an insular, "impotent Cambridge set," a literary Eden sustained on endless private trust funds. Although he was Oxford-educated, Murry's lower-middle-class origins sparked Bloomsbury's class snobbery, which branded him and Katherine the "Underworld," permanent social outsiders—writers grubbing for a living. While Virginia described a first *Athenaeum* lunch in her diary as "a long single file of insignificant brain workers eating bad courses," Katherine sided with her friend D. H. Lawrence's dismissal of the "Bloomsberries."

Katherine, as early as 1917, had implored Virginia to ignore Bloomsbury's gossip: "dont let THEM ever persuade you that I spend any of my precious time swapping hats or committing adultery." The real target of attack, though, was Katherine's influential husband, John Middleton Murry. The Murrys were seen as notoriously close, and Katherine suffered by association with the ambitious, gushingly self-absorbed Murry. Perpetually on her guard, she shielded the partner she'd met in 1912, first as her editor, soon her lodger and lover, the man for whom she'd left a note his first morning: "This is your egg. You must boil it. K.M." Years later, Leonard Woolf, an admirer of Mansfield, explained Katherine's increasing irritation with Murry. "She was a very serious writer, but her gifts were those of an intense realist, with a superb sense of ironic humour . . . She got emeshed in the sticky sentimentality of Murry and wrote against the grain of her own nature. At the bottom of her mind she knew this, I think, and it enraged her."

But as she packed for another artificial cycle of English springs and foreign winters, Katherine's bitterness went deeper. Murry possessed none of Leonard Woolf's stern protectiveness. Katherine often found herself forced to mother Murry, the boyishly handsome intellectual who, as her agent, was eager to promote her work—

something he'd make a lifelong career of—but was curiously impassive in coping with the crisis of tuberculosis. In her story "The Man Without a Temperament," she captured Murry's emotional diffidence—a man twisting a signet ring, covering his face as his ailing wife coughed. Condemned to winters alone, and forced to repay Murry any loaned money, Katherine rued, "How I envy Virginia; no wonder she can write. There is always in her writing a calm freedom of expression as though she were at peace—her roof over her head, her own possessions round her, and her man somewhere within call . . . what have I done . . . that I should have all the handicaps."

Arriving in foreign hotel rooms, asking to go to bed immediately, Katherine listened to the drum of the Mediterranean or the creak of wicker in her room, and compared literary marriages and fates. In England, Virginia was unaware she served as a compass point of envy in Katherine's foreign letters. But as early as 1917 it was Virginia who had privately set the tone for their uneasy alliance. In her diary her socially spiteful remark that the perfumed Katherine stank like a "cat that had taken to street walking" was followed almost immediately by a description of Katherine as "so intelligent" that friendship was inevitable. From reading their predecessors' diaries, both writers knew that the nineteenth century had parceled its rewards in small lots. But early in twentieth-century literary life, rivalry had begun to wear the hauntingly familiar face of another woman. If Virginia and her sister had kept ambition safe in different creative professions—Vanessa illustrating all Virginia's books— Katherine was all too similar. Childless, ambitious, more star than outsider, she inconveniently proved herself Virginia's blood equal. "Katherine is the very best of women writers," Virginia wrote a friend, slyly adding, "always of course passing over one fine but very modest example." From 1919 on, Woolf kept Mansfield firmly, if superstitiously, checked in her side vision, aware of the rival who'd once practiced signatures in a diary as if already autographing books.

Years later, remembering the long afternoons of talk over milky tea spent at her yellow table, Katherine wrote Virginia, "I wonder if you know what your visits were to me—or how much I miss them. You are the only woman with whom I long to talk *work*. There will never be another." Virginia later mused on Katherine: "Probably we had more in common which I shall never find in anyone else. (This I say in so many words . . . again & again.)" But until that final hard-won understanding, they wrestled, writers locked in a struggle of fear, envy, bad faith, private judgments, all worked out through the high-wire act of public professional lives.

On November 21, 1919, Katherine was the first to cross the line.

That autumn Murry sent Katherine, then recovering in Italy, Virginia's second novel, *Night and Day*, for review. As Katherine's search for cures turned from the mild sea air of Cornwall to the pure oxygen of Switzerland, she thanklessly tried to write reviews to offset mounting medical bills. Instead of writing fiction, for nearly eighteen months she'd spent her energies on reviewing. Unbeknownst to her, when her shockingly cynical story "Bliss" first appeared in 1918, Virginia had privately reviewed it in her diary. "Her mind is very thin soil," she wrote after flinging down the story. "For Bliss is long enough to give her a chance of going deeper. Instead she is content with superficial smartness; & the whole conception is poor, cheap . . . She'll go on doing this sort of thing, perfectly to her & Murry's satisfaction . . . Or is it absurd to read all this criticism of her personally into a story?"

Alone in Italy, burning for letters and for the printed English word, Katherine found the long, conventionally told *Night and Day* a failure, a judgment Leonard Woolf later privately concurred with. She called it "a lie in the soul" for its omission of the war that had killed her brother, but most damning in Katherine's appraisal was how far it fell short of the new modernist fiction she and Virginia had championed as reviewers. For Katherine, World War I had shattered the old order forever. Modern life—and new ways of writing—were being given their difficult birth. But Katherine's anxiety over health quickly gave way to anxiety over her review. A panicked flurry of nine letters to Murry in sixteen days. "My review of Virginia haunts me," she confessed, offering to rewrite it. Scattered among the muted praise of "exquisite" and "cultivated" was Katherine's fatal subconscious code for Virginia herself. Comparing the novel to a ship coming full sail into harbor, Katherine wrote, "The strangeness lies in her aloofness, her air of quiet perfection, her lack of any sign that she has made a perilous voyage—the absence of any scars."

On a morning of dripping English rain, November 28, 1919, Virginia Woolf reread the review by the friend to whom, only four months earlier, she had prayed in her diary, "Don't do mine!" Stung to the core, she turned to her diary. "She let her wish for my failure have its way with her pen," she wrote, imagining Katherine's motive. " 'I'm not going to call this a success—or if I must, I'll call it the wrong kind of success.' " Only later would the review-phobic Virginia admit her own need as a published writer: "I want to appear a success even to myself." But much in her life was soon to change: a move back into London itself; writing essays that illuminated "the obscure, the fragmentary, the failure"; and, in September 1920, beginning her third novel, *Jacob's Room*. In it and all the novels to follow, she cracked the creative code of her own voice. After the tedium of *Night and Day* she let images embedded deep in her subconscious surface, images of the ten idyllic childhood summers she'd spent in St. Ives, Cornwall: rolling a cricket ball covered in luminous paint late into the night; Talland House, with its thick escallonia hedge and stone urns; children, their mouths stained crimson from currants, watching afternoon shadows lengthen on the sloping knoll. One memory stood out: herself at six, falling asleep to the sound of the sea and to an acorn tethered to a blind that dragged across the nursery's wooden floor in the night wind. The details appeared soon as clues in the notebooks, "shivering fragments" of memory and desire that coalesced into lyrical flights of language—a writer possessed finally and inescapably of her own voice.

*L*ike a first draft, friendship itself is subject to endless revisions. And in the spring of 1920, despite Katherine's stinging review, Virginia Woolf once again traced her steps to North London to Katherine Mansfield's familiar door shaded by willow trees. After an initial chilliness, Virginia found "we fell into step, & as usual, talked as easily as though 8 months were minutes." Just beyond the open windows, views of Hampstead Heath beckoned. Katherine's illness was unmistakably clear, and with it, the canker of competition dissolved. Sitting across from Virginia, the once fat New Zealand schoolgirl was now painfully thin. Dressed in tartan woolens during a mild English May, she moved stiffly, her face worn with the waxy pallor of the consumptive. Her rings slid loose on her fingers. But, she told Virginia, she was beginning stories in a new style.

Studying Katherine's sunken, wide-set brown eyes, Virginia again realized that Katherine's hard composure was on the surface. "I feel a common certain understanding between us—a queer sense of being 'like'—not only about literature—& I think it's independent of gratified vanity. I can talk straight out to her." And for a brief English spring and summer in 1920, they did just that. In June, Virginia recorded "2 hours priceless talk." With the exception of her diary and Leonard, "to no one else can I talk in the same disembodied way about writing; without altering my thought." Their voices lowered—out of earshot of Murry, in the next room—Katherine confessed the price of foreign exile: Murry's inadequacies in crisis, her own lashing out at Ida Baker, her faithful nurse and warden. A terrifying winter alone, bedridden, a gun by her bed.

"We talked about solitude," Virginia recalled, "& I found her expressing my feelings, as I never heard them expressed." In Mansfield's tidy, book-stacked house, Virginia told Katherine that she had changed, had mastered a strange self-command where "subterfuges were no longer necessary." But, knees pressed against the common space of a tea table, Katherine still withheld much: the shame of her room being fumigated in Italy; the spate of failed injections and cures since coughing up blood in 1919; the haunting memory from her early Cornwall diary: "The man in the room next to mine has the same complaint . . . And after a silence I cough. And he coughs again. This goes on a long time. Until I feel we are like two roosters calling to each other at false dawn."

Illness had pared her body to a terrible translucence, but it had also winnowed the writing—spare, direct, clear-eyed. What she still couldn't say, she'd write instead. At thirty she was composing in a whole new manner—using inner shifts of time, letting subtle character detail and metaphor carry a story's deeper meaning. Reviewing fiction had deepened her own stories, giving them a new authority and tone. Between 1920 and 1921, in France, Italy and Switzerland, she wrote her best work, an astonishing surge of stories, among them: "Je ne parle pas français," "Miss Brill," "Poison," "The Daughters of the Late Colonel," "The Life of Ma Parker," "The Doll's House," "At the Bay" (a sequel to "Prelude") and "Marriage à la Mode."

In a series of rented houses nestled in dry hills in France and Italy, Katherine Mansfield worked against the clock—Keats and Chehkov, fellow consumptives, constants on her night table. In letters, Katherine conjured the heat and health of Mediterranean life: bougainvillea latticing stone walls, acres of almond and orange groves. But, increasingly, exhaustion, anxiety, bitter loneliness, set in. Illness had tempered her impetuous nature with a fierce patience. Forced to write paragraphs as short as the catch of her breath, in 1920 she revived the idea of publishing "a minute notebook." The black notebook she'd kept to record black days of fatigue and writer's block might be edited, showing breakthroughs such as writing "The Man Without a Temperament" in a single day, finishing at midnight. Her private journal had become an invalid's insurance policy, tiny premiums for future stories. "One must write about a doctor's waiting room," she'd note. "The glass doors with the sun from outside shining through; the autumn trees pale and fine; the cyclamen, like wax." Long fearful of all the still unwritten stories, she rued, "How unbearable it would be to die—leave 'scraps', 'bits' . . . nothing real finished." In 1917 she had noted that "to be alive and to be a 'writer' is enough." But by 1920 "even the *appearance* of the world is not the same . . . *Everything had its shadow.*"

In December 1920 Katherine burst into the world with her story collection *Bliss*, published not by the Hogarth Press but by the more prestigious Constable. Stronger stories followed. In February 1922 her third collection, *The Garden Party*, also published by Constable, went through three editions in just three months. In the interval, as Katherine was coping abroad, Virginia struggled with jealousy, imagining soaring sales. Unaware of just how frail Katherine had become, Virginia still jockeyed for position. "I've plucked out my jealousy of Katherine by writing her an insincere-sincere letter. Her books praised for a column in the Lit Sup—the prelude of paeans to come. I foresee editions; then the Hawthornden prize next summer . . . I've had my little nettle growing in me, & plucked it out . . . I've revived my affection for her somehow, & don't mind, in fact enjoy."

In August 1920, before either of Mansfield's collections had appeared, Virginia journeyed to Hampstead to say goodbye to Katherine, off for two years. They agreed to correspond. "She will send me her diary. Shall we? Will she?" Virginia wondered. "If I were left to myself I should; being the simpler, the more direct of the two." In a strange bid for openness, Katherine pressed a reluctant Virginia to review *Bliss*. Wondering if she meant it, Virginia mused, "Strange how little we know our friends."

On August 23, 1920, as Virginia left, winding her way down Hampstead's narrow shady streets, Katherine was about to embark on a path of "the soul's desperate choice." Illness, like writing, had focused difficult questions of identity. "The question is always 'Who am I?' and until that is discovered I don't see how one can really direct anything." In Switzerland from June 1921 to January 1922, Katherine worked nonstop on stories. While inventing characters, she reinvented her own. The clever falseness, the lying and disguises, were replaced by a sense of urgency "to become a conscious direct human being." In Switzerland, Murry was finally at her side, but the bleak prospect of expensive X rays in Paris still loomed. "Everything in life that we really accept undergoes a change," she wrote in her journal. "So suffering must become Love. That is the mystery." In 1922 Katherine struggled to get the psyche's final wording as right as possible. Despite the bitter memory of how her own father had once burned a published story she'd sent him, she continued to write stories, often about family, with nimble speed. On January 24, 1922, she wrote "Taking the Veil" in three hours. On July 7, a final story, "The Canary." On August 4 she signed a will. On October 16, 1922, she traveled from Paris to Fontainebleau, seeking a spiritual cure at Gurdjieff's Institute for the Harmonious Development of Man. Among her possessions was her passport, issued in 1919. Inside, in the second space at the top, next to "Profession," was a long blank line.

"*K*.M. bursts upon the world in glory next week," Virginia monitored just before *The Garden Party* was published. "I have to hold over Jacob's Room till October; & I somehow fear that by that time it will appear to me sterile acrobatics." Still measuring her own work by Katherine's, by 1922 Virginia had nonetheless achieved a life to be envied. The Hogarth Press flourished. Freud, T. S. Eliot, E. M. Forster, headed its list. Weekends were spent at Monk's House, the weatherboard cottage the Woolfs had bought in 1919. Nestled deep in the Sussex Downs, it had low flint walls, a tangle of a garden and carp knifing the pond's dark waters. Relaxation and concentration, twin aids to her productivity, were spurred by a quietly robust life—walking, playing lawn bowls, putting up marmalade. "Quiet brings me cool clear quick mornings, in which I dispose of a good deal of work and toss my brain into the air when I take a walk." She flourished at the essay-reviewing work Katherine had abandoned. Refining an intimate armchair style, she'd leave a unique imprint as one of the twentieth century's finest literary essayists. But it was her breakthrough novel that seized her imagination. Like Katherine's "Prelude," *Jacob's Room* was conceived as a homage to a dead brother. Also like "Prelude," it pioneered stream of consciousness technique. Puzzled and hurt that Katherine hadn't replied to her last letter, Virginia put the final touches on *Jacob's Room*.

On January 12, 1923, Nelly Boxall, the Woolf's cook at that first dinner in January 1917, burst in: " 'Mrs. Murry's dead! It says so in the paper!' " In her diary Virginia wrote:

At that one feels—what? A shock of relief—a rival the less? Then confusion at feeling so little—then, gradually, blankness & disappointment; then a depression which I could not rouse myself from all that day. When I began to write, it seemed to me there was no point in writing. Katherine wont read it. Katherine's my rival no longer. More generously I felt, But though I can do this better than she could, where is she, who could do what I can't! . . . Sometimes we looked very steadfastly at each other, as though we had reached some durable relationship, independent of the changes of the body . . . Yet I certainly expected that we should meet next summer, & start fresh. And I was jealous of her writing—the only writing I have ever been jealous of. This made it harder to write to her . . . Yet I have the feeling that I shall think of her at intervals all through life.

Katherine had died at thirty-four, exactly Virginia's age when they'd first met. Up to two months before Virginia's own death in 1941, Katherine still figured in her diary, the eighth to last entry. In 1923, at Murry's request, Virginia typed up Katherine's letters to her for a collected volume. Widower turned literary impresario, Murry had begun the hugely successful business of Mansfield's posthumous work. Coalescing fragments from her many journals and exercise books, he published them as a single journal in 1927. A royalty check from *The Doves' Nest*, collected stories, netted Murry ten times more than Katherine had earned in her career. Murry's careful but shrewd editing presented a romantically distorted portrait of Katherine as suffering artist, a legacy that overshadowed her work. But by 1927 the cult of Katherine was in full swing. Pale imitators later included Murry's second wife, who copied Katherine's bobbed fringe and dress style. Hearing that she too had tuberculosis, she gushed to Murry, "I wanted you to love me as much as you loved Katherine—and how could you, without this?"

In September 1927 Virginia Woolf quietly read in the Tavistock Square house she'd moved into a year after Katherine's death. On her lap sat the review copy of Katherine's edited journal. In her review Virginia acknowledged Katherine as a born writer: "Everything she feels and hears and sees is not fragmentary and separate; it belongs together as writing." While admiring the journal's sketches and details for unfinished stories, "we feel we are watching a mind alone with itself . . . There is no literary gossip; no vanity; no jealousy." Titling her review, "A Terribly Sensitive Mind," Virginia hinted at a strange cloudiness in Katherine's thinking. But seven years later Virginia wrote a friend, "She had a quality I adored and needed; I think her sharpness and reality." Despite false steps in friendship, each writer had profited from struggling with another so like and unlike herself. At opposite ends of 1922, Virginia Woolf and Katherine Mansfield were linked in one final pairing. *The Garden Party* and *Jacob's Room* joined T. S. Eliot's *The Waste Land* and James Joyce's *Ulysses* in the creative conjunction of a year in which modern literature was born.

"Still there are things about writing I think of & want to tell Katherine," Virginia wrote days after Mansfield's death. Katherine never read *Jacob's Room*, the novel she'd helped spark. Without a rival to spur her, Virginia turned competition back to its source: with herself. Over the next eighteen years she'd produce a steady succession of novels, some six in all, among them her masterpieces, *Mrs. Dalloway*, *To the Lighthouse* and *The Waves*. Throughout, she used her diary to note the intricate process of discovery in writing. "As for my next book," she wrote after *Orlando*, "I am going to hold myself from writing till I have it impending in me: grown heavy in my mind like a ripe pear; pendant, gravid, asking to be cut or it will fall." In the late afternoon she'd reflect on the morning's work—fiction, biography or essays. Her writer's diary, later excerpted and published by Leonard Woolf, provided an incisive working commentary on the furious hopes and irritations of creative life, work ruined by migraine or interruption, salvaged by the unexpected connection.

With the same unflinching eye she trained on her work, so, in midlife, she examined the fault lines in her own life. "Vanessa. Children. Failure" became shorthand for the failure she felt next to her sister's domestic and creative success. As with Katherine, not having children haunted Virginia. Both not only gave literature some of its most indelible images of children but, in giving birth to themselves as writers, gave birth to others who followed. The legacy of Mansfield's and Woolf's friendship wasn't rivalry so much as the way influence works in writers' lives, a bond as stubbornly potent as family. Creativity, for Woolf, was an invisible web where ideas were connected and "fertilized only by other peoples . . . thinking it too."

From 1925 on, she honored that connection, reading Alice James, publishing Sonya Tolstoy's autobiography, writing essays on writers' lives, collected into the two *Common Reader* series. Her creative debt to literary ancestors culminated in *A Room of One's Own*, her brilliant meditation on the circumstances needed for "the habit of freedom and the courage to write." What had been difficult with a contemporary like Katherine Mansfield could be shared with those who came before and after. To future generations of writers Virginia Woolf noted, "Masterpieces are not single and solitary births; they are the outcome of many years of thinking in common, of thinking by the body of a people, so that the experience of the mass is behind a single voice."

But in 1932 she began the singular torture of writing *The Years*, her novel chronicling a London family from 1880 to 1918. Going through ten titles, she labored five years, much of it spent in nightmarish revision, cutting down from 700 to 420 pages. While *The Years* was hailed as a success, becoming her first American bestseller, the strain of compulsive rewriting triggered a breakdown. The rise of fascism, the death of friends such as Lytton Strachey, as well as her nephew (in the Spanish Civil War), had also soured the fruits of fame. By 1941, with the Battle of Britain destroying London, Virginia found herself increasingly isolated at Monk's House with "no public to echo back." Alone at her trestle table in her writer's lodge, she surveyed a countryside spiraled with barbed wire. "I mark Henry James' sentence: observe perpetually. Observe the oncome of age. Observe greed. Observe my own despondency." At fifty-nine, long wary of euphoria and depression swings, she wrote, "Occupation is essential," noting the value of writing even humble details of daily life—haddock and sausage for supper—in her diary. But three years into the war the final threat wasn't foreign invaders but interior ones: the dark racing voices she'd heard in youth at Hyde Park Gate now whispered once again. Death, she'd noted in her diary, was "the one experience I shall never describe." On March 28, 1941, leaving a note for Leonard on the mantle, she weighted her pockets with stones and headed toward the river Ouse.

As her tall back receded across the chalk-quarried South Downs, she was leaving behind seventeen books and shelves of diaries. In one for 1931, Virginia had written, "I had three [dreams] lately: one of Katherine Mansfield: how we met, beyond death, & shook hands; saying something by way of explanation, & friendship: yet I knew she was dead. A curious summing up, it seemed[,] of what had passed since she died." Their lives had strangely mirrored their works—Katherine's the intense brevity of the short story, Virginia's the longer rhythms of the novel. Two weeks after hearing of Katherine's death, Virginia once again took out her diary. "Go on writing of course: but into emptiness. There's no competitor . . . For our friendship had so much that was writing in it." But standing on the threshold that first January night in 1917, could Katherine Mansfield or Virginia Woolf have predicted how this strange current of connection would so mysteriously alter the other's life? Or were the two pairs of eyes too busy noting everything—the guest's pale masklike face, the hostess's extended ungloved hand, the smell of supper rushing into the wintry air, the way the cold sharpens the senses. As Katherine later observed, "It's always a kind of race to get in as much as one can before it *disappears*."

Virginia Woolf, an undated and rarely seen photograph of the successful writer. (The Hogarth Press, London)

Anaïs Nin and her diaries in the Brooklyn vault.
(Marlis Schwieger)

5

THE
PROFESSIONALLY
PRIVATE WRITER

I wonder if there exists a God of Writers whose
justice is distributed only according to what is for
the good or evil of literature.

—ANAÏS NIN (aged nineteen), *Diary*

What does the world need, the illusion I gave in
life, or the truth I give in writing?

—ANAÏS NIN (aged thirty), *Diary*

$\mathscr{I}$nside the vestibule at 215 West Thirteenth Street, a row of brass doorbells, as tiny as the buttons on a woman's blouse, awaited callers. The building, a five-story brownstone, was situated on one of the shady cross streets in New York City's Greenwich Village. On the top floor an artist's studio had skylights running the length of the ceiling. The glass panels had been painted to look like stained glass. The tenant, Anaïs Nin, had hand-painted them herself so that the afternoon light would fall in a prism of primary colors. Friends had helped her improve the studio's plain wood furniture. The chairs, worktables and chests had been crayoned in intricate waxy patterns, "tangled forests of flowers, leaves, mandalas, lace patterns, monsters out of nightmares, exotic birds, cosmic wheels." (Nin's lover, a half-Scottish, half-Peruvian revolutionary, would later upset the furniture in a drunken jealous rage, smearing the designs.) With its clusters of candles, its floor draped with American Indian serapes, the studio had the hushed brilliant hues of "a pagan cathedral."

In the autumn of 1940 Anaïs Nin sat inside the top-floor studio waiting for the buzzer to ring. Petite, with wrenlike wrists and collar bones, she still resembled her childhood nickname, Linotte, little bird. Her eyes, like the afternoon light, often changed color. In certain lights, they were green, flecked with gold; at other times, a deep brown. She dressed with the studied eclecticism of the bohemian world outside—flared skirts, lace blouses, chunky Spanish jewelry. Around her neck she often wore a tiny gold key. It dangled between the breasts she thought too small. The key fit a locked iron box. For over a decade she had used iron or safe deposit boxes to hide and protect her diaries. In a different New York apartment, she'd later actually erect a false closet wall to hide the accumulating diaries, certainly the most current but also the earliest, which she had kept since childhood. In time, she'd deposit all of them in two five-drawer file cabinets in a bank vault just across the East River in Brooklyn. Only in a bank vault would her diaries be safe from loss, safe from her recurrent nightmare of fire. "If the diaries burned, I would be left only with this persona, smiling, ever available, ever devoted."

It was the persona, though, that the individual men who stood outside her vestibule had come to see. Checking a watch, stubbing out a cigarette on the stone steps, each waited a moment before pressing the fifth-floor buzzer. The building had no elevator. Nin had devised a complicated system of rings so that one lover wouldn't meet another on the stairs to the walkup apartment. Long rings. Short, staccato rings. Multiple rings. Like distress signals, each had his own code. Nin's lovers—artists, poets, critics, the odd investment banker—each entered the studio with its strange, carnival-cathedral light. In the center stood Anaïs Nin, novelist, lay analyst and, rumor had it, keeper of a legendary diary. In 1932 her friend the novelist Henry Miller had written in T. S. Eliot's magazine, *The Criterion*, that, when published, the diary would stand beside "the revelations of St. Augustine, Petronius, Abelard, Rousseau, Proust."

But, of course, that was not why the various men climbed the long flight of stairs. Geisha, confidante, mistress, Anaïs Nin would smile, welcome each, her eye color shifting. In late afternoons she took her lovers and, like Scheherazade, spun endless stories of her childhood—Paris, city of her birth; New York, city of her adolescence. Still trilling her *r*'s, her voice had the faint breathy hint of a French accent. If asked, she'd tell each man, as she had her childhood diary, that Spanish "is the language of my ancestors, but French is the language of my heart, and English of my intellect." Even though she was in her late thirties, Nin's body could have been that of a young girl: a slender, supple one hundred and fifteen pounds. Nin shrewdly used the afternoon's quick warm couplings to study illicit desire. A collector had commissioned her to write erotica at a dollar a page. It paid the sixty dollars a month rent. The stories remained a secret to most of the men, who, as they finally descended the stairs, felt themselves bathed in the same intense attention she trained on her diary.

After each lover, sometimes between them, Anaïs Nin opened her current diary. In longhand slanting to the right, she mused on her favorite topic: the diary and her split self. "The false persona I had created for the enjoyment of my friends, the gaiety, the buoyant, the receptive, the healing person, always on call, always ready with sympathy, had to have its other existence elsewhere. In the diary I would reestablish the balance . . . *I could let out my demons.*" But the diary had already proved to be its own kind of demon. For over half a century Nin would wander "the labyrinth of my diary," a maze as complicated as the one-way and cul-de-sac Greenwich Village streets outside her window. Over the years, she transcribed, typed, retyped, edited, arranged, ordered and reordered the mounting volumes. The topic was always the same: the personal and creative struggle over love and vocation, love *as* vocation. Occasionally she let select readers see portions of the diary. But the readers were part of the diary's problem. They were also its subjects. So too, as she called them, her "children," the lovers, mostly aspiring artists like herself, whom she supported, squirreling away money from her household budget to pay their rents and, occasionally, their wives' medical bills. (Without a shred of irony, Nin once recorded finding for a lover's wife the very thing that might alert her to their affair: a hearing aid.)

The problem wasn't the wives, but their husbands—the lovers who urged she quit the diary. "I only regret that everybody wants to deprive me of the journal," she confessed of the habit others regarded as "my drug, my secret vice." The diary, they argued, siphoned vital creative energy away from the novels and short stories she should be writing. Like an odalisque in a harem, Nin admitted that the diary was "my kief, hashish, and opium pipe . . . Instead of writing a novel, I lie back with this book and a pen, and dream, and indulge in refractions and defractions." Nin, who gave her body so freely, also suffered from a kind of literary nymphomania, "writing on cafe tables while waiting for a friend, on the train, on the bus, in waiting rooms at the station, while my hair is being washed." (Her lovers discouraged the compulsive writing, not the sex.) For Nin, though, sex and writing were entwined. Even cataloguing her diary's traveling hiding places read like a list of furtive sexual trysts: "buses, subways, taxis, lecture-hall desks, brief cases, in doctors' offices, hospital waiting rooms, park benches . . . The pages often stained with coffee, wine, tears, lipstick. It has traveled in canoes, ships, hidden among dresses, underwear, and once lay on the window sill outside of a hotel window, once on a fire escape in New York."

"Drawn to my pen as if by a magnet," she "resolved to write, write, and write . . . not look back or I will be frightened by what *I am.*" Originally written in childhood French, the adult diary had long been kept in English, the one language her critical musician father couldn't read. Guarding the diaries against the "preoccupation from prying eyes, from outside judgments," she was torn between a simultaneous need to hide and to be revealed. So too a need to shape the diary—and her very identity—into a final creative statement. More careful in her diary selections than in her erotic partners, she amassed some 150 volumes, dozens of file folders stuffed with looseleaf entries, over 35,000 final pages of diary. In 1966, portions would finally be published in seven volumes, the first appearing when she was sixty-three. After her death in 1977 two books of erotica appeared, followed by four volumes of childhood diaries. Later, three volumes of "unexpurgated" diary surfaced. By the early 1980s over three million copies of her books were in print.

As the books climbed the bestseller lists, garnering foreign translation rights, Anaïs Nin's diaries gradually embodied her favorite vocabulary: mirrors, labyrinths, masks, doubles. Art or artifice? Had Nin violated the diary's most cardinal sin, not telling the truth? Could a diary lie and still have truth embedded within it? Is deception or self-deception worse? Nin left a creative legacy at once hothouse, controversial, and rigged as complexly as her lovers' doorbell signals. Even the posthumous publication of the diaries, carefully controlled by her estate, continued their artful selection, unveiling Nin in a slow literary and psychological striptease. Like one of her novel's titles, the diary's reader became a Spy in the House of Love. For many, fascinated or appalled by what had been left out of the originals, the Diary became "the Liary." Her cult status, as icon of feminine creative will, soon revealed a woman not only who couldn't say no to men but who couldn't say an unconflicted yes to her own creativity. But not before the successful seduction of millions of readers, election to the American Academy and Institute of Arts and Letters, and, in 1976, a year before her death, being named by the *Los Angeles Times* as Woman of the Year.

Keeping the stories and versions of herself straight was a lifelong battle. In 1932 she'd briefly kept two sets of diaries. One red, the other green. The latter, a kind of false green light, was kept for her husband, the patient financier who supported her and, unwittingly, all her "children"—the man left out of the first published diaries. As a banker, Hugh Guiler should have had an instinct for a false set of books. But he championed the creativity that had a gnawing erotic compulsiveness to it. Perhaps he knew that it was only to the diary that she'd ever be totally faithful, a wild fidelity as passionate as a lover's secret note, as chaste as a blank page.

From the start the diaries included drawings and photos. Often line drawings silhouetted the pages of school notebooks used for the earliest diaries. Skyscrapers bend over a stick figure of a little girl, dizzy from the newness of New York. A ship's anchor with *"mon journal"* written down its center is perched upon by two birds spelling *Anaïs* and *my soul.* Photos were inserted in the later, leather-bound volumes. They showed Nin's poised beauty, her wavy chestnut hair hanging to her waist or coiled in a chignon. Later, when she sent her novels out to publishers, Nin sometimes included a packet of photos like a pre-publicity kit. If the printed word didn't charm and seduce, the photos would. Startlingly exotic, they conjured Nin's bohemian adult life: a view of the Seine from her Parisian houseboat; Nin in costume as a Spanish dancer, a spit curl coiled on her forehead like an upside-down question mark. In all the photos, from youth to just before her death at seventy-three, the face is eerily the same: the wide-set, heavily kohled eyes, the heart-shaped face, the chin with the hard final point of a tapered valentine.

Of all the photos, though, three frame the official version of Anaïs Nin's life. In the first, taken in the mid 1930s, a thirty-two-year-old Nin sits in her garden in Louveciennes, on the outskirts of Paris. Seated at a table, she wears a cape she's designed and a bracelet studded with cat's-eyes. Her shoulder-length hair is pulled back by a wisp of a headband. Behind her are the thick, ivy-covered walls of her two-hundred-year-old house. Its garden is a rich tangle of greenery—blossoming acacia, wild strawberries. Just as, across the Channel, members of Bloomsbury sit gossiping in their gardens, so Nin and her guests—novelist Henry Miller, actor Antonin Artaud and, later, writer Lawrence Durrell—sit discussing the same subjects: literature, sex, analysis. Their work, though, has a gritty surrealist edge—a love of fragments and dreamlike imagery—so popular between the world wars. Nin's guest list also occasionally includes the analysts René Allendy and Otto Rank. As they've initiated her into analysis, so she'll help Miller publish his first novel, *The Tropic of Cancer*. All the guests have read parts of her diary. They share an uneasy admiration for it. (What isn't written on the back of the photo is that Miller is already her lover. So too, in time, her analysts, Allendy and Rank.)

In the second photo Anaïs Nin, aged forty-one, stands in a small Greenwich Village loft at 144 Macdougal Street. Her hair is swept up in a froth of soft curls so fashionable in the mid-1940s. She wears a canvas printer's smock over a sensible skirt and blouse. Her espadrilled foot pushes the pedal of the treadle printing press. Tired of being rejected by commercial publishers, she's started her own press, the Gemor Press. In 1944 *Under a Glass Bell*, her collection of stories, is reviewed in *The New Yorker* by critic Edmund Wilson. "The main thing to say," he writes, "is that Miss Nin is a very good artist, as perhaps none of the literary Surrealists is." The collection will sell out in three weeks. (Not written on back of the photo is that after the review Nin had a brief, fitful affair with Wilson, who declared, "I would love to be married to you, and I would teach you to write.")

In the final photo Anaïs Nin, aged sixty-seven, stands behind a lectern haloed in auditorium light. As is the style in 1971, her crown of braided hair is woven with ribbons. She wears a long empire-style Indian gauze dress. Nin, hand on chin, stares out at the vast audience, a thousand people. They have come to hear the writer who's survived decades of discouragement, resorting to small presses or often printing her own books: "Writing for a hostile world discouraged me. Writing for you [the diary] gave me the illusion of a warm ambience I needed to flower in." It's the message so many have come to hear, helping the diary's first print run of 5,000 sell out in a single week. Its huge success has made Anaïs Nin into a kind of literary earth mother, especially among college students who cluster around her feet. Her diary has become Harcourt Brace's number-one college seller. "Recording a thousand women," it has struck a chord in its themes: woman as her own creative muse; the diary as autobiography. Could this young audience, as Nin suggests, have both creative and sexual freedom? As early as 1954 *The Nation* had noted, "Miss Nin is one of the few women writers in our literary tradition to affirm the centrality of the biological impulses for her own sex and on the same terms as for men." By 1971 her message is firm: "Create a world, your world. Alone. Stand alone. Create." (Not written on the back of the photo—or any other—is that Nin's *New York Times* obituary will list Hugh Guiler as her husband; the *Los Angeles Times* will list Rupert Pole. Both obituaries will be right. In New York, Hugh, her husband of fifty-four years, has been responsible for enabling her to emerge as an artist; in Los Angeles, Rupert, her younger tandem husband, will witness her late phenomenon as a published diarist. Both men, intelligent and devoted, will protect her estate.)

Each of these photos, among many others, appeared in the seven official volumes of the diary published between 1966 and 1974. The only photo missing, though, is the one that began her long habit of diary keeping. But no photo exists of Anaïs Nin boarding the *Montserrat* as it set sail from Barcelona to New York on July 25,

1914. On board, eleven-year-old Anaïs carried a small basket with the notebook her mother had just given her. In that first diary's opening entry she recorded her sadness at leaving Europe, which had been "a lucky charm for us." Hardly. Her father, the Cuban-born concert pianist Joaquín Nin, had abandoned the family for a young cigar heiress. It was the final blow to her parents' ill-fated marriage. In 1902 Rosa Nin had married the penniless musician in Cuba after he'd fled Spain for seducing a student. The Nins soon settled in Paris, where Anaïs was born on February 21, 1903. The subsequent birth of two sons, as well as a host of European addresses, did nothing to slow her father's fevered concert and womanizing schedules. Claiming that Rosa and the children applauded at his concerts like peasants, he left them at home, before leaving them entirely. On a humid July morning, a thunderstorm in the forecast, Rosa Nin and her three children set sail for a new life in America.

"The diary began as a diary of a journey, to record everything for my father. It was written for him, and I had intended to send it to him. It was really a letter, so he could follow us into a strange land." Or so the adult Anaïs Nin recalled her diary's beginning. Also true was that her mother, fearing Anaïs's separation anxiety, gave the diary to distract her. Whatever the final truth, father, loss and introspection were firmly encoded in Nin's young mind. The family settled in New York, moving from apartment to apartment. In a diary self-portrait Anaïs described herself as thin, "with fingers that often are clenched from nervousness." Joaquín Nin had refused to pay child support, but sent blisteringly exact lists of how his children were to be raised. Pious, domineering, self-abnegating, Rosa Nin ignored the only man she'd ever love. Her sons sided with her. Joaquín, strategically, wrote only to Anaïs, the child who continued to speak French, her father's favorite language. From age eleven on, she basked in the illusionary claim of specialness, copying her letters to him into her diary. As an adult, Nin wrote, "My life has been one long strain to create, to make myself interesting, to develop my gifts, to make my father proud of me." Yet when she was a child, her "dearly beloved shadow" corrected his daughter's grammar and faulted her "chatty pen." One month into keeping her diary, Anaïs confided, "I am eleven years old, I know, and I am not serious enough."

The family's financial problems meant taking in lodgers, compounding Anaïs's social shame for being "badly dressed with the cast-off clothes my aunts sent me from Cuba. I had to go to American schools with clothes designed for the tropics, pastel colors, silks, and all of them burnt by the sun so that very often they would split and tear during a party." Anaïs took the diary everywhere—geology class, parks, the beach—as a kind of psychic charm. Its pages recorded her steady resolve to be a writer. The same girl who wondered if she could borrow the ship's typewriter now drafted and submitted stories to magazines. "I told myself I would *learn* to express and then share with the world all that lies now in me, whispering in a language I understand but *cannot yet translate* . . . I will make the *world listen.*"

Words became deeds. "For after writing, I feel *reasonable*, and before acting, I pause to ask myself: Will I be ashamed to write this in my Diary?" By sixteen the obediently submissive parochial school girl, fitfully imitating the saints, let her Catholicism lapse. Confession would be saved for the diary. Tired of "nothing but scoldings, shouts and requirements," Nin dropped out of high school, briefly enrolling at Columbia in 1921. "I can truthfully say I have studied four subjects at Columbia: Composition, Grammar, French and Boys. I am glad to rid myself of both grammar and boys." The girl her brother had once called "fish skeleton" and her father had cursed as ugly soon became aware of her power to charm. Sheer dresses, scented handkerchiefs, black stockings—the props of her later diary—were recorded alongside favorite authors and books. The diary's preoccupations quickly became writing, romance and money. To help support the family, Nin worked as an artist's model, her face appearing on the cover of the *Saturday Evening Post* and in dozens of paintings.

"Since I was a child I always had a gift for attitudes, poses, a way of walking, sitting, which satisfied the artists," Nin later wrote. But by nineteen she'd come to see her father's love as itself a pose. "The man who ceases to maintain and serve his home is like a creator who abandons his work," she scolded him in 1922. "We are carrying out the mission that you did not accomplish." In addition to the mission of her diary, she'd decided to carve out a role other than her mother's humiliating martyrdom. "Very early I was determined not to be like her but like the women who had enchanted and seduced my father, the mistresses who lured him away from us." But not before Anaïs herself married. In 1921 she began seeing Hugh Guiler, a handsome, poetry-loving trainee at the National City Bank of New York. The son of repressive Scottish parents, Guiler had traded in his literature degree from Columbia for the security of banking. In her diary Nin noted: "I believe Hugo controls and forces back much that is impulsive in him." But her "beloved puritan" also kept a diary. After they shared their diaries, love struck. "I am now in a golden cage which I have made for myself," Nin confided shortly before their engagement. They married in 1923. With steady goodwill, Hugh Guiler assumed the financial burden of his new wife and her family. His parents disinherited him. Putting an ocean between them, in 1924 he took a banking job in Paris, once again transplanting Anaïs and her family.

Nin initially felt alienated in Paris, a lifelong pattern of internal exile, stemmed only by the "faithful confidant" of the diary. Upon their arrival her father immediately served Rosa Nin with final divorce papers. While Anaïs and her husband settled in a series of increasingly luxurious apartments, she confessed, "A *good*, noble-natured man *bores* me." Increasingly, Hugh was "tied to the bank, is filled body and soul, with his work." Becoming "the typical 'businessman' we both hate," Hugh in the diary soon became the "Humorous Banker, who does not take banking humorously enough."

Unwilling to take a salaried job to help support her mother, Nin began a novel that would fail, as well as a book on journals that never materialized. Hugh corrected her syntax, urging a more concrete prose style. "He is critical of my writing, as I am of his life," she snapped. "His work keeps him from following ideas as I do, but why does he let me express everything? . . . He said that it was all as it should be. He had no time for spiritual life. When he had a little time, like last night, he was too tired; he was happier letting me *express him.*" No one, though, could quench Nin's need to express herself. After finishing an Edith Wharton novel, she felt *"the pain of letting others speak for me."* Her writing schedule intensified. "I can never resign myself to be the *audience.* I am immediately made desperately restless, with envy or desire, to emulate the *creator.*"

And so, casting back through the diaries she'd kept for nearly a decade and a half, Nin combed them for material. Since seventeen she'd edited them, occasionally sharpening scenes, honing the deeper emotional truth that had eluded her the first time. Likening the process to one which "acts as a strainer," she found that the diary forced her to examine "the love of the truth which is *not* in my character but which *you* have forced me to cultivate." Truth for Nin translated into what was emotionally but not necessarily always autobiographically true.

The strainer effect had its first serious consequences in the half-truths of her marriage. By 1928 the oxygen was slowly going out of it. Edited out of the early published diaries was that Nin's marriage had remained unconsummated for a year. Also consciously omitted was that late in 1928 Nin embarked on her first extramarital affair, with Hugh's former professor, visiting novelist John Erskine. To cover her tracks, she began locking up the diaries. But not before the stock market crash of 1929 forced the couple to move to Louvecien-nes, just outside Paris. There she discovered the sexually liberated novels of D. H. Lawrence, the subject of what would become her first published book. But as Hugh predicted, the diary "will be your whole life's work." In the two-hundred-year-old Louveciennes house, the stage was finally set for Anaïs Nin, newly aroused to the power of the senses, to act on the question she'd posed two years before her marriage: "Am I clever enough to be a woman and a writer? Is such a thing possible?"

*I*nvoking two of the world's great adulteresses and a nameless, decapitated male lover, Anaïs Nin opened the first volume of her famous published diary:

> Louveciennes resembles the village where Madame Bovary lived and died. It is old, untouched by modern life. It is built on a hill overlooking the Seine. On clear nights one can see Paris. It has an old church dominating a group of small houses, cobblestone streets, and several large properties, manor houses, a castle on the outskirts of the village. One of the properties belonged to Madame du Barry. During the revolution her lover was guillotined and his head thrown over the ivy-covered wall into her garden.

The seductive pull of the prose reads as the polished autobiography it was rather than the spontaneous diary it pretended to be. With cinematic skill, the diary slowly situates the village, establishing its literary credentials: the surrounding forest was owned by a miser out of Balzac; the nearby Seine brought diners like Maupassant; so too the tiny train carrying Parisians out "of Proust's novels." Inside its thick stone walls, Nin's garden smelled of "honeysuckle in the summer, of wet leaves in the winter." The house, its rooms each painted a different color, looked out on two green iron gates. It was a life others might envy: the security of a home in an ancient village, the completion of her first book, *D. H. Lawrence: An Unprofessional Study*. But in the winter of 1931 her life had "the air of a prison" about it. "The obstacle lies always within one's self," she admitted. And with this, she slowly hints at the first diary's true story: the psychic quest for wholeness and self-discovery; birth as a woman and as an artist; overcoming the "inner obstacles to a full, open life."

In the first published diary's dateless entries, covering 1931 to 1934, Nin sets up a drama of discovery and revelation, surface lies and deeper truths, that the diarist will uncover about herself and others. Like Nin, the reader becomes a cooly observant voyeur watching the Chinese boxes of stories within stories—all initially about others—unfold. To crack this first volume of Anaïs Nin's diary is to unlock the puzzle of all the others. In it, she sets up the themes woven through seven volumes: the psychology of creative life, the relation of love and work, the psyche's hidden dramas that sabotage both. To be plunged into this first volume of her adult diary is, at first, to accept its truth unquestioningly. And so we read on, already snared by Nin's narrated presentation of her life, the carefully edited version of how she wanted readers to see her. In 1931, as the diary opens, she has a profitable working relationship with fellow writer Henry Miller. Sharing craft, they influence each other's styles. "I have given him depth, and he gives me concreteness." With his full sensuous mouth and balding head, Miller "looked like a Buddhist monk." He is obsessed, though, with his estranged wife, June, and her tissue of protective lies about her childhood, money and possible lovers. "I ran into such complicated stories, intrigues, miraculous barters, that I gave up trying to understand," he tells a spellbound Nin, fascinated by Miller's stories of his torturous marriage.

Infidelity, passion, intrigue. The scene is seamlessly set for the arrival of the mysterious June at Louveciennes. The diary doesn't disappoint. Tall, voluptuous, with a "huntress profile," June Miller has phosphorescent skin, eyes kohled like "Egyptian frescoes." She hates daylight. Her pupils have a druggy sheen. Nin falls under her spell, but not before realizing June sorely lacks confidence, fearful of being caricatured in Henry's novels. In hypnotic detail, volume one describes the trio's descent into Paris's café and demimondaine worlds: Miller's hovel of an apartment in Clichy; visiting a brothel where "Henry's whores" sit in "a room which looks like a velvet-lined jewel casket." Nin, finally siding with Henry, soon finds June destructive, incapable of a true identity. "Anaïs was just bored with her life, so she took us up," June counters.

The Millers' hellish marriage triggers Nin's revelation about herself. "It is quite possible that I may be even more secretive than June," she confides. "I have always been tormented by the image of multiplicity of selves. Some days I call it richness, and other days I see it as a disease, a proliferation as dangerous as cancer." In 1932 she enters analysis with Dr. René Allendy. In a room soundproofed by a black Chinese curtain, Nin soon realizes he fails to take her identity as an artist seriously. The following year she begins analysis with Otto Rank, Freud's fallen disciple, an expert on creativity and neurosis. Together, they continue the earlier work of why she's "a woman giving to the point of self-annihilation," supporting Henry, giving him her typewriter when his broke, helping pay for *The Tropic of Cancer* to be published. Or why she needs her *mensonges vitals,* the white lies she tells "to lull others."

Early on, Nin's first diary quickly becomes an inner detective story. "I would not be concerned with the secrets, the lies, the mysteries, the facts," she corrects Miller about June's need for lies. "I would be concerned *with what makes them necessary.* What fear." In her earlier childhood diaries Nin had recorded her terror of the father who read during meals, "only interrupting himself to scold about the microbes on the silverware, which he passed over an alcohol lamp before using. He never ate the piece of biscuit his fingers had touched . . . We were taught to fear all but filtered water." A vegetarian who once killed a cat with a cane, Joaquín Nin flew into violent rages. "It was only through a great deal of acting that I escaped punishments," his daughter recalled. "I would do anything to keep him from lifting my dress and beating me."

In this first published diary, interwoven with therapy transcripts, Anaïs Nin reveals that when she was a child, "He liked to take photos of me while I bathed. He always wanted me naked . . . His eyes were partly concealed by heavy glasses (he was myopic) and then by the camera lens." Analysis was beginning to free her "of the EYE of the father, the eye of the camera which I have always feared and disliked as an *exposure.*" Her father's "passion for criticism and perfection paralyzed me," she confesses, "his hard blue eyes on us, looking for the flaws." The fault-finding father had lodged in her subconscious, subverting her creative life. "Neurosis itself does not nourish the artist," Nin quotes Rank, "he creates in spite of it." Rank advises that she disentangle herself from the diary, something all her father figures urge.

In June 1933 Nin journeys to Valescure-St.-Raphael in southern France to visit her ailing father. Still coldly formal, the fifty-four-year-old Joaquín Nin tells the hotel waiter that Anaïs is his fiancée. The father with tinted hair is soon bedridden with lumbago. Over several days, he presents his side of being married to the dowdy, demanding Rosa Nin. Anaïs is won over. On the bed in his sickroom they share stories about their liberated love lives and celebrate their mutual identity as artists. The temporary healing of their bond helps when, in 1934, Nin suffers the birth of a stillborn child. The incident is catalytic, triggering what she feels is the birth of her adult self.

"Through flesh and blood and love, I was made whole. I cannot say more."

By 1934, at the close of this first published diary, the reader shares the thrill of Nin's considerable triumphs: reuniting and setting equal terms with her father, surviving the trauma of a stillbirth, finishing her novel *Winter of Artifice*. We witness Nin on the trail of her own subconscious, discovering its problems and revelations along *with* her. Inner permission for "the *aggressive* act of creation" is still a struggle. "To create seemed to me such an assertion of the strongest part of me that I would no longer be able to give all those I love the feeling of their being stronger, and they would love me less. An act of independence would be punished by desertion." In therapy, Rank tells the thirty-one-year-old Nin, "When the neurotic woman gets cured, she becomes a woman. When the neurotic man gets cured, he becomes an artist. Let's see whether the woman or the artist will win out." Her life's work, she realizes, is probing the psychology of creative will. She'll "speak for many women" but as an artist. "I feel I am merely one of many, a symbol." In the diary she'd give voice to the "mute ones of the past, the inarticulate, who took refuge behind wordless institutions; and the women of today."

The camera—the object Nin feared and craved—needs to pause here for a moment. For, instinctively, the reader senses there's something wrong with the portrait that Nin presents of herself in this first published diary—the narrative's too smooth, the loose ends too neatly tied up. It reads more like a tightly plotted novel than a diary. It's only with information that surfaced after Nin's death in 1977 that we finally learn the truth about the material in this first diary and begin to reconcile its contradictions. On the second page of the diary Nin has casually mentioned a false shuttered room in her eleven-windowed house in Louveciennes: "One shutter in the middle was put there for symmetry only, but I often dream about this mysterious room which does not exist behind the closed shutter." It's the perfect metaphor for how to reread her first diary with its *trompe l'oeil*–like facade; we open the diary's false shutters one by one.

Here is the truth behind Nin's highly edited version of that first diary which so captivated millions of readers. When she boldly tells us "I carry away no secrets, as Henry reads the journal," referring to her red leather journal, she not only fails to mention a green "decoy" diary she kept for Hugh but omits her marriage entirely from the first published diary. (It surfaces only as a vague fact in volume six.) Nin's marital status is coyly blank. The diary's clinical, observant style suggests a chaste professional life. What Nin omits is the revolving door of lovers she entertained while Hugh was away on business trips. Only by the late 1980s, when her long-standing affair with Henry Miller came to light, do we realize why her descriptions of the Millers' lovemaking are so eerily precise. "I could understand and see, as if I had been there, the devastating charade lovers enter upon," Nin says in volume one as she "imagines" the Millers' lovemaking in their Clichy flat, "No time to turn down the coverlets, to close windows . . . Against the wall, on the carpet, on a chair, on a couch, in taxis, in elevators, in parks, on rivers, on boats, in woods, on balconies, in doorways at night." As would come to light when her "unexpurgated" diary of these same years was published in 1992, these were details familiar from her own sex life with Henry Miller. No mere "referee" in the Miller's marriage, Nin, like Henry, studied and used June for creative material.

Not that she had to look further than her own diary. Nin lifted from this first published diary her most famous short story, "Birth." "The doctor does not hear the breathing of the child," she says of her pregnancy in the diary's final, climactic scene. "The child is six months old. They might save it." For over ten pages she harrowingly details nightmarish injections, spasms, over two days of induced labor, a stillborn infant girl, her eyelashes glistening from the womb's birth waters. This "first dead creation," though, wasn't a stillbirth but an abortion. Pregnant, most likely by Henry, Nin actively sought injections to abort the six-month child. After three days of induced labor, she gave birth to a stillborn girl in the delivery room at Paris's Clinique Eugène Manuel. In the diary she rued the physical part of her "which refused to push, to kill, to separate, to lose."

But the diary's most violently disturbing omission still awaits. In her later, official diaries she tries to hint at it. "Rank told me that women practiced deception very badly," Nin cooly notes in diary two, "that many of the women he had analyzed . . . always left a 'clue.' " To those early cult readers of Nin's official diaries, she also left a cryptic clue in diary three—*"Guilts about exposing the father. Secrets. Need of disguises. Fear of consequences. Great conflict here. Division."* What guilt? Why the fear? After all, in her first published diary Nin writes how when she was visiting her ailing father in the south of France in 1933, he told her, " 'You are the synthesis of all the women I have loved. What a pity that you are my daughter!' " Certainly, it mirrored the same loving confusion she'd often felt about him. At twelve in her childhood diary, she'd written, "During Communion I just murmured, *God, France and Papa!* God knows what that means and like my diary, He will understand." But readers wouldn't. In 1992, when "unexpurgated" parts of the 1932–35 diary were published, titled *Incest*, the meaning was clear: the girl who had once confused God and her father, the Word made flesh, had taken his body in unholy communion. What readers of that first published diary didn't know at the time was that in 1933, Nin had done more than reconcile with her father on that trip to southern France. At age thirty she began an incestuous relationship with him that lasted roughly four months. After it, she continued her life's compulsive conquest of all father figures: analysts, editors, publishers, critics. " 'My only rival,' " her father said, sizing up the diary. He would be right. For the next forty years Anaïs Nin used her subsequent diaries to tell the world of the seductive selfishness of the father she'd finally watch collapse at his thousandth concert, the handsome dandy who died, exiled in Cuba, penniless, surrounded only by photographs of himself.

Thanks to the meteoric success of this first published volume of her diary and its successors, the opposite fate awaited his daughter. By the mid 1970s she'd become the world's most famous diarist, a black-caped literary sophisticate, darling of the Ivy League lecture circuit, her five novels published between 1940 and 1965 all reissued. Only after her death from cancer in 1977 would her early words come to haunt her. "My father said I angered him as a child because he felt I had a whole world of secret thoughts which I would not, or could not express, that I lied like an Arab . . . But I explained to him that the feeling I had was that no one was interested, and also that what I invented constantly was *fantasy*." After her "unexpurgated" diaries began appearing in the early 1990s, Anaïs Nin suddenly was seen as the world's most notorious diarist, the Hester Prynne of journal keeping, guilty of hoodwinking the public as well as the worse crime of counterfeiting creativity. Stunned that Nin had consciously violated the taboo of lying in a diary, the public felt the deeper psychic betrayal by a—*the*—creative role model they'd most trusted. The diary, after all, was the route to creative life for her as for millions of readers. But her diaries' huge success and the subsequent violence with which they've been attacked tell us not just about Nin's capacity for fantasy but about our own. For it is as much our own faces that shine back from the mirrored funhouse of Nin's diaries.

Anaïs Nin likened herself to a seer and her diaries to "crystal-gazing." In them, readers "see their fate, their potential self, secrets, their secret self." The phenomenon of the diaries can be explained only in part by their genius for timing. Nin's sexual provocativeness coincided with the era of mass production of the Pill. Throwing off the social shackles of their parents' late fifties lives, a generation came of age in an era of sexual freedom. Paralleling the rise and cult of psychoanalysis, Nin's diaries embraced it as the new secular religion. By the late sixties the talking cure was supplanted by the writing cure, a cheaper alternative to therapy. Nin foreshadowed and defined the culture of the self; as the sixties *we* culture devolved into the seventies *me* decade, self-absorption was given national license. Nin's diaries provided an ideal model with their mosaic of meditations on the working of the unconscious: recorded dreams, analysis sessions, letters to and from other creative seekers.

Every fantasy masks both a desire and a need. Both were stroked in the millions who flocked to Nin's diaries from the late sixties on. Exotic yet hip, the strangely ageless Nin mirrored her audiences: kohl-eyed, questing, seemingly independent of traditional ties. To those who'd grown up with absent, distant fifties fathers, Nin's diaries offered the fantasy of filial forgiveness. Or at least the fantasy of effortless analysis by wise, caring father figures. But it was her own inner life, the lack of confidence and fear of criticism, that spoke most directly, and in the very forum seekers valued—a diary. An entry Nin made at eighteen could easily have been their own: "I realize it is my Diary, my life, my self that I weave into a story . . . It all seems like a great circle to me; it is revolving around a central dot, I feel. I am it . . . You notice how small I am? How insignificant?"

Into dull suburban lives came Anaïs Nin—womanly, literary, French. No one before her had so seductively embodied the independent creative life of a woman who wanted to be a writer.

Late at night. I am in Louveciennes. I am sitting by the fire in my bedroom. The heavy curtains are drawn. The room feels heavy and deeply anchored in the earth. One can smell the odors of the wet trees, the wet grass outside. They are blown in by the wind through the chimney. The walls are a yard thick, thick enough to dig bookcases into them, beside the bed. The bed is wide and low.

Sleep, sex, books, solitude. To live in this room is to be safe, rooted, responsible only to the self. It's the literary version of the child's fantasy of miraculous orphanhood, safe from danger, all needs met, but without the burden of parents. How the heavy curtains or the burning logs are paid for is not the point. A bohemian life with bourgeois comfort is. The perfect fantasy for the free-spirited sixties and seventies generations raised in the prosperous post–World War II boom years.

To a young generation experiencing the chaotic protest war years, as well as the growing women's movement, Nin's diaries offered the fantasy of total control. Especially for women. In scene after scene Nin gains the upper hand. Most flagrant are those in which each analyst confesses *his* neuroses to her—the ultimate revenge fantasy for those who'd suffered Freudian analysts or husbands and fathers who wouldn't talk. Getting each man to confess his fear of passion, Nin dismantles the cold intellect she didn't want trained on her. "I began our session by making Allendy sit in the patient's armchair and by analyzing his 'omens' as expressions of his lack of confidence in life and in love. I used all his formulas and his lingo on him." Nin also psychologically castrates Otto Rank, who admits, " 'I denied myself life before, or it was denied me, first by my parents, then Freud, then my wife."

Just as Rank offers Nin equality by asking her to become his practicing colleague in New York, so the diary conjures one of its most alluring fantasies: inspired work collaboration between the sexes. Hip but platonic is how Nin presents her professional relations with René Allendy, Rank and Henry Miller, among others. Honesty, not sex, is the driving force. "I acted Allendy to Henry, pointed to his dependence on the criticism and opinion of others." Working elbow to elbow, she helped him "cut out extraneous material, change the order of chapters . . . We have much influence over each other's work." Nin paints similar portraits in her middle diaries of her then editor, the young Gore Vidal, with his "hazel, clear, open, mocking" eyes. Or Truman Capote "extending the softest and most boneless hand I had ever held, like a baby's," at one of her parties. (From the mid-1940s on, Nin tried to seduce the numerous gay men whom she befriended.) The diary erupts with compliments from the devoted, like psychic bulletins or paid commercials. " 'You have done it, the real female writing,' " Nin quotes novelist Lawrence Durrell on her diary. " 'We are all writing about the Womb, but you *are* the Womb.' "

"I live by impulse and improvisation, and want to write the same way," Nin declares in diary four. "I write like a medium. I fear criticism because I fear it will destroy my spontaneity." To a nation of diary keepers, she supplied the license for revenge on every composition teacher who'd ever told them their writing was incoherent. " 'Save paper!' " her brother once scolded, telling her to use only one diary page and erase it the next day. At twenty-two she attacked those "united in a conspiracy to teach me the discipline of writing, and while I wrote with the ease of a fountain, they brought me typewriters, dictionaries, the Technique of Columbia, the Point of View of Henry James, the Restraint and Compactness of Eugene Graves—endless rules and traffic regulations, sermons on the concrete, the Pictorial, Maturity—all of which, in a fit of rage, I metaphorically kicked into the river."

Millions of readers cheered. By 1971, Nin was receiving three hundred letters a week, "a furnace of love," from fans confessing their innermost lives. Six pages in the final diary quote from sample letters: " 'You are writing my life also.' " " 'You create for us the world in which we would like to live.' " " 'I am sixteen. In your

Diaries I see the person I am and the person I want to be.' " No doubt. Nin was seen as a kind of creative superwoman. Commanding the lecture circuit, she read at top colleges, corresponded with literary luminaries, received honorary degrees, had documentary films made about her. Not even cancer stopped her from twelve-hour workdays.

"They have been so often cheated and betrayed by the media, by their heroes," Nin noted of her trusting audiences. " 'I am a camera.' You, the reader, have the right to know the brand, range, quality of the diarist-camera." In the final published diary, she recorded how few facial lines she had, only "laugh wrinkles." But by then the cracks in the persona had already set in. Hissed by Smith College students after a 1969 lecture, Nin was taken to task for her "mistress sensibilities," her coquettish attitudes, for being an adult who played dress-up—going to a therapy session "dressed like royalty in exile" or painting her eyelashes during labor spasms. Her eye-rolling exhibitionism—bikini-clad in Mexico, velvet-robed in France—was less offensive than her self-confessed need to be a mother not "to children but to men." Playing creative handmaiden, ministering to the men in *men*tors, had contributed to her early reputation. Late in Nin's life, her diaries had become a narcissist's mirror rather than a window on a larger creative world.

"The diary is a blueprint for living, a Baedeker to freedom," she correctly observed. Yet in hers, Nin violated one of our secret needs for reading diaries: the hunger for creative models, for inspiration on how to live, to love, to work. Just as she confused her life and art, life *as* art, so readers were guilty of the same thing. Again. Autobiographical writing is notoriously unreliable: in his *Confessions*, Rousseau omitted his illegitimate children. Tolstoy thundered in *My Confession* on the virtue of celibacy after an early history of sleeping with his estate's peasants. Rilke wrote *Letters to a Young Poet*, among literature's most eloquent advice on creative and personal life, after abandoning his wife and infant. In her celebrated memoir, *Memories of a Catholic Girlhood*, Mary McCarthy inserted italicized sections discussing what wasn't true or possibly misremembered in the previous chapter. Her rival, Lillian Hellman, later admitted that Julia, the inspirational figure in her book of personal portraits, *Pentimento*, was someone she'd never met. Late in their careers McCarthy and Hellman waged a bitter dogfight of a lawsuit over each other's capacity for truth-telling.

But a diary, of course, has a different standard of truth applied to it than an autobiography. Like a spider spinning thread out of its own belly, a diary is a lifeline to an innermost self. Often it is the *only* place someone can be honest. In violating the truth forum of the diary, Nin was guilty of a kind of psychic incest, violating the taboo of lying to oneself. Lying to the world was inevitable after that—selectively using "transcripts" of therapy sessions or inserting an italicized factual bracket to validate the diary's overall authenticity. Public hatred of Nin exposes our own secret difficulty not only in keeping diaries honestly but in keeping them at all. "Everyone of us carries a deforming mirror where he sees himself too small or too large," she wrote, hitting upon the reason thousands of diaries are abandoned each year.

At sixty-seven Nin summed up her diary's odyssey: "A letter to my father, a letter to the world." But as the truth about the diary slowly surfaced, it became a letter the world returned to its sender. Its nagging vagueness had always been perplexing. Whom was she with, for example, on all those foreign trips whose photos crowd the late published diaries? Her notational style conveniently omitted pronouns. "Vera Cruz. Shrimps sold at the cafe served on a piece of toilet paper. At the market an American girl asked for brains. The butcher took a cow head off the hook and shook brains into a market bag." In the 1990s Nin's bicoastal, bigamous marriages was made public. Beginning in 1950 she had embarked on a nearly thirteen-year "trapeze" life, shuttling between Hugh Guiler in New York and Rupert Pole in Los Angeles. Her illegal marriage to Pole, a teacher sixteen years her junior, was later voided, though he remains her executor. (The two husbands would finally meet after Nin's death.) Nin, ironically, had made the fantasy of her diaries come true— being adored by two caring, intelligent men who championed her creativity. The price was not only keeping a literal lie box, the stash of index cards to keep her stories straight, but a punishing routine every two to three months of eleven-hour plane rides, insomnia and nightly sleeping pills.

Today, young readers still gravitate to Nin. College students read her erotica and steamy "unexpurgated" diaries for the century's final fantasy: safe, abundant sex in the age of AIDS. But her cult following—later dubbed the Ninnies—is diminished. Adult readers are no longer as sucked into the foggy vortex of psychobabble ("I write emotional algebra") or its mystification of creative life. For many, Nin remains a grotesque parody of herself, the personification of her costume at a 1953 party whose theme was to come as your madness:

> I wore a skin-colored leotard, leopard-fur earrings glued to the tips of my naked breasts, and a leopard-fur belt around my waist . . . I wore eyelashes two inches long. My hair was dusted with gold powder. My head was inside a birdcage. From within the cage, through the open gate, I pulled out an endless roll of paper on which I had written from my books. The ticker tape of the unconscious. I unwound this and handed everyone a strip with a message.

"No writer I can think of has more passionately embraced thin air," Elizabeth Hardwick observed in *Partisan Review* as early as

1948. Is there anything still to learn from the ticker tape of Nin's diaries? How to question truth in autobiographical writing. Nin's lies, omissions and half-truths turn the diaries into a parlor detective game. Hugh, for example, is Ian Hugo, *his* creative alias for his later career as an engraver and filmmaker. Nin's gay cousin, Eduardo Sánchez, at his request, is Nin's friend Marguerite in the diary. But just as a photo negative reveals the same picture in shaded reverse, so the diary's truth lies below the surface. Envy, professional jealousy, marital disillusionment, raw ambition, craving for recognition—these are the diary's real subjects. Nin gave us their fantasy opposites. Part of the reason for this, of course, is the period in which she was publishing, decades before the phenomenon of memoir and talk show confession. Had she been able to write honestly about these more complex truths, the diaries today would indeed be creative models for "all the obscure routes of the soul and a body seeking truth and never receiving medals for its courage." Instead, failed by the diaries, we're once again turned back to the stubborn corner of our own diaries, to the tedious, necessary discipline of inventing ourselves.

"You have hampered me as an artist," Nin admitted to her diary. "While I write in the diary I cannot write a book." As the heroine of her diary, Nin became the loser in fiction, unable to imagine a character other than herself. She had a recurrent dream of being a spoke stuck on a turning wheel. It was prophetic. The wheel of childhood and the diary. The little girl unable to let go of her diary sabotaged the woman and the artist who struggled to be born in it. Nin's inability during labor to "thrust out the child" was the perfect metaphor for her own stillborn creative life. Unable to kill her past, she aborted all her pregnancies instead, mothering legions of men, only to complain how they drained her creativity.

The diary brims with excellent psychiatric advice Nin failed to heed, but readers can still benefit from: creative assertion, identity independent of outside approval, the taking of financial and emotional responsibility for one's life. "What we call our destiny is truly our character, and that character can be altered," she noted soon after discovering analysis. But a diary colludes in this final fantasy: a belief that the self is mutable, its identity ever negotiable. It's far easier to say Anaïs Nin never changed than to admit we might not either. The diary—with its hidden insights that might suddenly, magically, transform our lives—is the self's gambling chip we play day after day. But insight, as Nin's diaries show, is nothing without action. Her life, a maze of missteps and wrong turns, produced a counterfeit map of a diary, one destined to lead only to the dead end of a bank vault.

"The failed artist," Nin quotes Otto Rank, is "one in whom the creative spark exists but is deformed, arrested, feeble, hindered in some way, by some disorder of the creative faculties which succeeds in creating only neurosis." Nin's neuroses clattered as noisily as the bangle bracelets snaking her thin arms. If she didn't pass the creative test she set up in her diaries, the reason is buried deep in her childhood diaries. Copying a letter to her father into her 1917 diary, she wrote, "I am sure that the first time you heard applause that was a little bit for you, you too felt a wish to hear it again." Mistaking applause for identity, fame for the filling of a gnawing inner void, Nin made a fatal creative pact: letting the parading adult persona she'd invented in her diaries win out over the shivering child who'd first sheltered herself in them.

On January 11, 1921, Anaïs Nin used the final page in her notebook to record a small incident of daily life. She had just planted twelve bulbs, each named after a favorite author or heroine, into a dish filled with white gravel. She worried that the flowers would soon overcrowd, "spreading and leaning over, without symmetry and order." Unbeknownst to her, the bulbs would become the perfect metaphor for her life's work. Just like her diary, they'd have a showy, short-lived blossom, anchored in a shallow dish. But at the time, seventeen-year-old Anaïs Nin merely wrote, "I am writing a chronicle of my garden of Narcissus in the last page of this Diary."

Anaïs Nin peering over a mountain of diaries stacked in the letter A. *(Marlis Schwieger)*

May Sarton at Wild Knoll looking out toward the Atlantic.
(Beverly Hallam)

6

A WRITER
IN THE
UNCERTAIN SEASONS

Oh and I thought, as I was dressing, how interesting
it would be to describe the approach of age, and the
gradual coming of death. As people describe love.
To note every symptom of failure: but why failure?
To treat age as an experience that is different from
others; and to detect every one of the gradual stages
towards death which is a tremendous experience,
and not as unconscious, at least as it approaches, as
birth is.

— VIRGINIA WOOLF, *A Writer's Diary*

I wonder whether it is possible at nearly sixty to
change oneself radically.

— MAY SARTON, *Journal of a Solitude*

I had lived my way into all this house is and holds for me eight years before I brought "the ancestor" home. As I stood on a stool and hammered in a hook strong enough to support the plain, heavy oak frame and the portrait itself, I knew I was performing a symbolic act, and this is the way it has been from the beginning, so that everything I do here reverberates, and if, out of fatigue or not paying attention, I strike a false note, it hurts the house and the mystique by which I live.

The family portrait that had been ferried across the Atlantic in 1919 was now positioned directly above a Flemish chest. The first-time house owner examined her eighteenth-century ancestor: the jowly Norman face, powdered wig, red jacket. The portrait had found its final home in the small village of Nelson, New Hampshire. To this remote village the new owner had brought her heritage, "at last . . . woven together into a whole—the threads of the English and Belgian families from which I spring," and her own split between a European birth and an American upbringing.

On June 7, 1958, poet and novelist May Sarton signed the deed for an abandoned house in "a village of which I knew absolutely nothing." She was forty-six. She had moved from Cambridge, Massachusetts, where her father, George Sarton, a Harvard historian of science, had instilled in her the rigor of work, and her mother, Mabel, a furniture designer, a quiet appreciation for nature. Jumbled in the basement of Sarton's childhood home on Channing Place was the heavy Belgian furniture that would find its permanent place in Nelson. Her parents, former war refugees, had both died. So too had her early career in theater, first as an actress and later as an Off-Broadway director in New York. Having traded a scholarship to Vassar for Eva Le Gallienne's Civic Repertory Theatre, she'd formed her own company, which failed during the Depression. From twenty-four on, she cobbled together a life as a poet and novelist. In 1939, "I simply wrote to fifty colleges and offered to read for twenty-five dollars if they would put me up for a few days."

Petite, dark-haired, a determined point to her chin, Sarton had spent her thirties and early forties on the lecture and teaching circuit from New Orleans to Santa Fe. What drove her was the need to be taken seriously as a writer. Ever aware of her intellectually demanding father and her artistic mother, who'd sorely compromised her gifts, Sarton published eleven novels and six books of poetry in less than two decades. Not all of them met with success. But in 1958, the year she moved to Nelson, she'd been nominated for a National Book Award in both poetry and fiction, and had decided to risk "that form of gambling called 'writing for a living.'" Except for the occasional lecture, or brief stint as college writer-in-residence, her livelihood would come exclusively from the writing itself.

She had come to Nelson alone. Turning her back on the early years of rootless pleasure—travel, affairs, a huge appetite for living in the moment—she settled into a life she'd long craved. "Borrowing other people's lives, other people's families," was now left behind. "I was beginning a new life in middle age." The house that would contain the life was an eighteenth-century farmhouse with five fireplaces and thirty-six acres of land. Poised on the edge of a village green, it fronted a tiny library and an abandoned brick schoolhouse. All around was wild acreage: hemlocks, "skirt-tearing blackberry bushes," fields dense with outcroppings of granite. In time, much of it would be cleared, and a lush garden seeded. But until then, "I felt then no responsibility except to a talent."

It was the house itself that first required Sarton's imaginative talents. Its former owner, an "indomitable, tragic hunchedback," had passionately loved gardens. But she'd let the house go. Four of the five upstairs rooms were heaped with rubbish. "Did I have the courage to lift it out of its depression?" Sarton made plans. "I was held by it, as one is held by a poem that has not quite jelled, that haunts the nights. I first had to dream the house alive inside myself." Downstairs a wall was knocked down, opening up the main room into a large kitchen–living room. The wood floor, tilting slightly like a ship's deck, was painted a soft yellow to catch the winter light. A kitchen area was sketched out on the back of an old envelope. The fireplaces choked with soot were cleared.

Finally setting up her study, Sarton got down to work at the desk designed and hand-painted by her mother. "The writer, at his desk alone, must create his own momentum, draw enthusiasm up out of his own substance, not just once, when he may feel inspired, but day after day when he does not." Coming to Nelson had been "no act of renunciation, only the opening of a door into this new silence." The quiet rhythms of a writing life. "For alone here, I first must give up the world and all its dear, tantalizing human questions, first close myself away, and then, and only then, open to that other tide, the inner life, the life of solitude, which rises very slowly until, like the anemone, I am open to receive whatever it may bring."

Outside her study hung a Hokusai print. At seventy-five the Japanese artist had said of himself, "I have drawn things since I was

six. All that I made before the age of sixty-five is not worth counting. At seventy-three I began to understand the true construction of
animals, plants, trees, birds, fishes, and insects. At ninety I will enter
into the secret of things. At a hundred and ten, everything—every
dot, every dash—will live." It would serve as more than a motto for
the writer herself. In dozens of small ways, she would see it practiced daily in the community around her.

In Nelson, Sarton at first "knew the dead better than the living,"
memorizing the names carved into soft slate in the cemetery atop the
hill. But in some of Nelson's living descendants she'd soon find a
community, individuals all in their late sixties or seventies, who
shared her "respect for the professional craftsman." Solitary, taci-
turn, careful of privacy, each prized work, no matter how commonplace. Diffident strangers soon became friends: Horace Upton, the
eighty-year-old mailman; Quig, the painter and frame restorer who
worked night shifts at the woolen mills; seventy-year-old Perley
Cole, who helped Sarton first plant phlox, delphinium, cosmos and
plum trees. The rough-hewn Cole was usually scything waist-high
grass or "somewhere off in the woods cutting brush, and here I am
at my desk pruning out a thicket of words."

But more than Yankee pragmatism spurred her. Aware of crossing the meridian of middle age, Sarton was "deliberately cutting life
back to the marrow." Over the seasons, she'd try to eliminate the
inessential, both personally and professionally. The world outside
her study windows was a tangible reminder of survival and renewal.
In summer, the garden yielded lettuce, beets, eggplant. In fall, there
was cider from harvested village apples. In winter, sparrows and
cardinals fed under boughs shrouded in snow. "Silence was the food
I was after, silence and the country itself—trees, meadows, hills, the
open sky." So too "something like New England itself—struggle,
occasional triumph over adversity, above all the power to be renewed. For here the roses grow beside the granite."

It all waited: the cord of wood stacked neatly on the back porch, the cups grouped in newly papered cabinets, the books lined on their shelves. "Everything has been prepared as if for a guest, and I am the guest of the house."

*B*ut, of course, this was only part of the story. The most important part had been left out. In 1968 when Sarton's memoir of her first eight years in Nelson, *Plant Dreaming Deep*, appeared, it won her admirers. Like her earlier *I Knew a Phoenix*, portraits of family and mentors partly written for *The New Yorker*, this second memoir was skillfully crafted. In writing about Nelson, Sarton evoked a kind of solitary Eden, a hymn to rural life: freshly mown hayfields, long hours of summer gardening, chill autumn nights. She set her solitary creative life against the background of community solidarity, a shared passion for individual craft. Just as she gave Perley Cole work well into his late seventies, so in late middle age she had begun a second career as a writer. Inspired, Sarton's fans flocked to Nelson by the carload, crossing the tiny green hoping to catch a glimpse of her and her neighbors. They'd become minor celebrities, familiar from the memoir's accompanying black-and-white photos, which also offered glimpses of Sarton's house, its simple, Quaker-like interiors.

In 1971 May Sarton sat down to write about the same experience of creative solitude in Nelson, but this time putting in all she'd left out. She abandoned the seductive, polished style of memoir, stripping the prose and, in the process, the life. For this, she chose a journal. In the very first entry she confronted the issue squarely:

> *Plant Dreaming Deep* has brought me many friends of the work (and also, harder to respond to, people who think they have found in me an intimate friend). But I have begun to realize that, without

my own intention, that book gives a false view. The anguish of my life here—its rages—is hardly mentioned. Now I hope to break through into the rough rocky depths, to the matrix itself.

Nearing sixty, she was painfully aware of more than the body's steady betrayals—age spots flecking the backs of her hands, joints aching in damp weather. In her journal's opening pages she catalogued other facts with brutal simplicity: no one had quite replaced the intense friendship of Quig, her Nelson neighbor, who had long since died. Handyman Perley Cole had separated from his wife. In his eighties he now lay dying in a squalid nursing home. Sarton herself was bitterly despondent over past failed love affairs. Critics had savagely attacked her recent work. Eden had suffered the Fall.

"Autobiography," she later wrote, "is 'what I remember' whereas a journal has to do with 'what I am now, in this instant.'" Five years after she'd written *Plant Dreaming Deep*, Sarton realized she had only hinted at her private demons: self-doubt as a writer, fear of failure, the precarious daily act of improvising a vocation, keeping hope alive. In her new journal she decided to record not just her creative life but its underside: solitude, illness, growing old. Her working title alone suggested how radical a change Sarton intended—the sentimental optimism of *Plant Dreaming Deep* yielded to the bare fact of a life: *Journal of a Solitude*.

By the time it was published in 1973, Sarton had moved from Nelson to an even more remote location: a stark, windswept landscape off the Maine coast. Wild Knoll was a three-story colonial set on a spur, its terraced garden opening out to an expanse of meadow that jutted over the sea. Sarton would spend the remaining decades writing in York, Maine, chronicling creativity against the odds. "Adversity is my climate," she observed. Yet *Journal of a Solitude*, published at sixty, would make her famous. It and the eight journals to follow spanned generations of readers either fascinated or annoyed by her quarrel with destiny. In her sixties Sarton began a complex dialogue with herself, readers, and the community she'd both shunned and often been shunned by. In intending the journals for publication, she created a culture of diary writers as interested in how to live as in how to write. Every year thousands of letters from around the world—from men and women, old and young, writers and creative tourists—interrupted the solitude she had made so tantalizingly famous.

But on that sodden September morning in 1971, rain sheeting the windows of her Nelson study, May Sarton had simply believed she was beginning a journal to combat severe depression. Originally triggered by a failed love affair, the journal quickly evolved into a self-portrait of a writer risking creativity and passion late in life. The struggle only confirmed Sarton's need for a solitary creative life. "I am alone here for the first time in weeks, to take up my 'real' life at last. That is what is strange—that friends, even passionate love, are not my real life unless there is time alone in which to explore and discover what is happening or has happened." As she wrote those words, she unknowingly voiced the credo of all the journals to follow—the impulse to uncover and reveal, the psyche's quest to "make sense of one's life and discover one's usefulness." Since her twenties Sarton had doubted her talent but never questioned its vocation, and the value of journals themselves.

> I cannot always believe even in my work. But I have come in these last days to feel the validity of my struggle here, that it is meaningful whether I ever "succeed" as a writer or not, and that even its failures, failures due to a difficult temperament, can be meaningful . . . The fact that a middle-aged single woman, without any vestige of family left, lives in this house in a silent village and is

responsible only to her own soul means something. The fact that she is a writer and can tell where she is and what it is like on the pilgrimage inward can be of comfort.

That pilgrimage was all the more interesting for its paradox: a writer who'd starkly renounced the world, only to chronicle its tantalizing sensuousness. In photos her houses beckoned with earthly pleasures—tall vases choked with fresh flowers, baskets of bone-white shells scooped up on walks, a night side table anchored with books. At Wild Knoll the solitary house seemed fit for the very things she lacked: children, a marriage partner. But she had chosen her fate: sitting at a desk day after day, responsible only to a talent about which she often had serious doubts. In 1971, just as women took to the streets in protest, Sarton retreated into a contemplative, creative life. Intrigued by her independent writing life, the world would envy her talent for self-reliance. Over the next three decades May Sarton's journals, almost all chronicling a single year in the writer's life, offered millions of readers a window on a creative world many secretly craved. Written on her small portable typewriter, on a desk later looking out on the wild, granite-strewn Maine coastline, the journals sprang "from my isolation to the isolation of someone somewhere." In the journals Sarton was seen as a kind of Everywriter, a fellow traveler improvising creativity in the uncertain seasons of a life, a hard-won confidence earned page by page.

Beginning with her life in Nelson and later at Wild Knoll, she fashioned an intimately detailed portrait of a writer's routine: rising in winter at six-thirty; juggling the poetry, novels and journals; being interviewed; worrying if advances would cover the house's endless repairs. But her journals also provided an unfailingly human face: a woman who quit smoking in her sixties, went on a diet in her seventies, bemoaned into her eighties the curse of her own fame—

the avalanche of mail and unsolicited manuscripts, the needy fans. Willful, practical, impatient with small talk, Sarton in her journals was a writer as worried about the pipes freezing as about keeping her reputation alive.

"The move to Nelson," she later recalled, "putting down roots in a small, lonely village where I knew no one, did, after fifteen years, season and toughen me. There began my real life; from then on I did not need to know 'famous people' and had a hunger for people like myself who had to struggle to keep their heads above water." The outside world formed a muted backdrop to the deceptively unchanging order of her world—Nixon, Ford, Carter, Reagan noted almost as if odd sproutings in Sarton's lush garden. Her eye was held by the hard, certain cycles of the natural world, the seasons she minutely catalogued, and by her own keeping "busy with survival." The journals caught the reassuring rhythms of routine in a world chaotic with change. Tiny details soon became familiar touchstones: Sarton bent over a bed of irises, thinking out a sonnet; slipping Wellington boots over pajama bottoms and shoveling a path to the birdfeeders; roaming the salt marshes with her sheltie. The seductive calm of daily routines—writing, gardening, walking—was carefully caught in the numerous black-and-white photos woven through each journal. The photos satisfied readers' natural curiosity about this most private life, and intensified its mystique of solitude: the house's roomy interiors, the cluttered third-floor study, the cascade of exotic winter plants visible in a small windowed solarium, the heavy wooden dining table set for a meal. This and her interior life were what she had come to record.

As she sat alone at her desk, the daily—for centuries the diary's cornerstone—soon became Sarton's psychic domain. Routine became a way to master the personal uncertainty that had plagued her since childhood. Written between sixty and eighty-three, the journals focused on daily work—of all kinds—as the way to stem internal chaos. "I have learned in these last few years to forget the desk and everything on it as soon as I leave this room." "The key," she later noted, "seems to be for me to do each thing with absolute concentration, to garden as though that were essential, then to write in the same way." Just as Dorothy Wordsworth cored apples, stitched seams, seeded her tiny kitchen garden, so May Sarton used the natural world to order her inner life. Nursing a hurt—a rejection, a failed morning's work—she weeded her garden, stripped the sheets, opened the windows wide. And recording it all, page by page, she invented her freedom.

The writer who had first settled in a remote New Hampshire village was busy building an audience fascinated that a woman could both celebrate and shun traditional domestic life. For an ever-growing audience, Sarton's most daring act was combining rather than separating details of daily life. The pair of hands that had typed a poem had also cooked stuffed eggplant surrounded by sweet potatoes, and recorded it all in the same journal entry. In her journal Sarton brought centuries of quiet but manifold creativity into a new light. In 1973, with the publication of *Journal of a Solitude*, she also hit upon a phenomenon waiting to happen. She wrote about what her audience most craved: the forbidden fruit of solitude. Her largest audience was either married women with children, or older readers in caretaking roles. "The cry," she noted, wasn't "so much for 'a room of one's own' as time of one's own." With each passing year, that would only grow. Over the next three decades Sarton's journals provided readers with a vicarious solitude: the sheer novelty of time alone, unmarked time to watch how the light shifts in seasons or how a house settles, its sounds as familiar as the friction of one's own bones.

On that wet September morning in 1971, as she wrote *Journal of a Solitude*'s first sentence, "Begin here," Sarton unknowingly also gave her future readers—diarists and potential writers—the license to begin, to use a journal as work. Spurred by the civil rights and later the women's movement, she used her journals, long the means of the outsider, as a way to discover voice and vocation. Candid about her own doubts and failures, she was always beginning life anew. Each journal would become a kind of instruction manual: for some readers, how to work; for others, how to live or how to love. Whatever their reasons, in *Journal of a Solitude* readers recognized its cry of loneliness and spiritual conflict, a human being like themselves, often riddled with self-doubt or buffeted by depressions. "Every grief or inexplicable seizure by weather, woe, or work can— if we discipline ourselves and think hard enough—be turned to account . . . And the discipline of work provides an exercise bar, so that the wild, irrational motions of the soul become formal and creative." Before their eyes, readers watched Sarton, beginning at sixty, reinvent herself over and over through disciplined work. Grappling with her demons of boredom, panic and impatience, she observed, "There is nothing to be done but go ahead with life moment by moment and hour by hour—put out birdseed, tidy the rooms, try to create order and peace around me even if I cannot achieve it inside me . . . And here in my study the sunlight is that autumn white, so clear, it calls . . . clarify, clarify."

In Nelson and later in the third-floor study at Wild Knoll, treetops brushing the windows, May Sarton strove to clarify a lifelong impatience with herself. "I hardly ever sit still without being haunted by the 'undone' and the 'unsent.' I often feel exhausted, but it is not my work that tires (work is a rest); it is the effort of pushing away the lives and needs of others before I can come to the work with any freshness and zest." Alone, surrounded by photos of Colette and other writers in old age, she regained balance in quiet hours of walks and reading. W. H. Auden, Flannery O'Connor, Simone Weil were for long stretches the house's only company. In *Journal of a Solitude*, she copied out T. S. Eliot:

Teach us to care and not to care
Teach us to sit still.

Year after year, scores of readers, hoping to imitate her sitting still, copied the Eliot into their own journals as well as Sarton's own words:

> I always forget how important the empty days are, how important it may be sometimes not to expect to produce anything, even a few lines in a journal. I am still pursued by a neurosis about work inherited from my father. A day where one has not pushed oneself to the limit seems a damaged damaging day, a sinful day. Not so! The most valuable thing we can do for the psyche, occasionally, is to let it rest, wander, live in the changing light of a room.

In May 1973 May Sarton settled permanently at Wild Knoll. In Nelson she "began to feel I lived in a museum and had become a target for public curiosity." The move to York, Maine, assured independence and privacy in a house overlooking a "stretch of wild woodland, rocky coast, meadows running to the sea." At Wild Knoll she quickly settled into new routines: seeding a garden, planting clusters of daffodils, cosmos, Japanese anemones, peonies. Music once again filled the house. She adopted a tawny-colored sheltie named Tamas to accompany her on solitary afternoon walks.

"Without tension, it has been the happiest year I can remember." Since *Journal of a Solitude*, it had also been a year and a half without a journal. "Was it that happiness is harder to communicate, or that when one is happy enough there is little incentive even to try to sort out daily experience as it happens?" But Sarton the writer slowly stirred. "I became haunted by something I read years ago to the effect that when the Japanese were in a period of peace they painted only fans." Writing, she'd long known, had at its core a tension, a hidden agenda brought to light only sentence by sentence. "Writing for me is a way of understanding what is happening to me, of thinking hard things out. I have never written a book that was not born out of a question I needed to answer for myself."

At Wild Knoll, May Sarton wrote a succession of books, each with its own question: the novels *Crucial Conversations* and *Anger* probed the artistic and domestic tensions within marriage; *The Magnificent Spinster* imagined the possibilities of work in late middle age; *A Reckoning* explored the psychic price of illness and old age. Poetry, Sarton's first and deepest love, continued its celebration of the immediate natural world. But in September 1974 she once again began a journal. *The House by the Sea*, covering 1974 through the summer of 1976, chronicled the return of her creativity. She began several books simultaneously: the journal, a new book of poems and a collection of portraits.

As she sat down to write *The House by the Sea*, she imagined a journal finally illuminating the contented side of solitude: a robust Bordeaux waiting on a table set for one with good china. Mornings of writing, evenings of reading. There was Bramble, the wild cat tamed in Nelson, curled on warm flagstones; in the garden dozens of tendrils shot up from dark soil as, upstairs, words blossomed quietly on the page. It was a life of planting, tending, pruning—in the study, the garden, the psyche. "But a journal cannot be planned ahead, written as it is on the pulse of the moment." The year, though, brought the deaths of three of her oldest friends; her closest living friend, Judy Matlock, was lost to Alzheimer's disease; and Sarton herself, plagued by a viral throat infection, was often unable to work. Sitting in her upstairs study, she sorted out these painful events in the new journal. In the long hours, she grappled with the questions she'd spend the rest of her writing life examining: illness, old age, adversity, independence and the stubborn creativity of being human.

In the winter of 1974, at sixty-two, Sarton looked back on her own long creative journey—how she'd come to Wild Knoll and where she was going. Memories of years spent in London in her late twenties—sitting in Katherine Mansfield's old garden or visiting Virginia Woolf—were ever on her mind. Simultaneously, she kept her journal, *The House by the Sea*, as well as beginning *A World of Light*, a collection of portraits of key creative influences up to age forty-five. In each she wanted to trace: "How does one grow? How does one change?" On long walks along the icy Atlantic, she reflected on her central life experiences: fleeing war-torn Belgium, arriving in America in 1916 at age three; her divided allegiances between Europe and America. How her parents' polar creative strengths, discipline and passion, had proved essential to her early theater and literary careers. How in 1936 her first two books had brought her to the notice of Elizabeth Bowen and Virginia Woolf—those early years of creative promise, when the sloe-eyed Sarton, her dark hair swept back, sleek as a seal, believed that anything was still possible.

But in 1974 the hair was gray; glasses magnified astigmatic eyes; tweeds and beat-up sneakers replaced the well-cut suits of early New York days, when she lived in a series of hotels. Those early years filled the pages of both the journal and the memoir. With the sea constant in the distance, Sarton examined the bittersweet legacy of creative mentors: novelist Elizabeth Bowen, translator S. S. Koteliansky, *New Yorker* poet and critic Louise Bogan. If *A World of Light* was a memoir of what she remembered, the early promise of career, then *The House by the Sea* caught what she was living: the fears and problems of the aging artist.

"If there is an art to the keeping of a journal for publication yet at the same time a very personal record, it may be in what E[lizabeth] Bowen said: 'One must regard oneself impersonally as an instrument.' " Just as *Journal of a Solitude* had been an experiment in brutal honesty, a public document of private but human doubts, so in

The House by the Sea Sarton refused to spiritualize away the pain of friends recently or long since dead. The journal's raw immediacy balanced the carefully crafted formal portraits in *A World of Light*—the memoirist's temptation to romanticize, round off corners, present a socially acceptable public face of oneself and others. Sarton showed the journal to be memoir's invaluable shadow side, exposing the darker, truer textures of a life. In the memoir Sarton's parents sit contentedly in their leafy Cambridge garden, she in her Chinese shawl, he in a battered straw hat. It is a portrait of a latter-day Tolstoyan marriage: a work-driven husband warning his wife, " 'I shall always put my work before you or any child we may have' "; a migraine-prone wife's "capacity to compromise many times with her own gifts for the sake of his work." In the journal Sarton acidly jotted, "My mother buried her anger . . . so she beat herself inside—and he never grew up." Journal writing helped Sarton exorcise the rages she'd internalized watching her parent's marriage. It also clarified the struggle she'd inherited: how to keep a work life humane. "No writer," she concluded, "can justify ruthlessness for the sake of his work because being human to the fullest possible extent is what his work demands of him."

Being fully human, staring clear-eyed at failure and risk, soon became her journals' signature. Failure had long been a familiar shadow in Sarton's life, beginning as early as 1935 with the demise of her Off-Broadway repertory company. At twenty-four she was already on a second career. Critical literary success, achieved early on in England, had been more fitful in America, suspicious of a writer working in three distinct genres. While friends with many of the top writers of her generation, she confessed to a failure of character: "I have shied away from my peers, partly because writing, as a trade, is so competitive, and I am a bad loser. Any meeting with a successful writer opens wounds."

In her mid-sixties, Sarton calculated the price of her self-imposed professional isolation. If *A World of Light* depicted her crucial friendship with Louise Bogan, poetry critic for *The New Yorker*, in her journals she trained an unsparing eye on the underside of creative alliances—criticism, betrayal, conflict. A private but not often public supporter of Sarton's work, Bogan cited sentimentality as a lie at the heart of it, admonishing, "You keep the Hell out of your work.' " Sarton had finally begun to put it into her journals instead. Unlike centuries of diarists nursing hurts in private, in publishing her journals she let the public decide. In *The House by the Sea* she starkly confronted her own limitations as a writer. "Only very recently have I come to see and to accept that Louise Bogan really never believed in my work as poet or as novelist. I couldn't face this even a few years ago, and never did while I knew her, for I always hoped for the saving word then. Now I can accept it, partly because I have a firmer hold on my work and far more self-assurance than I did." But it would still take another eleven years, with her fifth journal, written in her seventies, before she could admit, "It has taken me a long time to be honest about Louise Bogan because I loved and admired her so much. But now at nearly seventy-five I must admit that the explanation may well be jealousy. At the time when she almost ceased to write poems, I was producing a lot, in three fields. Chapters of *I Knew a Phoenix* were appearing in *The New Yorker* the year after I began seeing her."

With each passing year, Sarton's unflinching self-scrutiny, the anatomy of her failures, were second only to her capacity to rebound and reinvent herself. From *Journal of a Solitude* on, she became for many a link in the creative chain of literary mentors. Just as she had sat at tea in 1938 waiting to hear what, if anything, Virginia Woolf thought of her first novel, she knew what a few kind words meant to an aspiring writer. "Praise for the middle-aged or old has always come too late; it cannot come too soon. Young talent thrives on it." In publishing her journals, Sarton offered writers of all ages advice, praise and free criticism. As Woolf had written for the Common Reader, so Sarton spoke to the Common Writer: the diarist, the novice, the uncelebrated writer. In doing so, her journals' lasting contribution would be their legacy of confidence. It was part of a tradition that had long built on itself: writers who moved forward by reading backward—Katherine Mansfield reading Dorothy Wordsworth's journals, Virginia Woolf reading Mansfield's, Sarton reading Woolf's. And so it would continue, generation after generation of diarists, a coded helix of creative voice.

May Sarton had lived long enough not only to write about Virginia Woolf in her journals but to read what Woolf had written about Sarton in *her* diaries. In volume five of Woolf's diaries, published in 1984, Sarton recognized her anxious, ambitious twenty-six-year-old self. So too Woolf's testy shorthand in the diary—a famous writer flattered but annoyed by a younger writer's "silly but clever imitation" of her style. Now in old age, Sarton herself was besieged by legions of writers and journal keepers, each eagerly awaiting a verdict on their work or life. Before the appearance of a new journal, she braced herself for those who threatened to flock to her doorstep

> with their fervors, their problems, their hopes, who come to me, I suppose, to reaffirm a vision of life or a way of living that appeals to them. But they cannot know what such a life costs. They take so much for granted, and when I look back at myself at twenty-five or thirty, I am newly aware that so did I. Youth is a kind of genius in itself and knows it. Old age is often expected to recognize that genius and forget its own, so much subtler and gentler, so much wiser. But it is possible to keep the genius of youth into old age, the curiosity, the intense interest in everything from a bird to a book.

On weekends Sarton met with the occasional reader, offering generosity or her notoriously scrappy temper. She soon began incorporating passages from readers' letters into her journals as a way to respond to the sheer volume of mail and to correct misconceptions. Often her opinions shocked readers. A journal, with its lure of narcissism, was not for the young. Nor was a life of solitude. "I do not see that you have a *vocation* powerful enough in its pulls to justify a life of solitude," Sarton told one reader (and therefore a million), citing a necessary commitment to work first. On a filmmaker who had mastered the discipline of craft: "I gather she has some doubts about the solitary life. I told her that I feel it is not for the young (she is thirty-three). I did not begin to live alone till I was forty-five . . . I had a huge amount of life to think about and to digest, and, above all, I was a *person* by then and I knew what I wanted out of life."

As she edged toward seventy, what May Sarton craved was a more minute observing of life's late seasons: the bittersweet autumn of the body, the wintry silences of old age. In *The House by the Sea* she first recorded worrying about falling down four flights of stairs and not being found for days. In all the journals to follow, a new daily reality slowly surfaced: the solitude of illness. In 1980 Sarton underwent a mastectomy, its effect in her life discussed in her journal *Recovering*. In 1988 she suffered a stroke, the struggle to regain her creative powers becoming the subject of her journal *After the Stroke*. In the journals *Endgame* and *Encore*, Sarton, almost eighty and forced to dictate her entries into a Sony recorder, detailed the struggle with a fibrillating heart, a left lung filled with fluid, severe diverticulitis. Like Alice James before her, she used the body's steady betrayals to train a diarist's detached eye. "For one cannot probe pain or come to terms with what it has to teach without detachment. It is the sentimentalists who cannot bear to look at their pain, who wallow in it, and it is the cowards who simply shut it out . . . Pain is the great teacher if we can look at it coldly, examine it as a doctor examines a broken arm."

The older she got, the more Sarton held firm to her belief that "private dilemmas are, if deeply examined, universal, and so, if expressed, have a human value beyond the private." For many not familiar with or even partial to her novels, Sarton's later journals helped them cope with the numbing routines of new drugs, diffident doctors, experimental cures. So too her galled response to visitors' cheeriness: "I am thinking about making a list of things not to say to someone recovering from surgery," she wrote in *Recovering*. "One of them is surely 'count your blessings.' " Training herself to hold a pen, steady a glass, write a sentence, Sarton voiced what others couldn't: the humiliation of being left alone in a hospital corridor for hours; the helplessness of not being able to make a meal or button a sweater. For those isolated by illness or old age, she offered a sense of community. Often one of her journals was someone's only companion in illness, a secret on a hospital night stand; for caregivers, it was a model for their own journals, a way to understand the rage that comes with illness's sudden dependence.

"Sometimes I think the fits of rage are like a huge creative urge gone into reverse," she'd written in *Journal of a Solitude*. Five years later, *Recovering* examined the consequences of bottled-up pain, of life without that "built-in safety valve against madness or illness." Between 1978 and 1979 Sarton traced "the long excruciating journey . . . toward some regained sense of my self" following the mastectomy, mixed reviews of her latest novel, and a brief unhappy affair. If the journals had taught her anything, it was that "nothing that happens to us, even the most terrible shock, is unusable, and everything has somehow to be built into the fabric of the personality." Turning once again to "this familiar means" of her journal, she noted, "What keeping a journal again is helping me to do—is to make my peace with solitude once more, and to come back to work without ambition, for the joy of it."

Looking out on the stone sculpture of a phoenix anchored at the foot of her garden, Sarton knew that ambition in the years ahead meant the task of transforming rejection into renewal, hurt into hope. In quiet hours at Wild Knoll, its solitude interrupted only on weekends, she wrote out her late journals' lesson:

> Pain is the great teacher. I woke before dawn with this thought. Joy, happiness, are what we take and do not question. They are beyond question, maybe. A matter of being. But pain forces us to think, and to make connections, to sort out what is what, to discover what has been happening to cause it. And, curiously enough, pain draws us to other human beings in a significant way, whereas joy or happiness to some extent, isolates.

Soon the natural world—the garden long neglected, the sound of the sea outside the bedroom window—became a source of happiness. "There are great pleasures in not feeling well—I get up shockingly late for me, around seven-thirty . . . half-asleep, I listen to the morning sounds, a faint murmur of ocean . . . the goldfinches in flight, the wood pigeons' repeated coos, and the low 'frahnk' of the blue heron as he flies to the pond." In *Recovering*, Sarton was renewed once again in the quiet rhythms of Wild Knoll. Finally "on a rising curve," her appetite had returned not only for robust wines and fresh vegetables from neighbors' gardens but also for work. By the journal's close she looked back on the year's dividends: a film celebrating her life and work, a *Paris Review* interview, a sold-out poetry reading at the Library of Congress.

By 1982 Wild Knoll was once again an earthly paradise: the garden lush, the sea quicksilver beyond the fringe of salt marsh. Sarton for the first time ever began a journal in the spring, to celebrate turning seventy. "I have always longed to be old, and that is because all my life I have had such great exemplars of old age," she wrote, referring to her parents and teachers in Belgium and

Cambridge. *At Seventy* was an exuberant, confident salute to late life. If her journals minutely catalogued the stark realities of growing older, *At Seventy* also exploded the myths of old age: declining stamina, severed work life. Chronicling "a summer without solitude," the new journal became "a record of a runner who never catches up with herself." Crisscrossing the country, Sarton gave numerous readings, one night selling fifteen hundred dollars worth of books. She attended the birthdays of three close friends "all in full possession of their powers" at eighty-eight, ninety and ninety-one.

"One of the censors that has been at work," she'd written in *Recovering*, "has been the notion that to be in love at our age is ludicrous and somehow not proper, that passionate love can be banished after sixty shall we say? . . . Love at any age has its preposterous side—that is why it comes as a kind of miracle at any age." Increasingly, she turned outward toward community. At seventy Sarton recorded a renewed social activism—helping someone meet his or her medical bills, interest in the local H.O.M.E. project, which provided schooling and shelter for the indigent. "We have to find a way, religious or not, of sanctifying life again." Writing, difficult as it was, was her way. First published at twenty-six, she was having a second debut at seventy. "So in the end I have to accept myself as a useful creator (at least I can believe that now in my old age) and a difficult human being."

How one reads May Sarton's journals depends, over time, on whether one sees Sarton as the useful creator or the difficult human being. Pioneer or narcissist, or both? All the journals challenged her friend Louise Bogan's observation "At my present age, one is permitted hope but not ambition." Hope for Sarton took the ambitious form of the journal kept for publication. A contradiction in terms, a published journal is a calculated gamble that risks the world judging the life as well as the work, the life *as* the work. Sarton willingly took the risk.

Hoping the journals' readers would see beyond her immediate personality, she gambled that her fate as a writer depended on that of her readers. A journal casually picked up in a bookstore, or slipped off a library shelf and read in the dusty afternoon light, finds us in a moment either of curiosity or of need. The scoffer in a bookstore returns another day an admirer, picking up one of her journals after its subject has finally, often viscerally, entered his or her life: struggling with creative isolation, waiting on a hospital gurney, or suddenly finding oneself among the "widows, people to whom solitude had 'happened.' "

By the mid 1980s much had happened to May Sarton: fame and its whiplash. Her journals, she knew, either fascinated or annoyed the public. She was someone whose fame stemmed from solitude yet who often complained about the very isolation she'd chosen. A writer who in a public stage whisper lamented her work's lack of critical reception but whose books, all published by Norton, sell briskly. Whatever the contradictions, her legacy as a journal keeper was unique: Sarton was the outsider with an inside ticket: a well-established writer who wrote what it feels like to be outside the fray. Anticipating criticism, she posed questions about the journals themselves, wondering if their repetitions were merely carelessness or the innate pattern of diaries—a writer grappling over a lifetime with the same material from every possible angle. Creativity was a high-wire act that happened in intimate spaces: sitting at a desk as the outside world was banked deep with snow. "A lot of poetry of living, especially alone, takes place in the kitchen," she wrote in *The House by the Sea.* "I thought of this yesterday when I was cutting up green cherry tomatoes . . . and felt calmed by the domesticity, cutting up, finding cinnamon and ginger."

"How one lives as a private person is intimately bound into the work," Sarton wrote in *Journal of a Solitude*. "And at some point I believe one has to stop holding back for fear of alienating some imaginary reader or real relative or friend, and come out with personal truth." In many of the journals an X stood in lieu of a name. Like the chromosome, X was a code for female, a code for love affairs with "the fascinating but sometimes deadly Muses." Her honesty, not her actual choice in love, caused her public isolation. Only one of her books, *Mrs. Stevens Hears the Mermaids Singing*, published against the advice of her agent and editors in 1965, concerned an openly gay relationship. The other eighteen novels addressed questions of friendship, aging, politics, divorce.

May Sarton, unlike Anaïs Nin, kept her romantic life private in her journals. Interested less in the true identity of a specific individual, her readers sought another intimacy in Sarton's journals: their own fates. In her unsparing descriptions of Judy Matlock, Sarton's long-time companion before she moved to Nelson in 1958, readers poignantly glimpsed their own potential futures. By the time Sarton moved to Maine, Matlock had developed Alzheimer's disease. Beginning with *The House by the Sea*, Sarton showed the cruel fate of the Alzheimer's victim—Matlock, a once brilliant scholar visiting Sarton for the weekend, packing a suitcase over and over, throwing a nightgown into the wastebasket, pulling up lettuce instead of weeds. "An irritable, totally selfish infant has replaced the wise, dignified, loving person one loved, *and still loves,* and that is why the pain is so acute," Sarton wrote in *Recovering*. "I have been honest about all the horror of senility because there are many people who have to face it alone." Finally put into a nursing home, the frail Judy sat unaware she was in the Walden Nursing Home. Returning home, Sarton used her journal to record her thoughts: "The reason senility is so frightening is, of course, that it shakes the foundations of our belief in what life is all about, a long process of growth, a ripening that we hope may be only one step in the long evolution of each soul toward more light. Senility destroys this illusion or appears to."

Journals are meant to be read as they were written: slowly, in stages, left on the bedside table to allow time for digestion. Read at a clip, Sarton's journals can seem tediously self-involved, subject to vague, repetitive generalities. But her journals show less who she is than who her vast and varied readership had become over three tumultuous decades. On a reading tour in the early 1970s, Sarton first noted the trapped faces of suburban housewives: "Under the polite small talk, one sensed . . . the bored child who does not know what he lacks, but knows he is being deprived of something essential to his well-being." In each new journal she caught the scope and consequences of the life choices her readers had made over the decades. Over eighty percent of Sarton's readers were married women with children. A letter from one, reproduced in the journals, showed why letters were often so difficult for Sarton to respond to. A young mother, a painter, wrote:

I wonder which Hell is worse—the Hell of an entirely self-motivated life, or the hell of which I feel a part: myself struggling to come to terms with what I want to say, how I want to say it, the fear and doubt. So much holds me back. My own inertia, the choice I made ten years ago to be second in marriage, the children . . . Does one give up a measure of security, and whatever else is necessary, to develop? . . . I envy your solitude with all my heart, and your courage to live as you must.

In her journal Sarton reflected:

But there is something wrong when solitude such as mine can be "envied" by a happily married woman with children. Mine is not, I feel sure, the best human solution. Nor that I have ever thought it was. In my case it has perhaps made possible the creation of some works of art, but certainly it has done so at a high price in emotional maturity and in happiness. What I have is space around me and time around me. How they can be achieved in a marriage is the real question. It is not an easy one to answer.

For her legion of readers, Sarton's very initials—MS—parallel those for "manuscript" and also for that feminist symbol of independence and uneasy solidarity. In her journals those who feared saying the difficult, feared seeming shrill or too intimate, had found a potent creative model. "For a long time, for years, I have carried in my mind the excruciating image of plants, bulbs, in a cellar, trying to grow without light, putting out *white* shoots that will inevitably wither." The blind groping for voice—*how* to say it, how to root in fertile ground—is at the core of Sarton's journals. If they lack the edge and calculated rawness of Anne Sexton, who put into her poetry what Sarton left exclusively for her journals, Sarton remains the more widely read. Why? She wrote for those who didn't have the confidence for skepticism—the late bloomer, the writer who may or may not be an amateur but, being unwilling to test the work in public, remains one.

"If one writes only for one's own pleasure," Virginia Woolf observed in her diary, "I suppose the convention of writing is destroyed." For centuries the diary has been a hedge against literary perfectionism. But a published journal is held to public standards of judgment, its loose form no longer protection against charges of sloppy writing. As Sarton moved her journals into the public arena, questions inevitably arose: Is a journal a work of art or a work of therapy? Is it more concerned with the life or with the writing that *transforms* the life? Sarton's prolificness often had a suspicious fluency in the journals. Can something that looks so easy be complex?

Yet even in her eighties Sarton still worried about the quality of the current journal. In an earlier one, she confided, "The two sins I am accused of in the novels are 1) careless style and 2) over-idealism. 'Marriages are not like that.' 'People do not talk as your characters do.' " Such candor in public often backfired. In *At Seventy*, Sarton muses on a review of her latest novel in the *New York Times*:

> It was a thoughtful and generous review, although she considers *Anger* a failure. I am grateful. But I have to face the fact that by talking openly about the problems of the novel in the journal—in this case, *Recovering*—I expose myself. Ballantyne [the reviewer] collates some statements in the journal with the novel to buttress her argument that I failed to meet my own challenge in writing it.

Sarton's ability to rise phoenix-like in her journal was solace to the discouraged writer, often marginalized and without a literary network. "Real literature today must survive outside the media," she noted in *Recovering*, "and does so by means of a network of readers of sensitivity and good will who share their discoveries." The network worked both ways. If Sarton's journals shared and shored up others' confidence by providing experiences similar to their own, letters from readers sustained her through illness and adversity. "It is my solitude and what I have said about it that has made the link, and made so many women and men I do not know, regard me as a friend in whom they can confide."

Private confidences paraded in a public forum are a tricky bargain, anticipating the phenomenon of the confessional in late twentieth-century life—the competing tragedies of talk shows. How is the published journal different? Taking swipes at Anaïs Nin's "narcissistic evasions and distortions in her journals," Sarton acknowledged, "There is always the danger of bending over oneself like Narcissus and drowning in self-indulgence. If a journal is to have any value either for the writer or any potential reader, the writer must be objective about what he experiences on *the pulse.*" By making her journals public, Sarton left a subtler legacy, coaxing the aspiring writer into the public forum. "But it is troubling how many people expect applause, recognition, when they have not even begun to learn an art or craft. Instant success is the order of the day," she wrote in 1967, about the same time she reworked a single poem in over sixty-one drafts.

*W*hat tempts a writer to publish a journal? Exhibitionism, self-expression? Sarton's early theater life gave her a natural sense of audience, served her well at readings, where she heard poems *"land* in that special silence when a large audience is moved." In her journals readers witnessed a writer enacting the private drama of claiming her public self-worth. A creative business ledger, the journals noted that the Detroit Public Library rebound her books every six months; that she earned a minimum of $50,000, often $100,000, in royalties annually; that in the 1990s *Journal of a Solitude* had become a bestseller in Japan ("Of course. As a nation they have so little solitude"). As illness confined Sarton to home, the journals became her chance to set the record right: choosing her official biographer, evaluating the mounting list of books written about her. Long at the mercy of reviewers, in her journals she had found a way to control the reputation, to have the final word.

May Sarton once had a vivid dream years after Virginia Woolf's death. "I dreamt that I saw her walking in the streets of a provincial town, unrecognized, unknown, and somehow guessed that she had not committed suicide at all, but had decided that she had to disappear, go under as her famous self, and start again." The dream caught Sarton's unconscious wish for herself, fleeing not her failures but her journals' success. Ironically, she questioned the disproportionate success of her journals. "I suspect the journal as a form," she wrote in *Recovering*, "because it is too easy, too quick perhaps." Yet it will be for her journals that she'll be read well into the next century. The cameo details will still be familiar—a woman finally publishing her first book at ninety, a college student who writes, "Is keeping a journal selfish?" The universality of their desires is refracted through Sarton herself, "the solitary compulsive" who formalized grief into a sonnet; bought artichokes after a stroke, "enamored of the slow progress" they require; tape-recorded the journal at seventy-eight, "a door opening to work again."

"At this very moment somebody is discovering me in a public library," she wrote in *Endgame*. "Many of these letters say, 'I've never heard of you before but I saw the title of your book'—*Journal of a Solitude*—'and I took it home.' " A psychic orphan who in her journals kept re-creating home and herself, Sarton gave readers dispossessed by life or temperament a sense of home. As she created the mystique of a literary Eden and the reality of a personal purgatory, her lessons were clear: learning to accept dependence in old age, to lean on "root friends," to rail against marginality in work or life.

Wild Knoll, for legions of journal readers, will always be cast in late autumnal light. The garden, otherwise stripped back, teems with the season's late blooms: sprays of aster, cosmos, a solitary rose. The sea, constant and singular as a heartbeat, sounds through open windows. Inside, photos of Isak Dinesen and Colette in old age grace the writer's desk. Downstairs the living room shelves house André Gide, Katherine Mansfield, Virginia Woolf, Nadine Gordimer, Alice Walker, a reconstituted family, a circle of influence—creative, not blood, lines.

One such influence was the critic S. S. Koteliansky, mentor to Sarton and, before her, to Katherine Mansfield. Sarton knew Mansfield's letter to him by heart: "I am glad you criticized me. It is right that you should have hated much in me. I was false in many things and *careless*—untrue in many ways. But I would like you to know that I recognized this and for a long time I have been trying to 'squeeze the slave out of my soul.' " Sarton would quote the letter and Chekhov's famous line in her first memoir. Before her death at eighty-three in 1995, she'd spend the remainder of her life squeezing the slave out of her soul and, in her journals, helping readers do the same. Like seeding a garden, it was never too late to begin. Planting bulbs over age sixty is, after all, "the work of hope." And for May Sarton it flourished best alone. "Solitude, like long love, deepens with time, and, I trust, will not fail me if my own powers of creation diminish. For growing into solitude is one way of growing to the end."

EPILOGUE:
FIRST PERSON
SINGULAR

Is it not possible that the rage for confession,

autobiography . . . especially for memories of

earliest childhood, is explained by our persistent yet

mysterious belief in a self which is continuous and

permanent.

—KATHERINE MANSFIELD, *Journal*, 1920

NOVEMBER 7

I often sit here imagining how the walls must have been a pale dusty brown, the color of a dried moth's wing. Or that's how I picture them. But the walls of the original house were torn down years ago. The spot where I now sit belonged to the house where Alice James and her family finally settled after moving to Cambridge, Massachusetts, in 1866. It was here that the five James siblings returned exhausted after the family's nomadic years in Europe. Dragging steamer trunks up narrow flights of stairs, they had far more than clothes to unpack. In Europe, they had filled their minds and imaginations the way others fattened pockets with souvenirs or strange coins. The hard work of their own destinies lay before them: finding ways to give voice to newly tapped creative and intellectual talents.

It was here at 20 Quincy Street that Alice's favorite brother, Henry, locked himself in his upstairs room for hours on end, trying to write. At twenty-two he summoned a furious, tortured concentration, willing himself into a writer. At forty he'd still be complaining in his notebooks, "If only I could concentrate myself: this is the greatest lesson of life. I have hours of unspeakable reaction against the smallness of my production; my wretched habits of work—or unwork . . . my vagueness of mind, my perpetual failure to focus my attention." Ever aware of his brother William's success, Henry, like Alice after him, had had to leave home in order to write. Over the next four decades, his imagination competing only with itself, he produced endless stories and novels, barely exhausting his fund of memories. Or his frantic need to write them out as fast as he could.

Now, in death, all the famous Jameses are joined, their graves two miles west of here in Cambridge Cemetery. Tourists often picnic amid the fragile tombstones, a respite before reboarding buses bound for Concord, to the sites of Thoreau, Emerson and Alcott. As one stands in front of the tight row of graves, it's as if the Jameses were still squabbling over a crowded foreign breakfast table. Not even death stems their competition. William's paragraph of accomplishment, as Henry feared, is etched larger than his own. Alice's stone bears an epitaph her brothers chose from Dante: FROM MARTYRDOM AND EXILE TO THIS PEACE. For them, death, not a diary, was her final accomplishment.

But outside the site of their old Cambridge house, a blue oval plaque finally yokes their achievements: ON THIS SITE LIVED WILLIAM JAMES, PHILOSOPHER, HENRY JAMES, NOVELIST, ALICE JAMES, DIARIST. The two other brothers, alcoholics or failures, are quietly omitted. But like the shadows darkening the nearby brick pathway, they too haunt the spot Henry once described as "about as lively as an inner sepulchre." The James threshold that Emerson and Hawthorne crossed on their way to dinner is now the site of Harvard's Faculty Club into which an endless parade of people wander for weddings, business seminars or to use the bathroom. Despite its staged comfort, the discreet accent of faded armchairs worn like pairs of old shoes, the spot is still charged with the James children's legacy of self-consciousness. The faces of strangers and undergraduates alike all wear the same quiet anxiety, as if Alice's father, Henry Sr., were standing at the door invisibly exhorting them, as he once did his gifted children, "to *be* something."

Certainly, while sitting here on odd Monday afternoons, I always feel as if I were taking an exam I'm ill-prepared for. From the walls stare down pale nineteenth-century faces, eyebrows arched as if amused by the jagged line of my salt-stained boots, or that I carry papers in a shopping bag. I often sit here for a quiet hour in the late afternoon waiting to teach a writing seminar. Across the street, classroom lights burn day and night, a frantic industry of college and adult education students: mothers returning to school, people learning foreign languages at seventy. Alice's father, no doubt, would have applauded this perpetual quest for self-improvement, seen it as intrinsically American, expansive in its optimistic belief in potential. Nowhere does that sense of potential surface more visibly than in the mania for self-expression. As the millennium nears, the list of offered writing classes lengthens. Creative writing classes, journal classes, essay and composition classes, seminars in how to write memoir or publish books, crowd catalogs. It is the passion of the first person singular—to have its say, leave a mark, not lose itself in a world wired into global plurality, a world at once connected and alienating.

Like many writers, I've often supported a writing life by teaching. It gives me odd corners of time, like today, when I can sit in borrowed quiet and scribble in this notebook. I've never mastered the distracting formality of hard-spined journals, or the ones with creamy handmade paper shimmering with watermarks. Journal as artifact. I've owned all of them at some time. But the ones that fill themselves quickly with images or observations or odd bits of overheard dialogue are those that cost under two dollars. My shelves are lined with these small spiral notebooks, part journal, part writer's notebook. I buy them in ordinary stationery stores, soothed by the familiar covers soon to be smudged with my own fingerprints. Those of us who haunt stationery stores quietly take in the possibility of all that paper, all those pens, savoring them like a secret vice.

Today, in the last few pages of this notebook, I'm thinking about notes for a final chapter on diaries. But, as always, my eye is drawn to a painting directly across from me. It's a late-nineteenth-century portrait of a man in a starched wing collar, his shirt even whiter against the contrasting dark backdrop. It's not his face but that solid black background that continually holds my eye. It's as if everything I'm interested in were hidden behind that black curtain. I imagine that as the sitter posed for this portrait, his wife sat unseen near a window, diary in her lap, secretly writing. Or that a floor below, or three above in a cramped attic with low slanting ceilings, hired help with no leisure or confidence to write kept mental notes instead. Like all outsiders, their eyes were sharpened by daily watchfulness, their ears alert to stories they'd never have time to write. The man in the portrait is now nameless, his darkly handsome face lent solely to decorate a room. But whenever I stare at his portrait, I can't help but sense the invisible crowd hovering just behind him: centuries of outsiders willing themselves out from behind the curtain.

My bag bulges with writing. Others' writing. In just twenty minutes, fifteen of us will be seated around a seminar table, listening intently, as if in a séance, for sounds: murmurs of praise or criticism. The class is in memoir—short weekly autobiographical sketches. Everyone in the class wants to move out of private writing, out of the diaries the women have kept from childhood, the men since college. Of the fifteen students, almost all still keep some form of a notebook. The men call theirs journals; the women call theirs diaries. "I've kept a diary as long as I can remember," many write on their class information sheets. "Since nine." "Beginning at eleven." "From the time I could hold a pen." All the students want to break out into some final, longer creative work. A diary, they know, is a process. They want a product. One woman always carries her note-book to class, fingering its thick spine, as if anticipating how the book she hopes will emerge from it one day will feel, a fine, satisfying weight in the hand.

Every week someone asks a variant of the same two questions: How does one become a writer? How does one find a voice? Read. Write. Keep writing, I say. Rewrite. Read more. Study how someone else did it. Some stare blankly as if I've asked them to bisect a star. Joan Didion, I tell them, typed out Hemingway. Mary Gordon copied Virginia Woolf onto index cards. Cynthia Ozick dissected Henry James sentence by sentence. I give them great prose stylists like M. F. K. Fisher to learn from, the deceptive ease with which she writes about the natural world—the salty pleasure of a fresh oyster; standing in open markets watching eels slithering in white porcelain basins; the dry hills of Provence; spiky artichokes or strawberries as large as a child's fist; searching for shoes for her daughters' blistered feet.

I don't give them Fisher's journals, *Stay Me, Oh Comfort Me*, a title some might find ironic. Her honesty can seem meanspirited. "I know after correcting several thousand themes from every kind of class, Junior League to freshman, that there are countless, yes, countless people who *could* write. They could write much better than I. But they don't. I do. I don't know why. I seem to have no special interest, *no* interest really, in selling things and seeing them printed," she wrote at the start of her career. Already in 1936 she was weary: "I believe there are too many books, too many people writing."

While Fisher later won success, especially for her *New Yorker* pieces on food, her real subject was always our deeper hunger: the famished loss of a failed love affair; the loneliness of boiled egg suppers in a studio apartment; the slow, daily ways we starve ourselves. Hunger is deep in the class that awaits me: a hunger to be heard. But also, for some, to be vindicated and recognized. I teach that newest oxymoron: creative nonfiction, the rage of memoir where honesty has become a fetish, and revelation, a strategy. The sly catalogue of nursed grievances is no longer found just in diaries; their pages are being combed with an eye to writing memoir. Material that just ten years ago would have stayed hidden in a diary is now shaped into memoir. Injury has become an industry. But so too a whole new breed of writers certain that their stories voice identical ones long locked up in private diaries.

"What would be gained, what lost, in moving out of a diary into memoir?" I ask on the information sheet the first day. The answers vary. Most who've signed up for the class, though, are still afraid of writing about someone they're close to. Anticipating that person's hurt or anger has given many of them serious writer's block. Some show up with lists of pseudonyms. (On that first day as they write, I resist my own writer's tic, the very psychic trespassing they fear doing to others, namely, recording stray impressions of *them*—the oddly patterned sweater or the lipstick that looks like dried blood—into a notebook.) Most have come to clarify something for themselves, to give formal, final shape to some nagging story from their past, or some pattern they've noticed in their journals. The best writers know it will take more than this single course to achieve their goal, to move out of self-therapy into well-crafted prose. Their favorite memoirists have all had success first in other genres: as poets—Maya Angelou, Mary Karr, Lucy Grealy; or as novelists—Susanna Kaysen, Tobias Wolff, Geoffrey Wolff, Mary McCarthy, James Carroll, Mary Gordon. Memoir, I tell the class, is not transcribing a life from a diary. Nor is revelation necessarily the same thing as illumination. Shocking a public is not as important as shocking oneself, using writing, as Joan Didion says, "to find out what I'm thinking, what I'm looking at, what it means. What I want and what I fear." Often I suspect some of the students that first day aren't quite honest, not so much to me as to themselves. In an age of information and revelation, they still want to be famous first, writers second.

How could it be otherwise? The windows of local bookstores are filled with celebrity memoirs ghostwritten by others. But the secret lust for recognition is as old as writing itself. In the corners of his illuminated manuscript, an ambitious but anonymous medieval Irish monk scribbled, "Oh God be gracious to my soul and grant me better handwriting." Not that the itch to record doesn't have its traps—or fame its miscalculated notoriety. Often I've sat in this room as someone chuckles at headlines detailing the latest political career torpedoed by a diary. Up on ethics charges of sexual misconduct, former Senator Bob Packwood no doubt rued his willful naïveté—30,000 subpoenaed diary pages revealing his private intent to record "nothing about being a rejected suitor, only my successful exploits."

As I sit writing this, those who wander in here on their way to law school interviews or career counseling are more careful. Out the corner of my eye, I study the identical bulging Filofaxes, suggestive of the confidence their owners so want to project. Late at night, do they jot their fears on odd scraps of paper, confused that the public self they're so determined to persuade future bosses is real is, in fact, less solid than the one privately recording its doubts. I suspect many who come here are unaware of the history of this house. How William James, paralyzed by indecision, reluctantly yielded to his father's wishes, giving up painting for medical school. How, at forty, he finally shattered years of terrible writer's block immediately after his father's death. How he wouldn't write his greatest books until into his fifties. Or how a portly and celibate Henry wrote his masterpieces alone in his house in the mild English port town of Rye, struggling till the end with the "surging chaos of the unexpressed." Or how Alice waited almost until she lay dying to record a childhood anecdote with self-defeating, affectionate irony. In her diary she recalled Emerson asking what the Jameses' only daughter was like. Told she had a moral nature, he delighted, " 'How in the world does her father get on with her?' "

A final note before going off to class. It's almost cocktail time, that dusky hour when this room slowly begins to fill. For many wandering in now, planning their futures with Napoleonic precision, William James is merely a nearby ugly modern hall; Henry James, a writer obsessed with semicolons; Alice James, the name of a local press specializing in first-time writers. A trio of young women sits nearby. Despite their independent minds, all echo "me too" immediately after the first one orders the obligatory glass of Chardonnay. I imagine these three tried keeping diaries, however briefly, at some point in youth. Or fervently read Anne Frank in suburban bedrooms, safe from the horror she described with impossible clarity. In her, they found what they couldn't quite get right in their own diaries—the consistent reliability of her voice, her trustworthiness as a narrator. The consistency of a self.

The diarist's practice of writing a page a day is ideal training for a writer. Eavesdropping on the trio's conversation, though, I know that none has turned out to be a writer. They'd no doubt smile at how Fanny Burney, before giving up writing for the seductions of court life, wrote her diary to "Nobody . . . since to Nobody can I be wholly unreserved." I wonder: as friends, how close do the real-life women sitting here measure up to the imaginary friend each may have invented to begin a first diary? My closest friends, I realize, are those whom I can still imagine as that friend from a childhood diary. I watch the three, their conspiratorial pleasure and ease as they lean closer to one another, swapping stories about children or work or the books they have no time to read. They mention some of my favorite writers—Toni Morrison, Maxine Hong Kingston, Alice Munro. *The Stone Diaries*, Carol Shields's Pulitzer Prize–winning novel, sits on two of their night tables. (Just as, I suspect, Doris

Lessing's *The Golden Notebook* once did on their mothers'.) I wonder if they realize how generation after generation instinctively gravitates to novels written in the form of a diary, unaware that readers are still searching for the plot of their own lives in the pages of others.

A century ago, these friends would have buried their stories in private diaries. I like listening to the three talk, especially the sassy redhead with the narrow Boston Irish face. She's funny and intelligent, someone I'd enjoy having in the class I'm just about to teach. Probably I'd spend the entire semester just trying to get her confidence up to the level of her ability. It's her laugh that gives it away—too quick, too willing. Her taut jawline has that telling translucency I often see in overachieving students. Her arms are fashionably thin. Too thin. The wrists look as though they'd snap if exposed too long to frost. I'm sure she'd be horrified by Alice James, horrified by Alice's wasting of talent, rightfully seeing a potential writer lost to migraine as privileged indulgence. But it's not lost on me that in the same spot that Alice James once paced in perfectionistic circles, so others now sit, still going through life using their diaries or bodies to transform themselves.

NOVEMBER 7 (CONTINUED). 11 P.M.

Notes to put in somewhere in a final chapter on diaries:

In Japan, those too busy to keep diaries can, for a fee, tape-record their thoughts over the telephone. Day or night. At the end of the month, a company sends the customer "a nicely bound transcription of their musings."

Ten million blank hard-spined journals are sold annually in America. (I suspect the greatest number sell in the first days of

January. Like New Year's resolutions, most will be abandoned after only a few weeks.)

I recently received a software flyer in the mail. Among its offerings was a "Dear Diary" kit for young girls, selling for $12.95. "Store your personal thoughts and memories under lock and key. Decorate and personalize the cover and pages with the material included."

Admiral Byrd's diary suggests he didn't discover the North Pole. A key entry that showed his coordinates before he turned his plane around was erased by an unknown hand.

"The life of every man is a diary to which he means to write one story, and writes another." J. M. Barrie

Novelist Raymond Radiguet's stole his lover's diary to write his novel *The Devil in the Flesh*. The passages Cocteau and other critics hailed as so insightful into a woman's mind were, in fact, taken directly from her diaries. It was too late to prosecute. Ever precocious, Radiguet died at twenty.

My local library subscribes to *The Diarists' Journal*, a quarterly that publishes selections from famous as well as contemporary diaries. Its publisher, Edward Gildea, told the *New York Times*, "There's an awful lot of writing going on that nobody knows about."

Books in Print lists two and a half single-spaced pages under the subject heading "Diaries."

In San Francisco, a television news program began broadcasting segments of an "on-the-air diary" of Paul Wynne's AIDS journal.

The oldest surviving diary in English was kept by a woman.

NOVEMBER 9. NOTES WHILE SITTING ON THE EDGE OF BOSTON COMMON

In the busy late afternoon while walking in downtown Boston, I always have the same sensation staring up at offices stacked floor to floor. The air hums with a bewildering congestion of words, millions of them zipping along invisible electronic circuits, competing over e-mail, Internet and fax lines. But within the same city, there's a parallel universe of words, private thoughts being logged into private notebooks. Crossing Boston Common, I thought of all these hands in motion—smoothing the new page of a journal or dragging a computer mouse across a screen. I imagine this identical movement all across the country: in schools, private homes, adult education centers. Often it's within the same room. The local adult education center, one of three in greater Boston, offers "Keeping a Personal Journal," that strangest of course paradoxes: groups of people sitting together in a room in order to write alone. "This series is for those who wish to begin their own journal or deepen their commitment to an established process," the catalogue notes, offering guidance in "creative process," "career and lifework directions" and "journal as spiritual practice." Unable to sit in a windowless classroom, diarists coast to coast talk over the Internet. "Home pages" lend a cozy feel to an otherwise icy electronic chat. At night, all across the nation, satellites probably pick up the lonely click of keyboards. Beamed into space, the sound is the same—like someone buried alive, furiously tapping their way out.

Who is this self so busy writing its way to the millennium? The same one that has always written. The one that yearns for a coherent narrative of inner life, a continuous sense of identity. And as I sit here on this quiet bench on the edge of Boston Common, watching the parade of seemingly self-contained lives stroll past, I'm reminded of how a harried Katherine Mansfield worried about her "hundreds of selves." In her journal she confessed, "There are moments when I feel I am nothing but the small clerk of some hotel without a proprietor, who has all his work cut out to enter the names and hand the keys to the willful guests." Mansfield jotted that in 1920. But I wonder if it's not more true now in this age of accelerated fragmentation as we strive for inward coherence. Instinctively, out of the fragments of a self, people still use diaries to momentarily render life whole. As it always has, a diary gives us the necessary illusion that the recording eye is the real I.

On this unseasonably mild fall afternoon, I'm thinking about the culture of diaries, how it invisibly infuses daily life, signaling like airwaves. I wonder if secrecy is the late twentieth century's final lust. The paradox of the Information Age is that the instantly accessed self needs to hide, to recoup, to escape from overexposure. In a world of instantaneous global information—vital statistics scanned and printed out at the press of a single button—diarists work hard to preserve a sense of privacy. But is has always been the case. "I must be private, secret, as anonymous and submerged as possible in order to write," Virginia Woolf wrote, voicing a sure solution to creative anxiety. What led Da Vinci to keep his journal in handwriting decipherable only when held up to a mirror is still best voiced by Katherine Mansfield, that most modern of writers: "one tries to go deep—to speak to the secret self we all have."

That secret self, though, is at daily psychic odds with a culture of confession. Looking up from this notebook at the nearby houses, TV antennae fixed like fetishes, I'm reminded that, for many, a diary may still be the last private refuge in a world gone globally public. But our whole notion of private and public is changing as fast as digital channels. Ours has become the world *as* diary, a vast confessional stage with us its eavesdropping audience. In daytime and prime time, we're lured into the cool darkness of the new confessional—the modern talk show, the diary gone electronic. How well

Anaïs Nin anticipated the calculated intimacy of the talk show. Her whispered rewritten secrets set the striptease tone of on-air revelation. It's easy to imagine her on a theme talk show, sitting next to a row of diarists: Elizabeth Freake, who kept her eighteenth-century diary as a forty-two-year complaint about her unhappy marriage; Raymond Radiguet, who stole his lover's diary to write his novel; the Goncourts, two French literary brothers who kept a single diary; Arthur Munby, a Victorian with a passion for literature and scullery maids, who got his secret housekeeper wife, Hannah Cullwick, to dress in men's clothes and keep a diary he alone read.

On air as they bleat about their naked hungers, the crushing shames once saved for private confession, do they know how ingeniously the modern talk show mirrors the original aim of diaries: to confess, atone, expiate. Those earliest diaries weren't instruments of self-discovery, but records of conscience, strict moral accountings kept by Quakers and English Puritans. Today, confessions are beamed by satellite to the same heavens once thought to judge or absolve stormy marriages, lusts and family dysfunctions. Now, television provides collective absolution for those same human dramas, played out before an audience of millions too busy to reread their own diaries.

As this planet spins towards the twenty-first century, the diary has entered its newest phase, the vehicle of choice in the culture of self-discovery, therapy and twelve-step expiation. Diary as quest. A one-day local workshop explores "four quests—survival, understanding, creation, and wisdom . . . in the context of journal writing." I wonder: Is there a twelve-step program for compulsive writers? For graphomaniacs like Anaïs Nin (who wrote in an early diary, "I am filling notebooks, covering envelopes, saturating all papers which fall into my hands. I write in the train, in streetcars, in Mother's office, in the kitchen—everywhere, anywhere, at any time")? Certainly, it would stem the notorious cottage industry of

convicted felons issuing "The Private Diary of . . ." books following the latest sensational criminal trial. But as *New York Times* col-
umnist Maureen Dowd writes about the hothouse industry of public
revelation, "Shame is fame."

And where does the private imagination fit in? How is it coaxed
into different public voices? Is it any wonder that *A Room of One's
Own*, Virginia Woolf's classic on "the habit of freedom . . . to
write," continues to sell 50,000 copies annually? Weary of confession, of the buzzing distractions of others' stories, we turn back to
diaries to sustain our own. Just as Woolf plotted her way to a public
voice first formed in her diary, so others quietly continue in their
own literary and personal transformation. "Writing," Toni Cade
Bambara noted, "is one of the ways I participate in the transformation . . . the human responsibility to define, transform, develop."
Recalling the long journey from his Irish childhood to the Nobel
Prize podium, poet Seamus Heaney mused, "I had already begun a
journey into the wideness of the world. This in turn became a
journey into the wideness of language, a journey where each point
of arrival—whether in one's poetry or one's life—turned out to be a
stepping-stone rather than a destination."

How hungry the world still is for clues about those stepping
stones, the final destination of a self transformed by creative life.
How is it accomplished? What is the imagination's link to the life?
Judging by the public fascination with diaries, we gravitate to what
writers tell us as they're still struggling with the creative process.
The all-fiction issues of *The New Yorker* now routinely feature passages from writers' notebooks and diaries—Richard Ford's, James
Atlas's, Joyce Carol Oates's. A rediscovered writer like Dawn Pow-
ell has her novel and diaries reviewed simultaneously in the *New
York Times Book Review*. A single issue of the *Book Review* contains
a cover review of Anne Frank's definitive diary; a full-page review
of the latest biography on diarist Anaïs Nin; a review of a memoir

written in the form of a journal. "Sheer information—the power of fact—" notes Phyllis Rose, "lifts the diary, even when crudely written, to a higher level . . . There is no bad diary, but if there were, I would rather read it any day than a bad poem, story or play." Why is it that we often trust others' journals more than our own? In them we listen for clues to how someone negotiated the obstacle course of a life and work. In "Memories of an Interrupted Writer," poet Mairi MacInnes reflects on the "journals and half-written poems" kept during fragmented years of marriage and motherhood. "I was the perpetual apprentice, beginning from scratch with each new poem. When publication and awards came, they were irrelevant. The best was that difficulties as I experienced them increasingly loaded the work with the life." Before then, "for years it was all I could do to find a few hours a week and a quiet place to write, that's all. Sometimes I'd stop the car on the side of the road and scribble."

On this mild fall afternoon as I finish writing this last entry, books on how to imitate the contemplative life—stories of executives turned weekend monks—flood the stores. Cloistered silence brought back to a society wired for connection. Silence, patience, quiet persistence are all too familiar to the creative vocation. Yet the anonymity shadowing most creative work is often what sends most people back into the busy world. How many creative lives, I wonder, are given up too soon simply because a novice writer never got past a diary? The seductions of being instantly heard—or seen—are great, inevitable when society itself seems set to disprove Fitzgerald's famous remark in his notebooks that there are no second acts in American life. Today, in a daily competition for dysfunction, third and fourth acts raise the stakes for ever stranger stories. What will be left for diaries? Illumination? Or will the recording self be in danger of recording nothing *but* itself? As a British book reviewer, weary of the mania for confession, quipped, "If [Philip Roth's] Portnoy were a boy today, he wouldn't be out behind the billboard making passionate love to the very piece of calf's liver his family will be eating for supper that night. He'd be sitting in a group therapy session, trying to decide whether to blame his mother or the butcher."

NOVEMBER 11

Waiting for my husband to get ready, there's still time before going to my friend S.'s. Our birthdays overlap by a day, and this year she and I will celebrate on hers. Yesterday I thought of getting her something from the paper store, as she loves beautiful paper items—except journals, which is strange, as she's the only person I know who not only writes first in longhand but refuses to use a computer. She's written her three books, one a huge seller, on a portable typewriter in a study whose decor can only be described as early monastic. I was tempted to get her a journal anyway so that she could compile into one spot all the quotes on Post-it notes festooning odd parts of the house. After years of writing books, she's claimed that unconscious intimacy with writers whose work she loves, casually speaking of Fitzgerald or Mann as if they were family members or neighbors just down the street.

She knows I've long kept a series of speckled notebooks, the kind kids conjugate irregular verbs into or use for lab reports. Over the years, I've kept them as a sort of collective writer's diary, pages filled with passages from writers in their most private moments. On long evenings I've scanned the notebook pages, inspired or consoled by Chekhov or Flaubert, Walker, Welty or Flannery O'Connor. Some are entries I copied out in my beginnings as a writer. Years later, though, I still find it strangely soothing listening to writers talking to themselves: confessing, coaxing, bargaining.

Could the party tonight ever be as interesting, or the conversa-

tion as frank, as listening to these voices? It's easy to imagine Katherine Anne Porter sitting in a corner ruing, once again, how her
writing had been interrupted by "anyone who could jimmy his way
into my life." Or, at midnight, Porter giving her bracing cautionary
advice to anyone full of regret at beginning a writing career late in
life:

> I've spent so much of my life teaching and lecturing and reading
> . . . that I had not time or energy to write the things that I have
> really begun. I have 3 unfinished books which were the main ob-
> jects of my life. I am 85 years old, I am working ferociously trying
> to make a deadline, being a little late of course, but this time, thank
> God, my deadline is my own. I rather enjoy driving myself. It
> brings back the old times . . . And, without seeming to grow
> roses on a past that was full of briars and cactus, it was not so bad;
> I did survive . . . I suggest that you go ahead and do your work
> and do it as you please and refuse to allow any force, any influence
> (that is to say, any editor or publisher) to tamper with your life
> . . . You are practicing an art and they are running a business and
> just keep that in mind.

But journals are so hard to keep, S. always says before I remind
her of the endless examples of writers busy writing in the journals
they've sworn off. "Why the journal distresses me, but also fasci-
nates," Joyce Carol Oates notes, "[is that] I'm required to use my
own voice. And to record only the truth. (But not to record *all* the
truth. There have been many things I've eliminated over the years
. . . or hinted at so slantwise no one could guess.) Still, what is
recorded is always true. At least at the time it is recorded."

Unlike the public faces we present at parties, the private regrets
and armada of doubts in journals make them invaluable records.
Often written in stormy, self-distorting moods, journals offer future

readers truths greater than the diarist's immediate angle of vision. At the height of his early *New Yorker* success, John Cheever despaired after a long gin-soaked lunch:

> As I approach my fortieth birthday without having accomplished any one of the things I intended to accomplish—without ever having achieved the deep creativity that I have worked toward for all this time—I feel that I take a minor, an obscure, a dim position that is not my destiny but that is my fault, as if I had lacked, somewhere along the line, the wit and courage to contain myself completely within the shapes at hand . . . It is not that these are stories of failure; that is not what is frightening. It is that they are dull annals; they are of no import . . . of no importance to anyone. It does not matter. It does not matter.

But of course it did. Cheever was writing the stories that would secure his fame. It is only his journals, published after his death, that give glimpses into the courage and heartbreak of that journey.

"I really only ask for time to write it all—time to write my books. Then I don't mind dying. I love to write . . . let me finish without hurrying—leaving all as fair as I can," Katherine Mansfield quietly noted in her notebook. So many different voices appear on a single page in my own notebooks it's as if they're on a strange party line, inadvertently answering one another's hesitations and reflections:

Katherine Mansfield: "Calm yourself. Clear yourself. And anything I write in this mood will be no good; it will be full of sediment . . . one must learn, one must practice, to forget oneself."

André Gide: "I never produced anything good except by a long succession of slight efforts. No one has more deeply meditated or better understood than I Buffon's remark about patience ["Genius is but a greater aptitude for patience."] I bring it not only to my work but also to the silent waiting that precedes good work."

Virginia Woolf: "A note: despair at the badness of the book [*The Years*]: cant think how I ever could write such stuff—& with such excitement: thats yesterday: today I think it good again. A note, by way of advising other Virginias with other books that this is the way of the thing: up down, up down." And then: "Odd how the creative power at once brings the whole universe to order. I can see the day whole, proportioned."

Unable to give S. a journal of her own, I'm giving her someone else's. *An Interrupted Life: The Diaries of Etty Hillesum 1941–1943* is one of my favorite books, a hauntingly luminous twentieth-century autobiography. Hillesum, a Dutch Jew, wrote at the exact time and less than a mile from where the Frank family were hidden behind a false bookcase in the Secret Annex. Etty Hillesum, some say, is the older Anne Frank. Twenty-seven and single, she was a fledgling writer and political activist who kept her diary through October 1942, when she was sent to Auschwitz. She died there at age twenty-nine. Like the very best diaries, hers defies neat definition. It is a unique ongoing portrait of a writer—striking in that someone surrounded by darkness and death could write with such astonishing intensity about life. She used the diary not to close off the world but to record her full participation in it. Most unusually, hers is a spiritual autobiography that includes the body, its passions and pleasures. Her voice, original and insistent, is fully present in the diary's opening:

Sunday, 9 March [1941]. Here goes, then. This is a painful and well-nigh insuperable step for me: yielding up so much that has been suppressed to a blank sheet of lined paper. The thoughts in my head are sometimes so clear and sharp and my feelings so deep, but writing about them comes hard. The main difficulty, I think, is a sense of shame. So many inhibitions, so much fear of letting go, of allowing things to pour out of me, and yet that is what I must

do if I am ever to give my life a reasonable and satisfactory pur-
pose. It is like the final, liberating scream that always sticks bash-
fully in your throat when you make love. I am accomplished in
bed, just about seasoned enough I should think to be counted
among the better lovers, and love does indeed suit me to perfection, and yet it remains a mere trifle, set apart from what is truly
essential, and deep inside me something is still locked away. The
rest of me is like that, too. I am blessed enough intellectually to be
able to fathom most subjects, to express myself clearly on most
things; I seem to be a match for most of life's problems, and yet
deep down something like a tightly-wound ball of twine binds me
relentlessly and at times I am nothing more or less than a miserable, frightened creature, despite the clarity with which I can express myself.

That self-expression only deepened with time. In the eight exercise books of her diary, she wrote with fierce clarity on life, the self,
politics, writing and love. In the end, she left a translucent record of
how the self instinctively seeks wholeness even in a world that fatally
interrupts it. In the diary's final lines she rued, "Sadly, in difficult
times we tend to shrug off the spiritual heritage of artists in an 'easier'
age, with 'What use is that sort of thing to us now?' It is an under-
standable but shortsighted reaction. And utterly impoverishing."

While we read backward to earlier writers' diaries to tell us who
we are, the diaries that every age most needs to read are those still
being written. At this very moment, all across the country, notebooks are being filled, chronicling for future generations what the
previous century of writers, male and female, left out—raising children, earning livings, negotiating the complexities of daily life. The
heroic of the everyday has always been the business of diaries, their
real subject. "Strong emotion," Virginia Woolf observed, "must
leave its trace; and it is only a question of discovering how we can

get ourselves attached to it, so that we shall be able to live our lives through from the start."

Tonight on our way to S.'s, we'll drive past windows lit in chill winter darkness. Inside all kinds of homes—shabby walk-up apartments or houses with narrow yards shrouded in snow—children sit on beds secretly writing in first diaries. Nearby, someone at seventy encodes an entire life's story onto a single microchip. Trying to get unstuck, someone else is probably copying Joan Didion into a notebook, a hand retracing her words "when the world seems drained of wonder, some day when I am only going through the motions of doing what I am supposed to do, which is write—on that bankrupt morning I will simply open my notebook and there it will all be, a forgotten account with accumulated interest, paid back to the world." Or maybe it's a line from poet Seamus Heaney, "Walk on air against your better judgement," for a separate notebook. I always think of the many lives inside, invisible to a car speeding late at night. Tonight, that sound of traffic outside will bring someone to a window—a break from the silence of sitting alone at a desk. Caught in the window's reflection is work and a stack of notebooks. Standing quietly at the window, listening to cars speeding in the dark, someone is staring into the night, still thinking about if and how to finally move the words out into the world.

NOTES

The following abbreviations have been used:

    MF Marjory Fleming

    AJ Alice James

    KM Katherine Mansfield

    AN Anaïs Nin

    MS May Sarton

    LT Leo Tolstoy

    SY Sonya Tolstoy

    VW Virginia Woolf

Prologue: From Eye to I

p. 4 "You've known": Anne Frank, *The Diary of a Young Girl* (New York: Doubleday, 1953), 210.

p. 6 "Living is an": Phyllis Rose, *Parallel Lives* (New York: Knopf, 1983), 5.

p. 9 "The false person": AN, "Genesis of the Diary," in *The Novel of the Future* (Athens, Ohio: Swallow Press, 1968), 143.

p. 12 "I have no": George Plimpton, ed., *Writers at Work: The Paris Review Interviews*, 2nd ser. (New York: Penguin, 1977), 146–147.

p. 14 "I remember": *Letters and Memorials of Jane Welsh Carlyle*, vol. 2, ed. James Anthony Froude (New York: Scribners, 1900), 37.

p. 15 "It strikes me": *The Diary of Virginia Woolf*, vol. 2, ed. Anne Oliver Bell (New York: Harcourt Brace, 1978), 319.

p. 15 "I write variations": Ibid., Vol. 3, 275.

p. 16 "Never let": VW, *The Death of the Moth* (London: Hogarth Press, 1942), 74.

p. 16 "Do you keep": Oscar Wilde, *Complete Works* (London: Collins, 1981), 357.

p. 16 "We don't think": Joyce Carol Oates, "Selections from a Journal: January 1985–January 1988," ed. Daniel Halpern, *Antaeus* 61 (Autumn, 1988), 347.

p. 17 "Of course I": *The Journal of Katherine Mansfield*, Definitive Edition, ed. J. M. Murry (London: Constable, 1954), 221.

p. 17 "It is worth": VW, *Diary*, vol. 2, 35.

p. 18 "for women": VW, *A Room of One's Own* (London: Hogarth Press, 1929), 131.

CHAPTER ONE: THE SHADOW WRITERS

p. 19 *"I* too am": *I Too Am Here, Selections from the Letters of Jane Welsh Carlyle*, ed. Alan and Mary McQueen Simpson (Cambridge: Cambridge University Press, 1977), 7.

p. 21 "little glass": Isabella Keith to Marjory Fleming, November 11, 1811.

p. 22 "semicolings and": While I have kept many of Marjory Fleming's misspelled words, for purposes of overall clarity, I have corrected many others. To study the original journal, misspellings and all, the two best sources are: *The Journals, Letters, & Verses of Marjory Fleming (Collotype Facsimile From The Original Manuscripts)*, ed. Arundell Esdaile of the British Museum (London: Sidgwick and Jackson, 1934); and *The Complete Marjory Fleming: Her Journals, Letters & Verses*, transcr. and ed. Frank Sidgwick (London: Sidgwick and Jackson, 1934).

p. 23 "I never read": *Complete Marjory Fleming*, 122.

p. 24 "quiet, friendship": Ibid., 23.

p. 24 "sunshine and": Mark Twain, "Marjorie Fleming," *Harper's Bazaar*, 1909.

p. 25 "show singular": Leslie Stephen, ed., *Dictionary of National Biography*, vol. 19 (London: Smith, Elder, 1889), 281.

p. 28 "This is the": *Complete Marjory Fleming*, 157–60.

p. 29 "I am very": Ibid., 6.

p. 29 "Isabella teaches": Ibid., 3.

p. 30 "This address": Ibid., 120.

p. 30 "into a bed": Ibid., 34.

p. 30 "I like loud": Ibid., 12.

p. 31 "I must begin": Ibid., 53.

p. 31 "Genius is a": Mme. De Genlis, *Adèle et Théodore. Letters sur l'éducation* (Paris: Chez M. Lambert and F. J. Baudouin, 1782), 42.

p. 32 "I am married": Quoted in Honoria, *The Female Mentor* (London: T. Cadell & W. Davies), 1802, 9.

p. 32 " 'Girl! Make' ": *Complete Marjory Fleming*, 162.

p. 33 "If you educate": *The Edinburgh Review*, no. 30 (January 1810), 314.

p. 33 "It is Malancholy": *Complete Marjory Fleming*, 63–64.

p. 33 "I wrote so": Ibid., 43–44.

p. 34 "For my part": Ibid., 56.

p. 34 "If those girls": Charlotte Brontë, *Roe Head Journal* (1836), Bonnell Collection 98 (8), Brontë Parsonage Museum.

p. 34 "I can never": *Complete Marjory Fleming*, 83.

p. 34 "I confess that": Ibid., 40.

p. 34 "My religion is": Ibid., 80–81.

p. 35 "I acknowledge that": Ibid., 55.

p. 35 "Isas health": Ibid., 83.

p. 35 "We should get": Ibid., 5.

p. 35 "I am studying": MF to Isabella Fleming, April 1, 1811.

p. 35 "I cannot say": Isabella Keith to Isabella Fleming, April 1, 1811.

p. 35 "A sailor called": *Complete Marjory Fleming*, 108.

p. 36 "In the love": Ibid., 103.

p. 36 "Isabella is always": Ibid., 109.

p. 36 "Love is a": Ibid., 109.

p. 36 "Heroick love": Ibid., 103.

p. 36 "I am now": MF to Isabella Keith, July 26, 1811.

p. 37 "I fear he": Isabella Fleming to Isabella Keith, January 9, 1812.

p. 37 "I have all": Isabella Keith to Isabella Fleming, January 15, 1812.

p. 37 "the constant theme": Isabella Fleming to Isabella Keith, January 9, 1812.

p. 37 "O Isa": poem written December 15, 1811, copied and sent to Isabella Keith.

p. 38 "painful restraint": Isabella Keith to Isabella Fleming, January 1812.

p. 38 "I will never": *Complete Marjory Fleming*, 82.

p. 39 "life of a": Henry Brougham Farnie, *Pet Marjorie: A Story of Child-Life Fifty Years Ago* (Edinburgh: William P. Nimmo, 1860), 26.

p. 39 "I am more": Dr. John Brown to Elizabeth Fleming, circa 1862.

p. 40 "Any further success": Farnie, *Pet Marjorie* (1863 edition), ii.

p. 40 "I owe my": John Brown, M.D., *Marjorie Fleming* (Edinburgh: Edmondston and Douglas, 1864), xi.

p. 40 "insisted on having": The invectives continued in prefaces well into the twentieth century. See John Brown, M.D., "Marjorie Fleming," in *Spare Hours* (Boston: Houghton Mifflin, 1908), 48.

p. 40 "Many of the": These and many other reviews appear at the end of Brown's 1864 edition of *Marjorie Fleming*.

p. 40 "Children at this": Samuel Taylor Coleridge, *Biographia Literaria*, vol. 2, ed. J. Shawcross (London: Oxford University Press, 1907), 112.

p. 41 "A great many": *Complete Marjory Fleming*, 105.

p. 42 "almost every day": Brown, *Marjorie Fleming*, 10.

p. 42 "in a moment": Ibid.

p. 42 "She was the": *London Mercury*. For a detailed discussion of the Scott legend, see Frank Gent, "Marjory Fleming and Her Biographers," *The Scottish Historical Review*, vol. 36, no. 102 (October, 1947).

p. 43 "and you know": *Letters of John Brown*, ed. D. W. Forrest (London: Adam and Charles Black, 1907), 163.

p. 43 "I very often": Isabella Keith to Marjory Fleming, November 1811.

p. 44 "Wife and children": James Hamilton, *Memoirs of the Life of James Wilson* (London: James Nisbet, 1859), 172.

p. 44 "to put the": Ibid., 154.

p. 44 "shut up in": Henrietta Wilson, *The Chronicles of a Garden* (London: James Nisbet, 1863), iv.

p. 44 "very superior": Hamilton, *Memoirs*, 113.

p. 44 "I have often": Farnie, *Pet Marjorie*, 60–61.

p. 45 "I wanted to": Brontë, *Roe Head Journal*, October 14, 1836.

p. 45 "Remember, dear": *The Journals of Louisa May Alcott*, ed. Joel Myerson and Daniel Shealy (Boston: Little, Brown, 1989), 47.

p. 46 "I have one": Anne Frank, *The Diary of a Young Girl* (New York: Doubleday, 1953), 234.

p. 47 "I understand": Ibid., 234.

p. 47 "I keep on": Ibid., 241.

p. 47 "the legacy from": Miep Gies, *Anne Frank Remembered* (New York: Simon and Schuster, 1987), 235.

p. 48 "I want to": Frank, *Diary*, 210.

p. 48 "You're going": Zlata Filipovic, *Zlata's Diary: A Child's Life in Sarajevo* (New York: Viking, 1994), 198.

p. 49 "Your note": *Letters of Robert Louis Stevenson* (letter to William Archer, March 27, 1894), vol. 4, ed. Sir Sidney Colvin (London: William Heinemann), 240.

CHAPTER TWO: THE MARRIED MUSE

p. 51 "Why do you": ST to LT, October 12, 1895.

p. 51 "Every man": *Tolstoy's Diaries*, vol. 2, ed. and transl. R. F. Christian (London: Athlone Press, 1985), 418.

p. 54 "My God!": Ibid., vol. 1, 166.

p. 54 "will never": Tatyana Kuzminskaya, *Tolstoy as I Knew Him* (New York: Macmillan, 1948), 34.

p. 56 "Will you": *Tolstoy's Letters*, vol. 1, ed. and transl. R. F. Christian (New York: Scribner's, 1978), 168.

p. 56 "On the wedding": LT, *Diaries*, vol. 1., 168.

p. 56 "Your youth": *Tolstoy's Letters*, vol. 1, 168.

p. 56 "living those": *The Diaries of Sophia Tolstoy*, ed. O. A. Golinenko et al., transl. Cathy Porter (New York: Random House, 1985), 834.

p. 57 "How stricken": Ibid., 839.

p. 57 "It's six": LT, *Diaries*, vol. 1, 4.

p. 57 "I came to": Ibid., 24.

p. 58 "What force": ST, *Diaries*, 835.

p. 58 "In his account": Ibid., 841.

p. 59 "What phase": Tikhon Polner, *Tolstoy and His Wife* (New York: Norton, 1945), 39.

p. 59 "It's no longer": LT, *Diaries*, vol. 1, 156.

p. 61 "My diary again": ST, *Diaries*, 3.

p. 61 "It makes me": Ibid., 45.

p. 61 "It is not": Ibid., 7.

p. 62 "One blow": Ibid., 9.

p. 62 "I should like": Ibid., 9–10.

p. 63 "Never before": LT, *Letters*, vol. 1, 182.

p. 64 "She used": Ilya Tolstoy, *Reminiscences of Tolstoy* (New York: Century, 1914), 137.

p. 64 "I shall never": LT, *Letters*, vol. 1, 190. For a fuller account, see Tatyana Tolstoy, *Tolstoy Remembered* (New York: McGraw-Hill, 1977), 22.

p. 65 "Make him": Kuzminskaya, *Tolstoy as I Knew Him*, 196.

p. 65 "I am a": ST, *Diaries*, 27.

p. 66 "Lyovochka has": Ibid., 11.

p. 66 "Where is it": LT, *Diaries*, vol. 1, 178.

p. 66 "After thirteen": Ibid., 192.

p. 67 "Sometimes I long": ST, *Diaries*, 8.

p. 67 "I am so": Ibid., 31.

p. 68 "You think": Polner, *Tolstoy and His Wife*, 70.

p. 71 "There is something": ST to her sister Tanya, November 1879.

p. 72 "From the fun-loving": Ilya Tolstoy, *Reminiscences*, 261–62.

p. 73 "I have accepted": Anne Edwards, *Sonya: The Life of Countess Tolstoy* (New York: Simon and Schuster, 1981), 275.

p. 74 "If I'd been": *The Autobiography of Countess Sophie Tolstoi*, transl. S. S. Koteliansky (London: Hogarth Press, 1922), 20.

p. 74 "Everybody in this": ST, *Diaries*, 74.

p. 79 "I have to": Ibid., 94.

p. 79 "How I regret": Ibid., 100.

p. 80 "Never have I": LT, *Letters*, vol. 2, 373.

p. 81 "Now I am": ST, *Diaries*, 75.

p. 82 "The samovar boiled": Valentin Bulgakov, *The Last Year of Lev Tolstoy* (New York, Dial, 1971), 161.

p. 84 "Many people": ST, *Diaries*, June 18, 1887.

p. 84 "I cannot help": ST, *Diaries*, 141.

CHAPTER THREE: THE HIDDEN WRITER IN A WRITING FAMILY

p. 87 "What an awful": *The Diary of Alice James*, ed. Leon Edel (New York: Dodd, Mead, 1964), 66.

p. 90 "I think that": Ibid., 25.

p. 92 "an extravagant": R. W. Lewis, *The Jameses: A Family Narrative* (New York: Farrar, Straus and Giroux, 1991), 32.

p. 93 "What enrichment": Ruth Bernard Yeazell, ed., *The Death and Letters of Alice James*, (Berkeley: University of California, 1981), 148.

p. 93 "some damnèd": Lewis, *Jameses*, 51.

p. 94 "Our parents": Henry James, *Notes of a Son and Brother* (New York: Scribners, 1914), 66.

p. 94 "Your sister": AJ to William James, August 6, 1876, Houghton Library, Harvard.

p. 95 "special and marketable": H. James, *Notes*, 49.

p. 95 "Our chief": Lewis, *Jameses*, 97.

p. 96 "The quiet little": Edward W. Emerson, *The Early Years of the Saturday Club, 1855–1870* (Boston: Houghton Mifflin, 1918), 328.

p. 96 "I had": AJ, *Diary*, 95–96.

p. 98 "well fitted": For an insightful and comprehensive discussion of nineteenth-century neurasthenia, see Jean Strouse's *Alice James: A Biography* (Boston: Houghton Mifflin, 1980), particularly the sixth chapter, "Nerves."

p. 99 "In those ghastly": AJ, *Diary*, 45.

p. 100 *"Your* letters": Yeazell, ed., *Death and Letters* of Alice James, 28.

p. 101 "I cannot make": AJ, *Diary*, 209.

p. 101 "a creature with": Strouse, *Alice James*, 272.

p. 102 "steady flame": AJ, *Diary*, 95–96.

p. 102 "The difficulty about": Ibid., 223.

p. 102 "I have seen": Ibid., 34.

p. 102 "How funny": Ibid., 62.

p. 103 "How grateful": Ibid., 31.

p. 103 "If I can": Ibid., 113.

p. 104 "It's rather": Ibid., 36.

p. 104 "William uses": Ibid., 148–49.

p. 105 "When the fancy": Ibid., 149.

p. 106 "Nurse asked": Ibid., 31.

p. 106 "There is no": Lewis, 183.

p. 107 "How sick": Ibid., 64.

p. 108 "It is an": Ibid., 66.

p. 109 "I wish you": Yeazell, ed., *Death and Letters of Alice James*, 82.

p. 111 "When will": AJ, *Diary*, 60.

p. 111 "What determines": Ibid., 127–129.

p. 112 "I was greatly": Ibid., 67.

p. 113 "While I think": Ibid., 61.

p. 113 "Ever since": Ibid., 207.

p. 114 "It is reassuring": Ibid., 227.

p. 114 "Whether it is": Ibid., 41.

p. 117 "I know you've": *The Letters of William James*, ed. Henry James (Boston: Atlantic Monthly Press, 1920), 310–11.

p. 117 "It is the": Yeazell, ed., *Death and Letters of Alice James*, 186–87.

p. 118 "Within the last": AJ, *Diary*, 211.

p. 119 "Alice James's diary": Strouse, *Alice James*, 324–26.

p. 120 "These long": AJ, *Diary*, 218.

CHAPTER FOUR: A PUBLIC OF TWO

p. 123 "We've got": *The Collected Letters of Katherine Mansfield*, vol. 1, ed. Vincent O'Sullivan and Margaret Scott (Oxford: Oxford University Press, 1984), 327.

p. 123 "What a queer": *The Diary of Virginia Woolf*, vol. 1, ed. Anne Oliver Bell (New York: Harcourt Brace, 1977), 222.

p. 127 "ALL those": KM, *Collected Letters*, vol. 1, 290.

p. 127 "Don't lower": Ibid., 318.

p. 127 "a little colonial": *The Journal of Katherine Mansfield*, Definitive Edition, ed., J. M. Murry (London: Constable, 1954), 157.

p. 128 "dogged my steps": *The Letters of Virginia Woolf*, vol. 2, ed. Nigel Nicolson and Joanne Trautmann (New York: Harcourt Brace, 1976), 107.

p. 130 "I really can't": KM to J. B. Pinker, May 3, 1922, cited in Claire Tomalin, *Katherine Mansfield: A Secret Life* (New York: St. Martin's Press, 1987), 209.

p. 130 "a woman caring": VW, *Diary*, vol. 2, 61.

p. 131 "the diary as": VW, *A Writer's Diary* (London: Hogarth Press, 1953), viii–ix.

p. 131 "All parties": KM, *Collected Letters*, vol. 2, 324.

p. 131 "There's no doubt": VW, *Diary*, vol. 2, July 26, 1922.

p. 132 "I'd far rather": KM, *Collected Letters*, vol. 1, 291.

p. 132 "It is the only": Ibid., 324.

p. 132 "Now really": KM, *Journal*, 93.

p. 134 "Decidedly an interesting": VW and Lytton Strachey, *Letters*, ed. Leonard Woolf and James Strachey (London: Hogarth Press, 1956), 61.

p. 134 "Oh, I want": KM, *Journal*, 94.

p. 135 "I want to": Ibid., 94.

p. 135 "The Prelude method": *The Letters of Katherine Mansfield*, ed. J. M. Murry (New York: Knopf, 1929), 359.

p. 135 "I am a recluse": KM, *Collected Letters*, vol. 1, 304.

p. 135 "By the way": Ibid., 339.

p. 135 "Our press": VW, *Letters*, vol. 2, 150.

p. 136 "As a child": VW, *Moments of Being*, ed. Jeanne Schulkind (New York: Harcourt Brace, 1976), 71.

p. 137 "By nature": Ibid., 127.

p. 137 "A shock is": Ibid., 72.

p. 138 "written up in": VW, *The Common Reader* (New York: Harcourt Brace, 1925), 1.

p. 139 "I do like": KM, *Collected Letters*, vol. 1, 315.

p. 139 "note-books of": KM, *Novels and Novelists* (London: Constable, 1930), 36.

p. 140 "I myself": VW, *Diary*, vol. 1, 167.

p. 140 "Illness, she": Ibid., 216.

p. 141 "I wonder why": KM, *Collected Letters*, vol. 2, 288.

p. 141 "I find with": VW, *Diary*, vol. 1, 258.

p. 141 "She's had every": VW, *Letters*, vol. 2, 248.

p. 142 "K. is back": VW, *Diary*, vol. 2, 34.

p. 142 "We were both": VW, *Letters*, vol. 4, 366.

p. 142 "Is the time": VW, *Diary*, vol. 1, 259.

p. 142 "I must be": Ibid., vol. 5, 148.

p. 143 "Unpraised, I find": Ibid., vol. 1, 271.

p. 143 "It strikes me": Ibid., vol. 2, 319.

p. 144 "I can trace": Ibid., vol. 1, 266.

p. 144 "sorted itself": Ibid., vol. 1, 266.

p. 144 "I write variations": Ibid., vol. 3, 275.

p. 145 "Katherine is now": Ibid., vol. 1, 258.

p. 145 "I do believe": KM, *Collected Letters*, vol. 2, 343.

p. 146 "don't let": Ibid., vol. 1, 327.

p. 146 "She was a": *The Autobiography of Leonard Woolf*, vol. 3 (London: Hogarth Press, 1964), 204.

p. 147 "How I envy": KM, *Collected Letters*, vol. 3, 127–28.

p. 147 "Katherine is the": VW, *Letters*, vol. 2, 241.

p. 148 "I wonder if": "Fifteen Letters from Katherine Mansfield to Virginia Woolf," *Adam International Review*, nos. 370–75. London, 1972, 24.

p. 148 "Probably we had": VW, *Diary*, vol. 2, 227.

p. 148 "Her mind": Ibid., vol. 1, 179.

p. 148 "a lie in": *Katherine Mansfield's Letters to John Middleton Murry 1913–1922*, ed. J. M. Murry (New York: Knopf, 1951), 380.

p. 149 "My review of": Ibid., 395.

p. 149 "The strangeness": KM, *Novels and Novelists*, 108.

p. 149 "She let": VW, *Diary*, vol. 1, 314.

p. 150 "we fell into": Ibid., vol. 2, 44.

p. 150 "I feel a": Ibid., 45.

p. 150 "to no one": Ibid., 45.

p. 151 "We talked about": Ibid., 44.

p. 151 "The man in": KM, *Journal*, 139.

p. 152 "How unbearable": Ibid., 129.

p. 152 "to be alive": Ibid., 123.

p. 152 "I've plucked": VW, *Diary*, vol. 2, 80.

p. 153 "She will send": Ibid., 62.

p. 153 "The question": KM, *Letters to John Middleton Murry*, 697.

p. 153 "to become a": KM, *Journal*, 333.

p. 153 "Everything in life": Ibid., 228.

p. 154 "K.M. bursts": VW, *Diary*, vol. 2, 161.

p. 154 "Quiet brings": Ibid., vol. 3, 140–41.

p. 154 "At that one": Ibid., vol. 2, 226–27.

p. 155 "I wanted you": F. A. Lee, *John Middleton Murry* (London: Meuthen, 1959), 143–44.

p. 155 "Everything she": VW, "A Terribly Sensitive Mind," in *Granite and Rainbow* (London: Hogarth Press, 1958), 74.

p. 156 "She had": VW, *Letters*, vol. 4, 366.

p. 156 "As for my": VW, *Diary*, vol. 3, 209.

p. 157 "Masterpieces are": VW, *A Room of One's Own* (London: Hogarth Press, 1929), 98.

p. 158 "I mark": VW, *Diary*, vol. 5, 357–58.

p. 158 "I had three": Ibid., vol. 4, 29.

p. 158 "Go on writing": Ibid., vol. 2, 228.

p. 158 "It's always a": KM, *Journal*, 287.

CHAPTER FIVE: THE PROFESSIONALLY PRIVATE
WRITER

p. 161 "I wonder if": *The Early Diary of Anaïs Nin*, vol. 2, ed. Rupert Pole (New York: Harcourt Brace, 1982), 511.

p. 161 "What does": *The Diary of Anaïs Nin*, vol. 6, ed. Gunther Stuhlmann (New York: Harcourt Brace, 1976), 242.

p. 170 "Writing for": AN, *Diary*, vol. 1, 260.

p. 170 "Miss Nin": Ibid., vol. 5, 157.

p. 170 "Create a world": Ibid., vol. 1, 185.

p. 171 "The diary began": Ibid., 202.

p. 171 "My life has": Ibid., 204.

p. 172 "I am eleven": *Linotte: The Early Diary of Anaïs Nin, 1914–1920*, transl. from the French by Jean L. Sherman. Preface by Joaquín Nin-Culmell. (New York: Harcourt Brace, 1978), 8.

p. 172 "badly dressed": AN, *Diary*, vol. 1, 111.

p. 172 "I told myself": AN, *Early Diary*, vol. 2, p. 139.

p. 172 "I can truthfully": Ibid., 197.

p. 173 "The man who": Ibid., 447.

p. 174 "He is critical": AN, *Early Diary*, vol. 3, 148.

p. 174 "His work": Ibid., 132–33.

p. 174 "I can never": Ibid., 133.

p. 175 "Am I clever": AN, *Early Diary*, vol. 2, 248.

p. 175 "Louveciennes resembles": AN, *Diary*, vol. 1, 3.

p. 176 "I ran into": Ibid, 9.

p. 177 "It is quite": Ibid, 47.

p. 178 "only interrupting" AN, *Early Diary*, vol. 2, 86.

p. 178 "He liked to": AN, *Diary*, vol. 1, 87.

p. 179 "Through flesh": Ibid., 348.

p. 179 "To create seemed": AN, *Diary*, vol. 3, 259–60.

p. 179 "When the neurotic": Ibid., vol. 1, 291.

p. 179 "mute ones": Ibid., 289.

p. 179 "One shutter": Ibid., 4.

p. 180 "No time to": Ibid., 50.

p. 180 "The doctor does": Ibid., 340.

p. 181 "Rank told": AN, *Diary*, vol. 2, 7.

p. 181 *"Guilts about"*: Ibid., vol. 3, 260.

p. 182 "My father said": Ibid., vol. 1, 238.

p. 183 "I realize it": AN, *Early Diary*, vol. 4, 120.

p. 183 "Late at night": AN, *Diary*, vol. 1, 105.

p. 185 "united in a": AN, *Early Diary*, vol. 3, 97.

p. 185 "You are writing": AN, *Diary*, vol. 7, 203.

p. 186 "They have been": Ibid., 108.

p. 186 "The diary is": AN, *Diary*, vol. 5, 216.

p. 187 "Everyone of us": Ibid., vol. 1, 105.

p. 187 "Vera Cruz": Ibid., vol. 5, 113.

p. 188 "I wore a": Ibid., 133.

p. 188 "No writer I": Ibid., 36.

p. 189 "all the obscure": AN, *Diary*, vol. 2, 252.

p. 190 "The failed artist": Ibid., vol. 1, 280–81.

p. 190 "I am sure": AN, *Linotte*, 177.

p. 191 "I am writing": AN, *Early Diary*, vol. 2, 125.

CHAPTER SIX: A WRITER IN THE UNCERTAIN SEASONS

p. 195 "I had lived": MS, *Plant Dreaming Deep* (New York: Norton, 1968), 15.

p. 195 "at last": Ibid., 19.

p. 196 "I simply wrote": Ibid., 20.

p. 197 "I felt then no": Ibid., 19.

p. 197 "I was held": Ibid., 30–31.

p. 197 "The writer": Ibid., 58.

p. 197 "For alone": Ibid., 60.

p. 197 "I have drawn": Ibid., 46.

p. 198 "somewhere off": Ibid., 114.

p. 198 "Silence was": Ibid., 55.

p. 199 "Everything has": Ibid., 61.

p. 199 *"Plant Dreaming"*: MS, *Journal of a Solitude* (New York: Norton, 1973), 12.

p. 200 "Autobiography": MS, *The House by the Sea* (New York: Norton, 1977), 79.

p. 200 "Adversity is": MS, *Journal of a Solitude*, 65.

p. 201 "I am alone": Ibid., 11.

p. 201 "I cannot always": Ibid., 40.

p. 202 "from my isolation": Ibid., 67.

p. 203 "The move": MS, *At Seventy: A Journal* (New York: Norton, 1984), 87.

p. 204 "I have learned": MS, *House*, 108.

p. 205 "Every grief": MS, *Journal of a Solitude*, 109.

p. 205 "There is nothing": Ibid., 33.

p. 205 "I hardly ever": Ibid., 13.

p. 206 "I always forget": Ibid., 89.

p. 206 "Without tension": MS, *House*, 17.

p. 207 "Writing for me": MS, *At Seventy*, 105.

p. 207 "But a journal": MS, *House*, 11.

p. 208 "If there is": Ibid., 28.

p. 209 " 'I shall always' ": MS, *A World of Light* (New York: Norton, 1976), 52.

p. 209 "capacity to compromise": Ibid., 52.

p. 209 "My mother buried": MS, *House*, 60.

p. 209 "I have shied": MS, *At Seventy*, 55.

p. 210 "You keep": MS, *Journal of a Solitude*, 30.

p. 210 "Only very": MS, *House*, 96.

p. 210 "Praise for": MS, *Plant Dreaming Deep*, 180–81.

p. 211 "with their": MS, *At Seventy*, 76.

p. 212 "I do not": MS, *Recovering: A Journal* (New York: Norton, 1980), 34.

p. 212 "For one": Ibid., 209.

p. 213 "private dilemmas": MS, *Journal of a Solitude*, 60.

p. 213 "I am thinking": MS, *Recovering*, 131.

p. 213 "Sometimes I think": MS, *Journal of a Solitude*, 27.

p. 213 "nothing that": MS, *Recovering*, 13.

p. 213 "What keeping": Ibid., 9.

p. 214 "Pain is the": Ibid., 208.

p. 214 "There are": Ibid., 137.

p. 214 "I have always": MS, *At Seventy*, 11.

p. 215 "One of the": MS, *Recovering*, 205.

p. 215 "We have to": MS, *At Seventy*, 196.

p. 215 "So in the": Ibid., 181.

p. 216 "A lot of": MS, *House*, 160.

p. 217 "An irritable": MS, *Recovering*, 196.

p. 217 "I have been": Ibid, 197.

p. 218 "Under the polite": MS, *Journal of a Solitude*, 51.

p. 218 "I wonder which": Ibid., 122–23.

p. 218 "But there": Ibid., 123.

p. 219 "For a long": Ibid., 57.

p. 219 "If one writes": VW, *A Writer's Diary* (London: Hogarth Press, 1953), 135.

p. 220 "The two sins": MS, *Recovering*, 77.

p. 220 "It was a": MS, *At Seventy*, 176.

p. 220 "It is my": MS, *Recovering*, 81.

p. 220 "There is always": MS, *House*, 78–79.

p. 221 "But it is": MS, *Journal of a Solitude*, 15.

p. 221 "I dreamt that": Ibid., 210.

p. 222 "At this very": MS, *Endgame* (New York: Norton, 1992), 195.

p. 222 "I am glad": MS, *I Knew a Phoenix* (New York: Rinehart and Company, 1959), 212.

EPILOGUE: FIRST PERSON SINGULAR

p. 225 "Is it not": *The Journal of Katherine Mansfield*, Definitive Edition, ed. J. M. Murry (London: Constable, 1954), 205.

p. 228 "If only I": *The Notebooks of Henry James*, ed. F. O. Matthiessen and Kenneth B. Murdock (New York: Oxford University Press, 1947), 44–45.

p. 231 "I know after": M. F. K. Fisher, *Stay Me, Oh Comfort Me: Journals and Stories, 1933–1941* (New York: Pantheon, 1993), 66.

p. 233 "Oh God be": Gail Godwin, "A Diarist on Diaries," *Antaeus* 61 (Autumn 1988), 9.

p. 235 "a nicely bound": Harriet Blodgett, "Dear Diary: How Do I Need You. Let Me Count the Ways," *New York Times Book Review*, September 22, 1991, 25.

p. 238 "There are": KM, *Journal*, 205.

p. 238 "I must be": *The Diary of Virginia Woolf*, vol. 5, ed. Anne Oliver Bell (New York: Harcourt Brace, 1984), 148.

p. 238 "one tries": *The Letters of Katherine Mansfield*, ed. J. M. Murry (New York: Knopf, 1929), 401.

p. 239 "I am filling": *The Early Diary of Anaïs Nin*, vol. 2, ed. Rupert Pole (New York: Harcourt Brace, 1982), 353.

p. 240 "Writing is one": Toni Cade Bambara, *The Writer on Her Work*, ed. Janet Sternburg (New York: Norton, 1980), 154.

p. 240 "I had already": Seamus Heaney, *Crediting Poetry: The Nobel Lecture* (New York: Farrar, Straus and Giroux, 1995), 8–9.

p. 241 "Sheer information": Phyllis Rose, "Personal Secrets," *Self*, May 1990, 260.

p. 241 "journals and": Mairi MacInnes, "Memoirs of an Interrupted Writer," *The New Yorker*, February 26/March 4, 1996, 92.

p. 241 "If Portnoy were": Mark Childress, *Times Literary Supplement*, March 22, 1996, 30.

p. 243 "I've spent": Tillie Olsen, *Silences* (New York: Delacorte, 1978), 175–76.

p. 243 "Why the journal": Joyce Carol Oates, "Selections from a Journal: January 1985–January 1988," ed. Daniel Halpern, *Antaeus* 61 (Autumn 1988): 342.

p. 244 "As I approach": *The Journals of John Cheever* (New York: Knopf, 1990), 7.

p. 244 "I really only": KM, *Journal*, 154.

p. 244 "Calm yourself": Ibid., 269.

p. 244 "I never produced": *The Journals of André Gide*, ed. and transl. Justin O'Brien (New York: Vintage, 1947), 207.

p. 245 "A note: despair": VW, *Diary*, vol. 4, 262.

p. 245 "Sunday, 9 March": *An Interrupted Life: The Diaries of Etty Hillesum 1941–1943*, transl. Arno Pomerans (New York: Pantheon, 1983), 1.

p. 246 "Sadly, in difficult": Ibid., 196.

p. 246 "Strong emotion": VW, *Moments of Being*, ed. Jeanne Schukind (New York: Harcourt Brace, 1976), 67.

p. 247 "when the world": Joan Didion, "On Keeping a Notebook," *Slouching Towards Bethlehem* (New York: Farrar, Straus and Giroux, 1968), 135.

DIARIES AND
AUTOBIOGRAPHICAL
WRITINGS

MARJORY FLEMING

The Journals, Letters, & Verses of Marjory Fleming (Collotype Facsimile From The Original Manuscripts), ed. Arundell Esdaile. London: Sidgwick and Jackson, 1934.

The Complete Marjory Fleming: Her Journals, Letters & Verses, transcr. and ed. Frank Sidgwick. London: Sidgwick and Jackson, 1934.

SONYA TOLSTOY

The Autobiography of Countess Sophie Tolstoi, transl. S. S. Koteliansky. London: Hogarth Press, 1922.

The Diaries of Sophia Tolstoy, ed. O. A. Golinenko et al., transl. Cathy Porter. New York: Random House, 1985.

ALICE JAMES

The Diary of Alice James, ed. Leon Edel. New York: Dodd, Mead, 1964.

KATHERINE MANSFIELD

The Letters of Katherine Mansfield, ed. J. M. Murry. London: Constable, 1928; New York: Knopf, 1929.

The Scrapbook of Katherine Mansfield, ed. J. M. Murry. London: Constable, 1939.

Katherine Mansfield's Letters to John Middleton Murry 1913–22. London: Constable, 1951; New York: Knopf, 1951.

The Journal of Katherine Mansfield, Definitive Edition, ed. J. M. Murry. London: Constable, 1954.

The Urewera Notebook, ed. Ian Gordon. Oxford: Oxford University Press, 1980.

The Collected Letters of Katherine Mansfield, 3 vols., ed. Vincent O'Sullivan and Margaret Scott. Oxford: Oxford University Press, 1984, 1993.

VIRGINIA WOOLF

A Writer's Diary, ed. Leonard Woolf. London: Hogarth Press, 1953.

The Letters of Virginia Woolf, 6 vols., ed. Nigel Nicolson and Joanne Trautman. New York: Harcourt Brace, 1975–80.

Moments of Being, ed. Jeanne Schulkind. New York: Harcourt Brace, 1976.

The Diary of Virginia Woolf, 5 vols., ed. Anne Oliver Bell. New York: Harcourt Brace, 1977–84.

A Passionate Apprentice: The Early Journals 1897–1909, ed. Mitchell A. Leaska. New York: Harcourt Brace, 1990.

ANAÏS NIN

The Diary of Anaïs Nin, 7 vols., ed. Gunther Stuhlmann. New York: Harcourt Brace, 1966–80.

Linotte: The Early Diary of Anaïs Nin, 1914–1920, transl. (from the French) Jean L. Sherman. Preface by Joaquín Nin-Culmell. New York: Harcourt Brace, 1978.

The Early Diary of Anaïs Nin, 4 vols., ed. Rupert Pole. New York: Harcourt Brace, 1982–85.

Incest, The Unexpurgated Diary of Anaïs Nin, 1934–1935. New York: Harcourt Brace, 1992.

MAY SARTON

Journal of a Solitude. New York: Norton, 1973.

The House by the Sea. New York: Norton, 1977.

Recovering: A Journal. New York: Norton, 1980.

At Seventy: A Journal. New York: Norton, 1984.

After the Stroke: A Journal. New York: Norton, 1988.

Endgame: A Journal of the Seventy-Ninth Year. New York: Norton, 1992.

Encore: A Journal of the Eightieth Year. New York: Norton, 1993.

At Eighty-Two. New York: Norton, 1996.

SELECT BIBLIOGRAPHY

Alcott, Louisa May. *The Journals of Louisa May Alcott*, ed. Joel Meyerson. Boston: Little, Brown, 1989.

Alpers, Antony. *The Life of Katherine Mansfield*. New York: Viking, 1980.

Asquith, Cynthia. *Married to Tolstoy*. London: Hutchinson, 1960.

Bair, Deirdre. *Anaïs Nin: A Biography*. New York: Putnam, 1995.

Baker, Ida. *Katherine Mansfield: The Memories of L.M.* London: Michael Joseph, 1971.

Bell, Quentin. *Virginia Woolf: A Biography*. London: Hogarth Press, 1972.

Blodgett, Harriet. *Centuries of Female Experience: Englishwomen's Private Diaries*. New Brunswick, N.J.: Rutgers University Press, 1988.

———. *Capacious Hold-All: An Anthology of Englishwomen's Diary Writings*. Charlottesville: University Press of Virginia, 1991.

Brown, John, M.D. *Marjorie Fleming*. Edinburgh: Edmonston and Douglas, 1864.

Cheever, John. *The Journals of John Cheever*. New York: Knopf, 1990.

Edwards, Anne. *Sonya: The Life of Countess Tolstoy*. New York: Simon and Schuster, 1981.

Farnie, Henry Brougham. *Pet Marjorie: A Story of Child-Life Fifty Years Ago*. Edinburgh: William P. Nimmo, 1860.

Filipovic, Zlata. *Zlata's Diaries*. New York: Viking, 1994.

Fisher, M. F. K., *Stay Me, Oh Comfort Me: Journals and Stories, 1933–1941*. New York, Pantheon, 1993.

Fitch, Noel Riley. *The Erotic Life of Anaïs Nin*. Boston: Little Brown, 1993.

Fothergill, Robert A. *Private Chronicles: A Study of English Diaries*. London: Oxford University Press, 1974.

Frank, Anne. *The Diary of a Young Girl: The Definitive Edition*, ed. Otto H. Frank and Mirjam Pressler, trans. Susan Massotty. New York: Doubleday, 1995.

Gide, André. *The Journals of André Gide*, ed. and transl. Justin O'Brien. New York: Vintage, 1947.

Gies, Miep. *Anne Frank Remembered*. New York: Simon and Schuster, 1987.

Gilman, Charlotte Perkins. *The Living Autobiography of Charlotte Perkins Gilman*. Madison: University of Wisconsin Press, 1990.

Gordon, Lyndall. *Virginia Woolf: A Writer's Life*. Oxford: Oxford University Press, 1984.

Grindea, Miron, ed. *Adam International Review*. London, 1972.

Halpern, Daniel, ed., "Journals, Notebooks & Diaries," *Antaeus*, no. 61 (Autumn 1988).

Hillesum, Etty. *An Interrupted Life: The Diaries of Etty Hillesum, 1941–1943*, transl. Arno Pomerans. New York: Pantheon, 1983.

James, Henry. *Notes of a Son and Brother*. New York: Scribners, 1914.

James, William. *The Letters of William James*, ed. Henry James. Boston: Atlantic Monthly Press, 1920.

Kafka, Franz. *Diaries, 1914–1923*. New York: Schocken, 1976.

Kuzminskaya, Tatyana. *Tolstoy as I Knew Him*. New York: Macmillan, 1948.

Lewis, R. W. *The Jameses: A Family Narrative*. New York: Farrar, Straus and Giroux, 1991.

Macbean, Lachlan. *The Story of Pet Marjorie*. London: Simpkin, Marshall, Hamilton Kent, 1914.

Mallon, Thomas. *A Book of One's Own: People and Their Diaries*. New York: Ticknor and Fields, 1984.

Matthiessen, F. O. *The James Family*. New York: Knopf, 1961.

Meyers, Jeffrey. *Katherine Mansfield: A Biography*. New York: New Directions, 1978.

Moffat, Mary Jane, and Painter, Charlotte. *Revelations: Diaries of Women*. New York: Random House, 1974.

Olsen, Tillie. *Silences*. New York: Delacorte, 1978.

Plath, Sylvia. *The Journals of Sylvia Plath*, ed. Frances McCullough (New York: Dial, 1982).

Polner, Tikhon. *Tolstoy and His Wife*. New York: Norton, 1945.

Rose, Phyllis. *Woman of Letters: A Life of Virginia Woolf*. New York: Oxford University Press, 1978.

——. *Parallel Lives: Five Victorian Marriages*. New York: Knopf, 1993.

Sherman, Susan, ed. *May Sarton: Among the Usual Days*. New York: Norton, 1993.

Shirer, William L. *Love and Hatred: The Troubled Marriage of Leo and Sonya Tolstoy*. New York: Simon and Schuster, 1994.

Simmons, Ernest J. *Leo Tolstoy*. Boston: Atlantic Monthly Press, 1946.

Simons, Judy. *Diaries and Journals of Literary Women, From Fanny Burney to Virginia Woolf*. London: Macmillan, 1990.

Spater, George, and Parsons, Ian. *A Marriage of True Minds: An Intimate Portrait of Leonard and Virginia Woolf*. New York: Harcourt Brace, 1977.

Sternburg, Janet, ed. *The Writer on Her Work*. New York: Norton, 1980.

Strouse, Jean. *Alice James: A Biography*. Boston: Houghton Mifflin, 1980.

Tolstoy, Ilya. *Reminiscences of Tolstoy*. New York: Century, 1914.

Tolstoy, Leo. *Tolstoy's Letters*, vol. 1, *1828–1879;* vol. 2, *1880–1910*, ed. R. F. Christian. New York: Scribners, 1978.

——. *Tolstoy's Diaries*, vol. 1, *1847–1894;* vol. 2, *1895–1910*, ed. R. F. Christian. London: Athlone Press, 1985.

Tolstoy, Tatyana. *Tolstoy Remembered*. New York: McGraw Hill, 1977.

Tomalin, Claire. *Katherine Mansfield: A Secret Life*. New York: St. Martin's Press, 1987.

Troyat, Henri. *Tolstoy*. New York: Doubleday, 1967.

Wordsworth, Dorothy. *The Journals of Dorothy Wordsworth*, ed. Mary Moorman. Oxford: Oxford University Press, 1971.

Yeazell, Ruth Bernard, ed., *The Death and Letters of Alice James*. Berkeley: University of California Press, 1981.

Young, Douglas. *Edinburgh in the Age of Reason*. Edinburgh: University Press, 1967.

PERMISSIONS

ABOUT THE AUTHOR

Alexandra Johnson won the PEN/Jerard Fund
Award Special Citation for *The Hidden Writer*.
The award is given to a nonfiction work-in-
progress. Her writing has been published in *The
New Yorker*, the *New York Times Book Review*,
The Nation, *Ms*. Magazine, *The Christian Science
Monitor* and the *Boston Review*, among other
national publications. She teaches memoir at
both Harvard and Wellesley College.

Aug
3rd

Owing to the change y[...]
new page. Twice a year [...]
October. My good resolut[...]
methodically, yet with th[...]
wisdom teaches me, good sen[...]
modern science teaches us [...]
my reading.

I shall make one [...]
there is a break. On t[...]
which I mean that pleasure [...]
rather successfully combin[...]
staying at home. O[...]
celebrities: L. would [...]
Logan's tea party, nor to [...]
my observation from othe[...]
accumulate though wa[...]